AF814436

QUE Bee

From Doubts to Distinction
Your ICSE 2026 Exams Partner

GIST OF THE TEXTBOOK
Crisp & Complete Theory - No need to go back to bulky textbooks!

ALL TYPES OF LATEST PATTERN QUESTIONS
MCQs | Assertion-Reason | Odd One Out All in one place!

KEYWORDS HIGHLIGHTED
Important points and Keywords are neatly highlighted; Never miss what matters

10 YEARS' PYQS ANSWERS
Previous Year Question Papers with solutions

COUNCIL-STYLE ANSWERS
Write responses like an examiner expects

SAMPLE QUESTION PAPER
Practice in real-exam mode. Perfect your timing, strategy, and confidence.

arihant
SUCCESS AND NOTHING LESS

ARIHANT PRAKASHAN
(School Division Series)

ADMINISTRATIVE & PRODUCTION OFFICES

Regd. Office
'Ramchhaya' 4577/15, Agarwal Road, Darya Ganj, New Delhi -110002
Tele: 011- 47630600, 43518550; Fax: 011- 23280316

Head Office
Kalindi, TP Nagar, Meerut (UP) - 250002, Tel: 0121-7156203, 7156204

SALES & SUPPORT OFFICES
Agra, Ahmedabad, Bengaluru, Bareilly, Chennai, Delhi, Guwahati, Hyderabad, Jaipur, Jhansi, Kolkata, Lucknow, Nagpur & Pune.

PO No : TXT-XX-XXXXXXX-X-XX

Published By Arihant Publications (India) Ltd.

For further information about the books published by Arihant, log on to www.arihantbooks.com or e-mail at info@arihantbooks.com

Follow us on

PRICE ₹ 225.00

PRODUCTION TEAM

Publishing Manager
Keshav Mohan

Project Head
Shruti Aggarwal

Cover Designer
Bilal Hashmi

Inner Designer
Ankit Tyagi

Page Layouting
Ravinder Kumar

QUE Bee

ICSE
Computer Applications
Class 10

Types of Questions & their Respective Number

Type of Questions	Total Number
Multiple Choice Questions	189
Assertion-Reason Type Questions	50
Odd One Out	49
Short Answer Type Questions (Output Based, Rewrite or Convert the Code)	298
Differentiate	33
Long Answer Type Questions	99
TOTAL NO. OF QUESTIONS	**718**

Created by

Abhishek Sharma
BCA

Lalita Kaler
MCA

From Learner to Leader

Step-Into the Spotlight

QUE Bee is more than just a book - it's a platform for young achievers like you to guide future toppers. If you've cracked the code to smart study or have insights that can make learning easier for others, this is your moment to shine!

What Can You Share?

- Your study techniques, time management tips, or motivation hacks
- Feedback or suggestions to make QUE Bee even better
- Real experiences that can guide other students through the exam maze

What's in It for You?

- Your name will be featured in our exclusive Student Panel in the next edition
- Win exciting & surprise rewards for impactful suggestions
- **Get published** - your photo, Ideas-or even interviews can be featured in the book
- **Become a student icon** - recognized and followed by peers across schools

Let your learning become someone else's ladder.
Be remembered. Be featured. Be the guide.

SCAN TO SHARE YOUR IDEA

QUE Bee

Index

Latest Course Structure

*There will be **one** written paper of **two hours** duration carrying 100 marks and Internal Assessment of 100 marks.*

Theory - 100 Marks

1. Revision of Class IX Syllabus

(i) Introduction to Object Oriented Programming concepts, (ii) Elementary Concept of Objects and Classes, (iii) Values and Data types, (iv) Operators in Java, (v) Input in Java, (vi) Mathematical Library Methods, (vii) Conditional constructs in Java, (viii) Iterative constructs in Java, (ix) Nested for loops.

2. Class as the Basis of all Computation

Objects and Classes

Objects encapsulate state and behaviour – numerous examples; member variables; attributes or features. Variables define state; member methods; Operations/methods/messages/ methods define behaviour.

Classes as abstractions for sets of objects; class as an object factory; primitive data types, composite data types. Variable declarations for both types; difference between the two types. Objects as instances of a class.

Consider real life examples for explaining the concept of class and object.

3. User - defined Methods

Need of methods, syntax of methods, forms of methods, method definition, method calling, method overloading, declaration of methods,

Ways to define a method, ways to invoke the methods – call by value [with programs] and call by reference [only definition with an example], Object creation - invoking the methods with respect to use of multiple methods with different names to implement modular programming, using data members and member methods, Actual parameters and formal parameters, Declaration of methods - static and non-static, method prototype / signature, - Pure and impure methods, - pass by value [with programs] and pass by reference [only definition with an example], Returning values from the methods , use of multiple methods and more than one method with the same name (polymorphism - method overloading).

4. Constructors

Definition of Constructor, characteristics, types of constructors, use of constructors, constructor overloading.

Default constructor, parameterized constructor, constructor overloading, Difference between constructor and method

5. Library classes

Introduction to wrapper classes, methods of wrapper class and their usage with respect to numeric and character data types. Autoboxing and Unboxing in wrapper classes.

Class as a composite type, distinction between primitive data type and composite data type or class types. Class may be considered as a new data type created by the user, that has its own functionality. The distinction between primitive and composite types should be discussed through examples. Show how classes allow user defined types in programs. All primitive types have corresponding class wrappers. Introduce Autoboxing and Unboxing with their definition and simple examples.

The following methods are to be covered:

int parseInt (String s),

long parse Long (String s),

float parse Float (String s),

double parse Double (String s),

boolean is Digit (char ch),
boolean is Letter (char ch),
boolean is Letter Or Digit (char ch),
boolean is Lower Case (char ch),
boolean is Upper Case (char ch),
boolean is White space (char ch),
char to Lower Case (char ch)
char to Upper Case (char ch)

6. Encapsulation

Access specifiers and its scope and visibility

Access specifiers – private, protected and public. Visibility rules for private, protected and public access specifiers. Scope of variables, class variables, instance variables, argument variables, local variables.

7. Arrays

Definition of an array, types of array, declaration, initialization and accepting data of single and double dimensional arrays, accessing the elements of single dimensional and double dimensional arrays.

Arrays and their uses, sorting technique - selection sort and bubble sort; Search techniques – linear search and binary search, Array as a composite type, length statement to find the size of the array (sorting and searching techniques using single dimensional array only).

Declaration, initialization, accepting data in a double dimensional array, sum of the elements in row, column and diagonal elements [right and left], display the elements of two-dimensional array in a matrix format.

8. String handling

String class, methods of String class, implementation of String class methods, String array

The following String class methods are to be covered:

String trim()
String toLowerCase()
String toUpperCase( )
int length( )
char charAt(int n)
int indexOf(char ch)
int lastIndexOf(char ch)
String concat(String str)
boolean equals(String str)
boolean equalsIgnoreCase(String str)
int compareTo(String str)
int compareToIgnoreCase(String str)
String replace(char old Char, char new Char)
String substring(int begin Index)
String substring(int begin Index, int endIndex)
boolean startsWith(String str)
boolean endsWith(String str)
String valueOf(all types)

Programs based on the above methods, extracting and modifying characters of a string.

Alphabetical order of the strings in an array [Bubble and Selection sort techniques], searching for a string using linear search technique.

01

REVISING BASIC JAVA CONCEPTS

Java is a versatile, object-oriented programming language known for its **platform independence** and **security**. Developed by **James Gosling** at **Sun Microsystems** (now owned by Oracle), it's used for many types of applications.

Flow of Java Programming

Java programs are firstly compiled and then interpreted. The flow of Java programming is shown in the following figure:

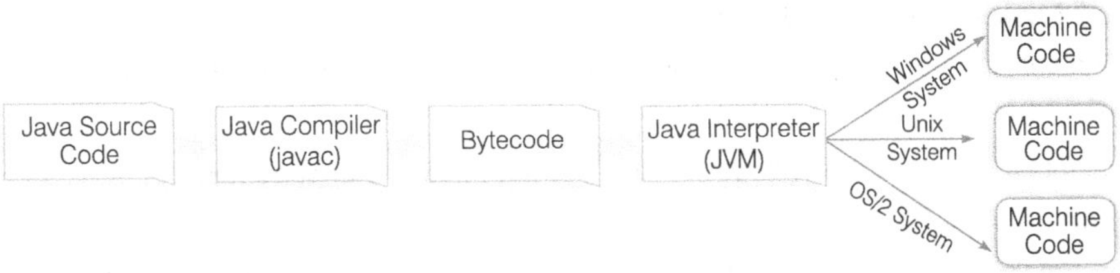

Java Source Code It is a collection of computer instructions built by the programmer using Java.

Java Compiler A Java compiler is a set of programs that transforms source code into bytecode.

Bytecode This bytecode is independent of the machine on which the program is to run. This makes a Java compiler highly portable.

Java Interpreter The Java interpreter decodes and executes bytecode for the Java Virtual Machine (JVM). The Java interpreter is actually a part of JVM. JVM is a platform-dependent execution environment that converts Java bytecode into machine code.

Machine Code JVM converts bytecode directly into machine code, that is designed to run on a specific microprocessor architecture or operating system such as Windows, UNIX, OS/2, etc.

Object Oriented Programming (OOP)

OOP is a programming paradigm centered around the concept of "objects," which are instances of classes. Objects can contain data, in the form of fields (often called **attributes**), and code, in the form of methods (**procedures** or **functions**). Essentially, OOP is about organizing your code around data, or objects, rather than actions and logic.

Features and characteristics of OOP's are as follows:

(i) Emphasis is given on data (objects) rather than function.

(ii) Programs are divided into entities known as objects.

(iii) Objects can communicate with each other through functions.

(iv) Functions that operate on data of an object are tied together.

(v) New data and functions can be easily added whenever necessary.

Elementary Concept of Objects and Classes

In object oriented programming technique, we design a program using objects and classes, which are as follows

Object

An object is a **real world entity**. It could be a person, place, table, chair or any item that the program may handle. Each object holds data and code to operate on the data.

Object	Student
Data:	Name RollNo Marks
Method:	Total( ) Percentage( )

Class

Class is a collection of objects of similar type. Each object of a class possesses same attributes and common behaviour defined within the same class. e.g. **Car**, **Truck**, **Bike** and **Cycle** are the objects of class **Vehicle**.

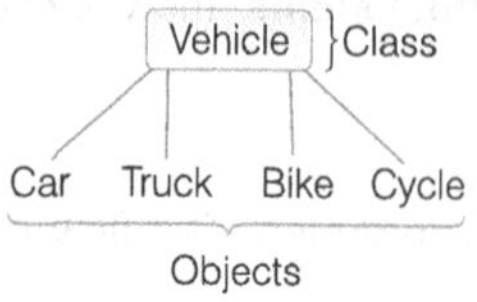

Principles of Object Oriented Programming

OOP works on the principles of encapsulation, abstraction, inheritance and polymorphism, which are as follows

Encapsulation

Process of wrapping up the data and methods in a single unit is known as **encapsulation**.

Data Abstraction

Data abstraction simplifies systems by **hiding complex details** and **exposing only essential features** for easier use and maintenance.

Inheritance

Inheritance allows a class to inherit **properties** and **behaviors** from another class, promoting code reuse and creating a hierarchy of related classes.

Polymorphism

Polymorphism in Java means **"one name, many forms."** It allows a single method or object to behave differently based on the context.

Character Set

- A character set in Java is a **set of alphabets**, **letters**, and **some special characters** that are valid in java programming language.
- In other words, characters are the smallest units (elements) of Java language that are used to write Java tokens.
- Java is a programming language it also has a set of characters used in forming tokens, instructions, programs, etc.

Character Sets in Java

Letters Both lowercase (a, b, c, d, e, etc.) and uppercase (A, B, C, D, E, etc.) letters.

Digits 0, 1, 2, 3, 4, 5, 6, 7, 8, 9.

Special symbols _, (,), {, }, [,], +, -, *, /, %, !, &, |, ~, ^, <, =, >, $, #, ?, Comma (,), Dot (.), Colon (:), Semi-colon (;), Single quote ('), Double quote ("), Back slash (\).

White space Space, Tab, New line.

Java program mostly uses ASCII code and Unicode for variable names, comments etc.

ASCII Character Set

- ASCII code stand for **American Standard Code for Information Interchange**.
- In ASCII format we use alphanumeric numbers.

- In this each character represented in 7 bits.
- It consists of total 128 (from 0 to 127) characters.
- The ASCII table includes:
  - **Control characters** (0–31) → \n (newline), \t (tab), \b (backspace)
  - **Printable characters** (32–126) → Letters (A-Z, a-z), digits (0-9), symbols (!@#$%^&*)
- It is also a small subset of Unicode because it contains 2 bytes while ASCII requires only one byte.

Unicode Character Set

In Java programming language, characters are defined by the Unicode character set.Unicode is a universal character encoding standard. This standard includes roughly 100000 characters to represent characters of different languages. Unicode uses 4 bytes to represent characters. Hence, it provides a very wide variety of encoding. It has three types namely UTF-8, UTF-16, UTF-32.

Unicode Encoding in Java

Unicode characters are represented in Java using Unicode escape sequences. These sequences start with \u followed by a 4-digit hexadecimal value that represents the Unicode of the character. This allows Java programs to include any character from the Unicode standard.

Escape Sequences in Java

Escape sequences in Java are special characters used to perform specific tasks, such as formatting or representing characters that cannot be directly included in a string. They begin with a backslash (\) followed by a specific character to denote their purpose. Escape sequences allow programmers to include special characters in their code, like newline, tab, or even a backslash itself.

List of Common Escape Sequences in Java

Escape Sequence	Meaning	Example Output
\n	New Line	Moves text to the next line
\t	Tab	Adds a tab space
\b	Backspace	Removes the previous character
\r	Carriage Return	Moves the cursor to the beginning of the line
\f	Form Feed	Used for page breaks in printing
\'	Single Quote	Prints ' inside a character or string
\"	Double Quote	Prints " inside a string
\\	Backslash	Prints \ inside a string

Tokens

Tokens are the smallest unit or single element of a Java program, which are identified by the compiler. It can also be defined as a individual character used in a Java program. There are five types of tokens, i.e. **literals**, **keywords**, **identifiers**, **operators** and **separators**.

Literals

These are the fixed values in a Java program. It can be any number, text or other information that represents a value. We can specify any value as a literal such as:

Integer Literals	It represents positive or negative value without decimal point. e.g. 14, –391, etc.
Floating Literals	Java have two kinds of floating point number: float and double. By default, floating literal is double. e.g. 0.01f is floating point literal and 6.5d is double-precision floating point literal.
Character Literals	These are constant valued character expressions embedded in a Java program. Character literals are expressed in Java within a pair of single quotes. These characters are termed as **ASCII characters**. e.g. 'A', '3', '*', etc.
String Literals	String is a set of alphanumeric characters. String literals are expressed within double quotes. e.g. "Hello", "100 pound", "TAJMAHAL", etc.
Boolean Literals	Boolean literals represent any one of the two values, either true or false and can be applied in a Java program to verify that whether the given condition is satisfied or not. e.g. boolean chosen = true;

Keywords

These are reserved words used within the program to specify a particular task.
Some keywords are as follows:

boolean	else	long	synchronized
break	extends	native	this
byte	final	new	throw
case	float	package	throws
catch	for	private	transient
char	goto	protected	try
class	if	public	void
const	implements	return	volatile
continue	import	short	while
default	instanceof	static	
do	int	super	
double	interface	switch	

Identifiers

This is a name given to a package, class, interface, method or variable. It allows a programmer to refer to the item from other places in the program. In Java, there are several points to remember about identifiers. They are as follows:

- An identifier can be any combination of alphabets (A to Z or a to z), digits (0 to 9), currency character ($) and underscore (_).
- The first character in identifier must be an alphabet, currency character or underscore.
- No commas or blanks are allowed within an identifier.
- Most importantly identifiers are case sensitive. e.g. foo and Foo are two different identifiers.
- A keyword cannot be used as an identifier.

e.g. **Legal identifiers** are : age, $salary, _value, _1_value

Illegal identifiers are : 123abc, -salary, auto

Operators

Operators in Java are symbols that perform operations on variables and values. Java provides different types of operators categorized based on their functionality.

Types of Operators in Java

Type	**Operator**
Arithmetic	+, −, *, /, %
Relational (Comparison)	==, !=, >, <, >=, <=
Logical	&&, || ,!
Bitwise	&, |, ^,~,<,>,>>
Assignment	=
Unary	+, −, ++, − −
Ternary	?:

Operator Precedence/Hierarchy of Operator

In Java, operator precedence (or hierarchy) determines the order in which operators are evaluated in an expression. Operators with higher precedence are evaluated before those with lower precedence.

If two operators have the same precedence, the evaluation order is determined by their associativity (left-to-right or right-to-left).

Precedence	Operator	Description	Associativity
1.	( )	Parenthesis	Left to Right
	[ ]	Array subscript	
	•	Access object method	
2.	++	Postfix increment	Left to Right
	– –	Postfix decrement	
3.	++	Prefix increment	Right to Left
	––	Prefix decrement	
	+, –	Unary plus/minus	
	!	Logical NOT	
	~	Bitwise NOT	
4.	*	Multiplication	Left to Right
	/	Division	
	%	Modulus	
5.	+	Addition	Left to Right
	–	Subtraction	
	+	String concatenation	
6.	<<	Bitwise left shift	Left to Right
	>>	Bitwise right shift	
	>>>	Bitwise right shift with zero extension(zero fill)	
7.	<, <=	Less than, less than or equal to	Left to Right
	>, >=	Greater than, greater than or equal to	
8.	= =	Equal to	Left to Right
	! =	Not equal to	
9.	&	Bitwise AND	Left to Right
10.	^	Bitwise XOR	Left to Right
11.	|	Bitwise OR	Left to Right
12.	&&	Logical AND	Left to Right
13.	||	Logical OR	Left to Right
14.	? :	Conditional	Right to Left
15.	=	Assignment	Right to Left

Separators/Punctuators

It helps to define the structure of a program. Some separators are as follows :

Separator	Symbol	Description
Parenthesis	( )	It holds method definition.
Braces	{ }	It is used to define block/scope of class, code, methods.
Brackets	[ ]	It is used in array declaration.
Period	.	It separates the package name from sub package.
Comma	,	It separates the consecutive variable of same type when declaration.
Semicolon	;	It is used to terminate the statement in Java.

Variables

- A variable is a container which holds the value while the Java program is executed. A variable is assigned with a data type.
- Variable is a name of memory location.

Constants

A constant value represents a named value that remains fixed throughout an entire program. A constant is declared in similar way as variable but with keyword final.

e.g., `final double TAXRATE = 0.25 ;`

Now , you will be able to use TAXRATE's value in your program but you will never be able to change its value again, because you created it with keyword final, which means that this named value will remain fixed for this name throughout the program where it has been created.

Data Types

In Java, data types define the type of data that variables can store. Java has two main types of data types:

1. Primitive Data Types (Built-in Types)

These are the basic types in Java:

- byte (1 byte) → Stores small integers (-128 to 127)
- short (2 bytes) → Stores medium-sized integers (-32,768 to 32,767)
- int (4 bytes) → Stores whole numbers (-2 billion to 2 billion)
- long (8 bytes) → Stores large whole numbers
- float (4 bytes) → Stores decimal numbers with less precision
- double (8 bytes) → Stores decimal numbers with high precision
- char (2 bytes) → Stores a single character ('A', '5', etc.)
- boolean (1 bit) → Stores true or false values

2. Non-Primitive Data Types (Reference Types)

These store references to objects:

- String → Stores sequences of characters ("Hello")
- Arrays → Stores multiple values of the same type
- Classes, Objects, Interfaces → Used in Object-Oriented Programming.

Expression

It is a construct mode of variables, operators and method invocations, which are raise according to the syntax of the language, that evaluates to a single value.

e.g. $$a = \frac{2 \cdot 34 - 2x^3}{x + y}$$

In Java, syntax of the above expression will be like:

```
a = (2·34- 2*x *x *x) / (x+ y);
```

Mathematical Library Functions

Java provides access to a lot of common mathematical functions as well as some of the more common irrational numbers using the Math class.

Function	Format	Description	Example
pow( )	Math.pow(x, y);	Returns double value of x^y.	Math.pow(2, 3) = 8
log( )	Math.log(x);	Returns double value of natural log (base e).	Math. log(3) = 1.0986122886681098
log10( )	Math.log10(x);	Returns the base 10 logarithm of a double value.	Math.log10(1000) = 3
sqrt( )	Math.sqrt(x);	Returns the square root of a positive number. It returns double data type.	Math.sqrt(25) =5
ceil( )	Math.ceil(x);	Returns the whole number greater than equal to the number.	Math.ceil(22.81) = 23 Math.ceil(1.1) = 2 Math.ceil(22.11) = 23
floor( )	Math.floor(x);	Returns the rounded value down to the nearest integer.	Math.floor(11.11) = 11.0 Math.floor(11.97) = 11.0
rint( )	Math.rint(x);	Returns the integer part of the number by removing fractional part (nearest integer value).	Math.rint(14.92) = 15 Math.rint(10.29) = 10
abs( )	Math.abs(a);	Returns absolute value, i.e. only magnitude of the number. It returns int/long/double.	Math.abs(–1.76) = 1.76 Math.abs(1.76) = 1.76

Function	Format	Description	Example
max( )	Math.max(a, b);	Returns the greater number between a and b. It returns int/float/double/long.	Math.max(2, 4) = 4 Math.max(4, 2) = 4
min( )	Math.min(a, b);	Returns the smaller number between a and b. It returns int/float/double/long.	Math.min(2, 4) = 2 Math.min(4, 2) = 2
random( )	Math.random( );	Returns a random number between 0 and 1. It returns a double type value.	
sin( ) cos( ) tan( )	Math.sin(x); Math.cos(x); Math.tan(x);	Returns the sin, cos, tan values respectively of a given angle in radian as an argument.	Math.sin (Math.PI/6) = .499999999 Math.cos (Math.PI/4) = 0.707106781 Math.tan (Math.PI/3) = 1.732050808

Type Conversion

Type conversion is a technique that is used either by the compiler or a programmer to convert one data type to another in Java. Type conversion is also known as **type casting**. For example, converting int to double, double to int, short to int, etc. There are two types of type casting allowed in Java programming:

Implicit Type Conversion

In this, a smaller type is converted to a larger type, this work is done automatically by the compiler.

Hierarchy of Implicit Type Conversion

From (Smaller Type) byte, short, char, int, long, float

To (Larger Type) short, int, int, long, float, double

Explicit Type Conversion

Explicit type conversion which is done by the programmer manually. In this conversion, a larger type can be converted into a smaller type.

When a programmer changes the variable type while writing the code. We can use the cast operator to change the type of the variable. For example, double to int or int to double.

Hierarchy of Explicit Type Conversion

From (Larger Type) double, float, long, int, short, char

To (Smaller Type) float, long, int, short, byte, int

Comments in Java

In Java, comments are used to add explanatory notes or remarks to your code. These comments are not executed by the program but serve as documentation for anyone reading the code. Java supports two types of comments:

- **Single-line Comments (//)** A single-line comment is used to add comments that span a single line. It is denoted by two forward slashes (//), and everything following the slashes on that line is treated as a comment. Single-line comments are useful for short descriptions or explanations.
- **Multi-line Comments (/* ... */)** A multi-line comment is used when the comment spans more than one line. It begins with /* and ends with */, allowing multiple lines of text between the start and end markers to be treated as comments. Multi-line comments are useful for adding longer explanations, block comments, or commenting out large sections of code.

Note *Both single line and multi-line types of comments improve code readability and help other developers (or your future self) understand the logic behind the code.*

Input/Output in Java

Input is any information that is needed by program to complete its execution.

Output is any information that the program must convey to the user.

Stream

A stream can be defined as a sequence of data. The InputStream is used to read data from a source and the OutputStream is used for writing data to a destination.

Byte Streams

Java byte streams are used to perform input and output of 8-bits (bytes) data in the byte format. There are many classes related to byte streams but the most frequently used classes are FileInputStream and FileOutputStream.

Character Streams

Java character streams are used to perform input and output for 16-bit unicode character in the character format. Character stream I/O automatically translates the internal format into the local character set and *vice-versa.*

Different Ways to Take Input in Java

There are two ways by which we can take input from the user as

(i) Using BufferedReader Class

(ii) Using Scanner Class

Using Scanner Class The Scanner class is a class, which allows the user to read values of various types. Scanner class is available in java.util system package. You must import java.util package to avail the facilities contained in Scanner class. The statement to import java.util package is : `import java.util.Scanner;`

After importing java.util package, create object which can hold a set of values of different types. The syntax to create a Scanner object is : `Scanner input = new Scanner(System.in);`

Methods to Read Tokens from Scanner Object

Methods	Returns
int nextInt( )	Returns the next token as an int.
long nextLong( )	Returns the next token as a long.
float nextFloat( )	Returns the next token as a float.
double nextDouble( )	Returns the next token as a double.
String next( )	Finds and returns the next complete token from the scanner object as a string.
String nextLine( )	Returns the rest part of the current line, excluding any line separator at the end.
void close( )	Closes the Scanner.

Printer Class

Printer classes are required when we need to create a formatted output stream.

There are two kinds of print statements:

- **System.out.print(argument)** prints its argument.
- **System.out.println(argument)** prints its argument and ends the line.

The print method just prints the string but does not move the cursor to a new line, while println( ) prints the string and moves the cursor to a new line.

Control Structure

Java control structures determine the order in which the code runs, enabling decisions, repetitions, and altering program flow.

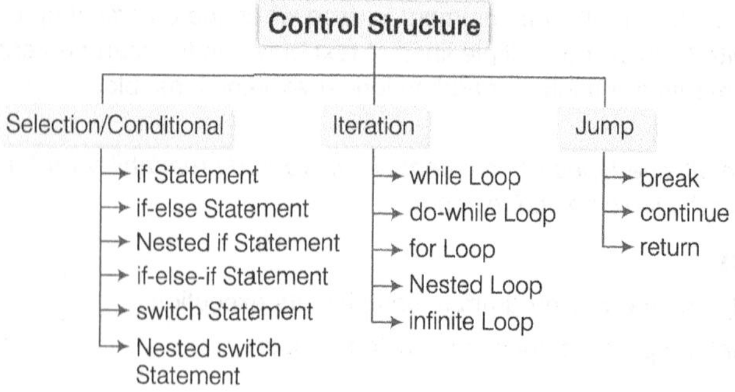

(i) Selection (Conditional)

These structures allow you to execute different blocks of code based on whether a condition is true or false. Java's selection statements are:

1. **if Statement** An if statement in Java runs a block of code only if a condition is true. If false, the code is skipped.

   Syntax
   ```
   if(Condition)
   {
      Statements;
   }
   ```

2. **if-else Statement** The if-else statement lets you run one block of code if a condition is true, and a different block of code if it's false.

   Syntax
   ```
   if(Condition)
   {
      Statement 1;
   }
   else
   {
      Statement 2;
   }
   ```

3. **Nested-if Statement** A nested if statement is an if or if-else statement inside another if or if-else statement.

   Syntax
   ```
   if(Condition 1)
   {
      if(Condition 2)
         Statement 1;
      else
         Statement 2;
   }
   else
   {
      Statement 3;
   }
   ```

4. **if-else-if Statement** The if-else-if statement lets you check multiple conditions in order. It's like a chain of if and else if statements.

   Syntax
   ```
   if(Condition 1)
      Statement 1;
   else if(Condition 2)
      Statement 2;
   else if(Condition 3)
      Statement 3;
   :
   :
   else
      Statement;
   ```

5. **switch Statement** The switch statement is a cleaner way to choose between multiple code blocks based on a single value, often better than a long chain of if-else-if statements.

   Syntax
   ```
   switch(expression)
   {
      case value 1:
         Statements;
         break;
      case value 2:
         Statements;
         break;
      :
      :
      default:
         Statements;
   }
   ```

6. **Nested switch Statement** Switch can also be used as a part of the statement sequence of an outer switch, which is called nested switch and is exactly the same idea as a nested if-else statement.

Syntax
```
switch(Expression 1)
{
   case value 1:
   switch(Expression 2)
   {
      case value A:
         Statements;
         break;
      case value B:
         Statements;
         break;
   }
   case value 2:
      Statements;
      break;
   :
   :
   :
   default:
      Statements;
}
```

(ii) Iteration

Iteration (or looping) repeats a block of code as long as a condition is true.

1. **while loop** A while loop repeats code as long as a condition is true, checking the condition before each loop run.

Syntax
```
while(Condition)
{
   Statements
}
```

2. **do-while loop** A do-while loop runs code at least once, then checks a condition. If true, it repeats; if false, it stops.

Syntax
```
do
{
   Statements
}
while(Condition);
```

3. **for loop** A for loop is a compact way to repeat code a specific number of times. It checks a condition before each loop run.

Syntax
```
for(initialization; condition;increment/decrement)
{
   Statements
}
```

4. **Nested loop** A nested loop is a loop inside another loop. The inner loop runs completely for each iteration of the outer loop.

Syntax

For a nested for loop
```
for(initialization; condition; increment/decrement)
{
   for(initialization; condition; increment/decrement)
   {
      Statement(s);
   }
   Statement(s);
}
```

For a nested while loop:

```
while(Condition)
{
   while(Condition)
   {
      Statement(s);
   }
   Statement(s);
}
```

5. **Infinite loop** An infinite loop repeats code endlessly because its condition is always true.

Syntax
```
for(initialization; ; increment/decrement)
{
   Statement;
}
```

(iii) Jump Statement

Jump statements transfer program control to different parts of the code, modifying the flow of loops and conditional statements. They let you exit loops, skip iterations, or go to specific locations.

1. **break Statement** The break statement exits a loop immediately, and the program continues with the code after the loop.

Syntax
```
while(Condition)
{
   Statement 1;
   if(Condition)
   {
      break;
   }
   Statement 2;
}
Statement 3;
```

2. **continue Statement** The continue statement skips the rest of the current loop iteration and jumps to the next iteration.

Syntax
```
do
{
   Statement 1;
   continue;
   :
   :
   :
}
while(Condition);
Statement 2;
```

3. **return Statement** The return statement immediately ends a method and sends program control back to where the method was called from.

Syntax
```
return(Expression);
```

Errors in Java

Errors are issues in the code that stop the program from running as expected. These errors can happen for many different reasons, and knowing the different types of errors can help you find and fix them more easily.

In Java (and most programming languages), errors can occur at different stages of the program execution process. These errors can broadly be categorized into three types:

- Syntax Errors
- Runtime Errors
- Logical Errors

Each type of error arises from different issues in the code, and understanding them is crucial to effectively debugging and writing error-free programs.

1. **Syntax Errors** Syntax errors occurs when the code doesn't follow the rules of the Java language. This includes things like missing semicolons, unmatched parentheses, incorrect keywords, or misspelled variable names.These errors are caught by the compiler at the time of compilation, before the program is executed.
2. **Runtime Errors** These errors occur during the execution of the program. The program compiles successfully, but an error happens when you run the code. This can happen when the program tries to perform illegal operations like dividing by zero, accessing a null object, or accessing an array index out of bounds.
3. **Logical Errors** Logical errors are bugs in the program that occur when the program runs without throwing any exceptions, but it produces incorrect results. These errors often occur due to incorrect algorithms, improper conditionals, or wrong assumptions. These errors happen due to flaws in the program's logic and are difficult to detect because the code compiles and runs without throwing exceptions. The program might execute without errors but produce incorrect results.

Exception Handling Keywords

Java provides specific keywords for exception handling purposes, these are:

- **throw** throw keyword is used to throw exception either user defined or java defined to the runtime to handle it.
- **throws** throws is used in a method's declaration to indicate it might throw exceptions that it doesn't handle. The calling code is then responsible for handling them or passing them on using throws.
- **try-catch** try-catch handles errors. try holds the code that might cause an error, and catch handles it. You can have multiple catch blocks and nest try-catch blocks. catch needs an Exception parameter.
- **finally** finally (optional, used with try-catch) always runs, even if an exception occurs, ensuring resources are closed.

EXAM ORIENTED QUESTIONS

TYPE - 1 01 Mark

Multiple Choice Questions

Q.1 The code obtained after compilation is known as **ICSE 2023; ICSE SQP 2022 (Sem I)**
(a) source code (b) object code
(c) machine code (d) java byte code

Q.2 The program code written in any high-level language to solve a problem is **ICSE 2022 (Sem I)**
(a) object code (b) source code
(c) machine code (d) bytecode

Q.3 The extension of a Java source code file is **ICSE 2024**
(a) .exe (b) .obj (c) .jvm (d) .java

Q.4 "Java compiled code (byte code) can run on all operating systems" – Name the feature. **ICSE SQP 2025**
(a) Robust and Secure
(b) Object Oriented
(c) Platform Independent
(d) Multithreaded

Q.5 A mechanism where one class acquires the properties of another class **ICSE 2023**
(a) Polymorphism (b) Inheritance
(c) Encapsulation (d) Abstraction

Q.6 The process of binding the data and method together as one unit is called as **ICSE SQP 2023; ICSE 2022 (Sem I)**
(a) encapsulation (b) inheritance
(c) polymorphism (d) dynamic binding

Q.7 The .... allows a class to use the properties and methods of another class. **ICSE SQP 2022 (Sem I)**
(a) Inheritance
(b) Polymorphism
(c) Encapsulation
(d) None of the above

Q.8

Name the feature of Java depicted in the above picture. **ICSE 2024**
(a) Encapsulation (b) Inheritance
(c) Abstraction (d) Polymorphism

Q.9 Which of the following is an escape sequence character in Java? **ICSE SQP 2024**
(a) /n (b) \t
(c) /t (d) //n

Q.10 The size of '\n' is: **ICSE SQP 2025**
(a) 2 bytes (b) 4 bytes
(c) 8 bytes (d) 16 bytes

Q.11 The keyword used to call package in the program **ICSE 2023**
(a) extends (b) export
(c) import (d) package

Q.12 Which of the following keyword is used to create symbolic constants in Java? **ICSE 2022 (Sem I)**
(a) final (b) Final (c) Constant (d) Const

Q.13 Among the following which is a keyword **ICSE SQP 2024**
(a) every (b) all
(c) case (d) each

Q.14 Which of the following is a valid Java keyword? **ICSE SQP 2025**
(a) If (b) BOOLEAN
(c) static (d) Switch

Q.15 The .... are the words which have special meaning **ICSE SQP 2022 (Sem I)**
(a) Keywords (b) Identifier
(c) Methods (d) Package

Q.16 Identify the type of operator && **ICSE 2023**
(a) ternary (b) unary
(c) logical (d) relational

Q.17 The logical operator which is an unary operator **ICSE SQP 2023**
(a) && (b) || (c) ! (d) >>

Q.18 The operator which acts on one operand is known as ...... **ICSE 2022 (Sem I), ICSE 2023**
(a) binary (b) ternary
(c) unary (d) relational

Q.19 If (a > b & & b > c) then largest number is **ICSE 2024**
(a) b (b) c
(c) a (d) wrong expression

Q.20 Identify the operator that gets the highest precedence while evaluating the given expression: **ICSE SQP 2025**

$$a + b \% c * d - e$$

(a) + (b) %
(c) – (d) *

Q.21 Ternary operator is a **ICSE SQP 2024**

(a) logical operator (b) arithmetic operator
(c) relational operator (d) conditional operator

Q.22 The expression which uses > = operator is known as **ICSE SQP 2024**

(a) relational (b) logical
(c) arithmetic (d) assignment

Q.23 String x = (a > = 90)? "excellent" : "best"; when a = 90 **ICSE SQP 2022 (Sem I)**

(a) best (b) excellent
(c) excellent best

Q.24 Give the output of the following, when x = 5 **ICSE SQP 2022 (Sem I)**

x + = x++ + ++ x + --x + x;

(a) 29 (b) 28 (c) 26

Q.25 Give the output of the following. **ICSE 2022 (Sem I)**

```
int  x = 2, y = 4, z = 1;
int result = (++z) +y + (++x) + (z++);
```

(a) 11 (b) 12 (c) 10 (d) 9

Q.26 A student executes the following code to increase the value of a variable 'x' by 2. **ICSE SQP 2025**

He has written the following statement, which is incorrect.

```
x = +2;
```

What will be the correct statement?

A. x + = 2;
B. x = 2;
C. x = x + 2;

(a) Only A (b) Only C
(c) All the three (d) Both A and C

Q.27 Give the output of the following. **ICSE 2022 (Sem I)**

```
int f=10,m=9;
String e=(m%f==9)? "YES": "NO";
System.out.print(e);
```

(a) YES (b) NO
(c) YESNO (d) NOYES

Q.28 The output 42/6% 2 is: **ICSE 2025**

(a) 1 (b) 10
(c) 2 (d) 0

Q.29 The data type which is specified that the method does not return a value is **ICSE SQP 2023**

(a) Void (b) void
(c) VOID (d) boolean

Q.30 The number of bytes occupied by the constant 45 are **ICSE SQP 2023**

(a) Four bytes (b) Two bytes
(c) Eight bytes (d) One byte

Q.31 The number of bits occupied by the value 'a' are: **ICSE 2023**

(a) 1 bit (b) 2 bits (c) 4 bits (d) 16 bits

Q.32 Which of the following data type cannot be used with switch case construct? **ICSE 2024**

(a) int (b) char (c) String (d) double

Q.33 Which of the following is a valid Integer constant? **ICSE SQP 2024**

1. 4 2. 4.0
3. 4.3f 4. "four"

(a) Only 1 (b) 1 and 3
(c) 2 and 4 (d) 1 and 2

Q.34 A data type which contains integer as well as fractional part and occupies 32 bits space is **ICSE 2022 (Sem I)**

(a) float (b) char
(c) double (d) byte

Q.35 The default value of a boolean variable is **ICSE SQP 2025**

(a) False (b) 0
(c) false (d) True

Q.36 int x = 98; char ch = (char)x; what is the value in ch? **ICSE 2024**

(a) b (b) A
(c) B (d) 97

Q.37 `int res='A';` What is the value of res? **ICSE SQP 2023**

(a) A (b) 66
(c) 65 (d) 97

Q.38 What is the final value stored in variable x? **ICSE SQP 2022 (Sem I)**

```
double a =-8.35;
double x =Math.abs(Math.floor(a));
```

(a) 9.0 (b) 7.0
(c) 6 (d) 7

Q.39 What is the final value stored in variable x? **ICSE 2022 (Sem I)**

```
double x=Math.ceil(Math.abs(-7.3));
```

(a) 7.0 (b) 8.0 (c) 6.0 (d) 9.0

Q.40 Give the output of the following statement

```
Math.pow(625, ½) + Math.sqrt(144)
```

ICSE SQP 2023

(a) 17.0 (b) 13.0 (c) 37.0 (d) 13

Q.41 What value will Math.sqrt (Math.ceil (15.3)) return? **ICSE 2023**

(a) 16.0 (b) 16 (c) 4.0 (d) 5.0

Q.42 What is the output of `Math. ceil(5.4)+ Math. ceil (4.5)`?

(a) 10.0 (b) 11.0 (c) 12.0 (d) 9.0

Q.43 Which of the following mathematical methods returns only an integer? **ICSE 2024**

(a) `Math.ceil(n)` (b) `Math.sqrt(n)`
(c) `Math.floor(n)` (d) `Math.round(n)`

Q.44 The output of Math.round(6.6) + Math.ceil(3.4) is **ICSE SQP 2024**

(a) 9.0 (b) 11.0
(c) 10.0 (d) 11

Q.45 The output of the following code is: **ICSE SQP 2025**

```
System.out.println(Math.ceil(6.4)
                    + Math.floor(-1 - 2));
```

(a) 3.0 (b) 4
(c) 3 (d) 4.0

Q.46 The output of Math.max(– 7, Math.min(–5, – 4)) is **ICSE 2025**

(a) – 5 (b) – 4
(c) – 7 (d) error

Q.47 int x=(int) 32.8; is an example of .... typecasting. **ICSE 2023**

(a) implicit (b) automatic
(c) explicit (d) coercion

Q.48 The style of expressing single line comment is **ICSE SQP 2023**

(a) /* comment*/ (b) * comment
(c) //comment (d) /* comment

Q.49 Which of the following are valid comments? **ICSE SQP 2022 (Sem I); ICSE 2014**

(i) /* comment */ (ii) /* comment
(iii) // comment (iv) */ comment */

(a) (i) & (iii) (b) (i) & (ii)
(c) All of these (d) None of these

Q.50 Method that accepts a string without any space is .... **ICSE SQP 2022 (Sem I)**

(a) next() (b) nextLine()
(c) nextInt() (d) None of these

Q.51 The Scanner class method used to accept words with space **ICSE 2023**

(a) next() (b) nextLine()
(c) Next() (d) nextString()

Q.52 The Scanner class is a .... class. **ICSE SQP 2023**

(a) Primitive (b) Derived
(c) Wrapper (d) Super

Q.53 The method of Scanner class used to accept a double value is: **ICSE SQP 2024**

(a) nextInt() (b) nextDouble()
(c) next() (d) nextInteger()

Q.54 `System.out.println('Z' + 32);` will display **ICSE 2025**

(a) z (b) Z
(c) 122 (d) 154

Q.55 `System.out.println("I said,\ "It\'s wise to obey elders.\"");`

The output of the above statement is:

(a) I said,'It is wise to obey elders'.
(b) I said, "It's wise to obey elders."
(c) I said, It's wise to elders.
(d) "'It's wise to obey elders."'

Q.56 Give the output of the following. When a = 5 and b = 7 **ICSE SQP 2022 (Sem I)**

```
if(a > b)
System.out.println(a+b);
System.out.println(a*b);
```

(a) 12, 35 (b) 35 (c) 35, 12

Q.57 The correct if statement for the following ternary operation statement is **ICSE SQP 2023**

```
System.out.println(n%2 == 0? "true":"false");
```

(a)
```
if(n%2==0)
    return true;
else
    return false;
```

(b)
```
if(n%2==0)
    return "true";
else
    return "false";
```

(c)
```
if(n%2==0)
    System.out.println("true");
else
    System.out.println("false");
```

(d)
```
if(n%2==0)
    return false;
else
    return false;
```

Q.58 Give the output of the following

```
switch(x)
{
    case 'a' : System.out.println
                        ("Discipline");
    case 'b' : System.out.println
                  ("Dedication"); break;
    case 'c' : System.out.println
                        ("Commitment");
    default : System.out.println("Success");
} when x='A'
```

ICSE SQP 2022 (Sem I)

(a) Discipline (b) Dedication
(c) Success

Q.59 Give the output of the following. **ICSE 2022 (Sem I)**

```
switch(x)
{
    case 'M':
      System.out.print("Microsoft Teams");
      break;
```

```
    case 'G':
        System.out.print("Google Meet");
    default:
        System.out.print("Any software");
        break;
    case 'W':
        System.out.print("Web Ex");
        break;
}
```

When x='g'

(a) Google Meet (b) Any software

(c) Google Meet
Any software (d) WebEx

Q.60 Consider the following program segment and select the output of the same when n=10 : **ICSE 2023**

```
switch(n)
{
    case 10 : System.out.println(n*2);
    case 4 : System.out.println(n*4);break;
    default : System.out.println(n);
}
```

(a) 20
40 (b) 10
4 (c) 20, 40 (d) 10
10

Q.61 Multiple branching statement of Java is **ICSE SQP 2023**

(a) for (b) while
(c) do ... while (d) switch

Q.62 Which of the following is not true with regards to a switch statement? **ICSE SQP 2025**

(a) checks for an equality between the input and the case labels
(b) supports floating point constants
(c) break is used to exit from the switch block
(d) case labels are unique

Q.63 A physical education teacher asks the students to do the side stretch as shown below, 10 times. Which programming construct the teacher uses? **ICSE 2025**

(a) if (b) switch (c) for (d) if else if

Q.64

```
n=1000;
while (n> 10)
{
    n=n/10;
}
System.out.println(n);
```

How many time the loop is executed and what is the output? **ICSE SQP 2022 (Sem I)**

(a) Loop is executed 2 times and the output is 100.
(b) Loop is executed 3 times and the output is 10.
(c) Loop is executed 2 times and the output is 10.

Q.65 Give the output of the following. **ICSE 2022 (Sem I)**

```
int v= 5;
while (--v>=0)
{
    System.out.print(v);
}
```

(a) 43210 (b) 54321 (c) 543210 (d) 4321

Q.66 Give the output of the following. **ICSE 2022 (Sem I)**

```
int x;
for ( x =1 ; x <=3; x++ );
System.out.print (x);
```

(a) 1 2 3 (b) 1 2 3 4
(c) 4 (d) 1

Q.67

```
for(k=1;k<=2;k++)
{ for(m=1;m<=4;m++)
    {
        System.out.println(m*2);
    }
}
```

How many times the inner loop is executed? **ICSE SQP 2023**

(a) 4 times (b) 8 times
(c) 2 times (d) 16 times

Q.68 do..... while loop is an **ICSE SQP 2023**

(a) entry controlled loop (b) infinite loop
(c) exit controlled loop (d) Finite loop

Q.69 State the type of loop in the given program segment **ICSE 2023**

```
for(inti=5;i!=0;i-=2)
System.out.println(i);
```

(a) finite (b) infinite (c) null (d) fixed

Q.70 Which of the following are entry controlled loops? **ICSE 2024**

1. for 2. while
3. do..while 4. switch

(a) Only 1 (b) 1 and 2
(c) 1 and 3 (d) 3 and 4

Q.71 To execute a loop 10 times, which of the following is correct? **ICSE SQP 2025**

(a) for (int i=11;i<=30;i+=2)
(b) for (int i=11;i<=30;i+=3)
(c) for (int i=11;i<20;i++)
(d) for (int i=11;i<=21;i++)

Q.72 Select the infinite loop: **ICSE 2025**

(a) for(int i = 1; i< = 10; i + +)
(b) for(int i = 2; i! = 0; i – = 3)
(c) for(int i = 5; i< = 5; i + +)
(d) for(int i = 1; i > = 1; i – –)

Q.73 Consider the program segment: **ICSE 2025**

```
int p=0;
for(p=4;p>0;p- =2);
System.out.print(p);
System.out.println(p);
```

The above statements will display:

(a) 42 (b) 4200
(c) 0
0 (d) 00

Q.74 Consider the following program segment in which the statements are jumbled.

Choose the correct order of statements to calculate and return the factorial of 4. **ICSE 2025**

```
for (k=1;k<=4;k+ +) ——→ 1
return fa; ——→        2
long fa=1, k; ——→     3
fa*=k; ——→            4
```

(a) 1, 2, 3, 4 (b) 3, 1, 4, 2
(c) 3, 1, 2, 4 (d) 1, 3, 2, 4

Q.75 The jump statement that is used inside a switch case construct to terminate a statement sequence. **ICSE 2022 (Sem I)**

(a) continue (b) break
(c) return (d) goto

Q.76 The absence of which statement leads to fall through situation in switch case statement? **ICSE 2023**

(a) continue
(b) break
(c) return
(d) System.exit(0)

Q.77 The statement that brings the control back to the calling method is: **ICSE SQP 2025**

(a) break (b) System.exit(0)
(c) continue (d) return

Q.78 Name the type of error in the statement given below **ICSE SQP 2022 (Sem I)**

```
int r=100/0;
```

(a) Syntax (b) Runtime
(c) Logical (d) None of these

Q.79 Name the type of error in the statement given below **ICSE 2022 (Sem I)**

```
double x; y; z;
```

(a) Logical error (b) Syntax error
(c) Runtime error (d) No error

Q.80 Missing a semicolon in a statement is what type of error? **ICSE 2023**

(a) Logical (b) Syntax
(c) Runtime (d) No error

Q.81 Name the type of error that occurs for the following statement **ICSE SQP 2023**

```
System.out.println(Math.sqrt(24-25));
```

(a) Syntax error (b) Runtime error
(c) Logical error (d) No error

Q.82 Name the type of error, if any in the following statement **ICSE SQP 2024**

```
System.out.print("HELLO")
```

(a) logical (b) no error
(c) runtime (d) syntax

Answers

1. (d)	**2.** (b)	**3.** (d)	**4.** (c)	**5.** (b)
6. (a)	**7.** (a)	**8.** (b)	**9.** (b)	**10.** (a)
11. (c)	**12.** (a)	**13.** (c)	**14.** (c)	**15.** (a)
16. (c)	**17.** (c)	**18.** (c)	**19.** (c)	**20.** (b)
21. (d)	**22.** (a)	**23.** (b)	**24.** (a)	**25.** (a)
26. (d)	**27.** (a)	**28.** (a)	**29.** (b)	**30.** (a)
31. (d)	**32.** (d)	**33.** (a)	**34.** (a)	**35.** (a)
36. (a)	**37.** (c)	**38.** (a)	**39.** (b)	**40.** (b)
41. (c)	**42.** (b)	**43.** (d)	**44.** (b)	**45.** (d)
46. (a)	**47.** (c)	**48.** (c)	**49.** (a)	**50.** (a)
51. (b)	**52.** (b)	**53.** (b)	**54.** (c)	**55.** (b)
56. (b)	**57.** (c)	**58.** (c)	**59.** (b)	**60.** (a)
61. (d)	**62.** (b)	**63.** (c)	**64.** (c)	**65.** (a)
66. (c)	**67.** (b)	**68.** (c)	**69.** (b)	**70.** (b)
71. (a)	**72.** (b)	**73.** (d)	**74.** (b)	**75.** (b)
76. (b)	**77.** (d)	**78.** (b)	**79.** (b)	**80.** (b)
81. (c)	**82.** (d)			

TYPE - 2 01 Mark

Assertion-Reason Type Questions

Directions (Q. Nos. 1-7) The following questions are Assertion-Reason based questions. Choose the answer based on the code given below

(a) Both Assertion (A) and Reason (R) are true and Reason (R) is a correct explanation of Assertion (A).
(b) Both Assertion (A) and Reason (R) are true and Reason (R) is not a correct explanation of Assertion (A).
(c) Assertion (A) is true and Reason (R) is false.
(d) Assertion (A) is false and Reason (R) is true.

Q.1 **Assertion (A)** In java statements written in lower case letter or upper case letter are treated as the same. **ICSE SQP 2024**

Reason (R) Java is a case sensitive language.

Q.2 **Assertion (A)** In Java, a method is a collection of statements that performs a specified task by directly modifying the data of the class.

Reason (R) A method in Java is used to define actions that operate on objects or data of a class.

Q.3 **Assertion (A)** Polymorphism in Java allows one object to take many forms based on the context.

Reason (R) The ability to make more than one method with same name enables polymorphism.

Q.4 **Assertion (A)** Data abstraction hides unnecessary details to simplify the system and expose essential functionality.

Reason (R) Data abstraction is achieved through the access specifier.

Q.5 **Assertion (A)** The Scanner class in Java is used for reading input data from various sources, including user input from the console.

Reason (R) The Scanner class can only read integer values from user input.

Q.6 **Assertion (A)** In switch case break statement avoids fall through. **ICSE 2025**

Reason (R) break statement helps to execute only one case at a time.

Q.7 **Assertion (A)** A clock is a real-life example of nested loops. **ICSE 2025**

Reason (R) The hour hand moves through 12 positions, while the minute hand moves through 60 positions within each hour.

Answers

1. (d) **2.** (d) **3.** (a) **4.** (a) **5.** (c)
6. (a) **7.** (a)

TYPE - 3 — 01 Mark

Odd One Out

Q.1 Choose the odd one. **ICSE 2022 (Sem I)**

(a) Robust (b) Platform Independent
(c) Inheritance (d) Multithreading

Q.2 Choose the odd one. **ICSE SQP 2022 (Sem I)**

(a) Encapsulation (b) Data abstraction
(c) Portable (d) Polymorphism

Q.3 Choose the odd one. **ICSE 2022 (Sem I)**

(a) > = (b) % (c) / (d) *

Q.4 Choose the odd one. **ICSE SQP 2022 (Sem I)**

(a) + (b) %
(c) / (d) ||

Q.5 Choose the odd one. **ICSE SQP 2022 (Sem I)**

(a) > (b) ==
(c) && (d) <

Q.6 Choose the odd one. **ICSE 2022 (Sem I); ICSE SQP 2022 (Sem I)**

(a) double (b) int
(c) char (d) String

Q.7 Choose the odd one. **ICSE SQP 2022 (Sem I)**

(a) return (b) break
(c) continue (d) System.exit(0)

Q.8 Choose the odd one. **ICSE 2022 (Sem I)**

(a) if else (b) if
(c) switch case (d) while( )

Answers

1. (c) **2.** (c) **3.** (a) **4.** (d) **5.** (c)
6. (d) **7.** (d) **8.** (d)

TYPE - 4 — 02 Marks

Short Answer Type Questions

Q.1 Name two types of Java programs.

Ans. Two types of Java programs are:

(i) Applets
(ii) Stand-alone applications

Q.2 Name any two basic principles of Object-Oriented Programming. **ICSE 2019**

Ans. Encapsulation, Data Abstraction, Polymorphism, Inheritance.

Q.3 Define abstraction. **ICSE 2018**

Or

What do you understand by the term data abstraction? Explain with an example.

Ans. Abstraction is a process of hiding the internal details or implementations from the user and showing only relevant or abstract(brief or short) information to user.

Example When we login to any social networking site like Facebook, Linkedin etc, we enter our user id and password and then we get logged in. Here we don't know how they are processing the data or what logic or algorithm they are using for login. Those informations are abstracted/hidden from us, since those are not essential for us. This is basically the abstraction.

Q.4 What is inheritance? **ICSE 2017**

Or

What is inheritance and how is it useful in Java?

Ans. Inheritance in Java is a cabability of one class (child class) inherit the properties of other class (parent class) in terms of parent class (superclass) and child class (subclass).

It helps in reusability in such a way that it adds some additional features to another class without modifying the contents of a parent class.

Q.5 Define encapsulation. **ICSE 2016**

Ans. Refer to text on page 2 (Encapsulation).

Q.6 State the Java concept that is implemented through

(i) a super class and a sub class.

(ii) the act of representing essential features without including background details. **ICSE 2013**

Ans. (i) Inheritance

(ii) Abstraction

Q.7 Define Java byte code. **ICSE 2020**

Ans. Java bytecode is the instruction set for the Java Virtual Machine (JVM). It's a platform-independent intermediate code generated by the Java compiler from Java source code. The JVM then executes this bytecode.

Q.8 What are literals? **ICSE SQP 2020; ICSE 2013**

Ans. Refer to text on page 3 (Literals).

Q.9 Identify and name the following tokens **ICSE 2019**

(i) public (ii) 'a' (iii) = = (iv) { }

Ans. (i) Keyword (ii) Literal

(iii) Operator (iv) Separator

Q.10 Name any four tokens of Java. **ICSE SQP 2017**

Ans. Four tokens in Java are

1. Keywords 2. Literals
3. Identifiers 4. Operators

Q.11 What is an identifier? **ICSE SQP 2017; ICSE 2015**

Ans. Refer to text on page 4 (Identifiers).

Q.12 Identify the literals listed below **ICSE 2015**

(i) 0.5 (ii) 'A' (iii) false (iv) "a"

Ans. (i) **0.5** is a double precision floating point literal.

(ii) **'A'** is a character literal.

(iii) **false** is a boolean literal.

(iv) **"a"** is a string literal.

Q.13 Explain the purpose of using a 'new' keyword in a Java program. **ICSE SQP 2020**

Ans. 'new' operator is used to create an instance of an object. It is also used to create an instance of a class.

Actually, it dynamically allocates memory in the heap with the reference, we define pointed from the stack.

e.g. `Myclass abc = new Myclass();`

Here, an instance of the class Myclass is created.

Q.14 Name the keyword which

(i) indicates that a method has no return type.

(ii) makes the variable as a class variable. **ICSE 2019**

Ans. (i) void (ii) static

Q.15 Name the following **ICSE 2017**

(i) A keyword used to call a package in the program.

(ii) Any one reference data type.

Ans. (i) import

(ii) class

Q.16 What are keywords? Give an example. **ICSE 2016**

Or

What does the token 'keyword' refer to, in the context of Java? Give an example for keyword. **ICSE 2011**

Ans. Keywords are special tokens which have reserved use in the language. It can not be used as identifier in Java and you can not declare a field whose name is keyword, for instance.

e.g. if, new, case, goto, int, etc.

Q.17 Name the Java keyword that

(i) indicates a method has no return type.

(ii) stores the address of the currently calling object. **ICSE 2013**

Ans. (i) The void keyword, it allows us to create functions that either do not require any parameters or do not return a value.

(ii) In Java, this keyword is a reference variable that refers to the current object.

Q.18 What is the use of the this keyword? **ICSE 2009**

Ans. The new keyword is used to create objects, which are instances of classes. It plays a crucial role in object creation and memory allocation.

Q.19 Name the following **ICSE 2020**

(i) The keyword which converts variable into constant.

(ii) The method which terminates the entire program from any stage.

Ans. (i) final (ii) System.exit()

Q.20 Name the operators listed below. **ICSE 2017**

(i) < (ii) + +

(iii) & & (iv) ? :

Ans. (i) < → Less than operator

(ii) + + → Postfix/Prefix Increment

(iii) & & → Logical AND Operator

(iv) ? : → Conditional Operator

Q.21 What is the value of x1 if x= 5? **ICSE 2017**

x1 = ++x − x++ + −− x

Ans. If x = 5

```
x1 = ++x - x +++ - - x
   = 6 - 6 + 6
x1 = 6
```

Q.22 int x=20, y=10, z; **ICSE SQP 2017**

What is the value of z in

z = ++x * (y– –) – y?

Show the steps.

Ans. z = ++x * (y - -) - y

⇒ z = 21 * 10 - y (given x=21, y=9)

⇒ z = 210 - 9

⇒ z = 201

Q.23 Evaluate the value of n if value of p = 5, q = 19 **ICSE 2015**

```
int n=(q–p)>(p–q)? (q–p):(p–q);
```

Ans. The value of n is 14.

Q.24 If int y = 10, then find int z = (+ +y * (y+ + +5)); **ICSE 2015**

Ans. int y = 10;

z = (++y * (y++ + 5);

= 11* (11+ 5)

= 11* 16 = 176

Q.25 Operators with higher precedence are evaluated before operators with relatively lower precedence. Arrange the operators given below in order of higher precedence to lower precedence. **ICSE 2014, ICSE SQP 2022 (sem 1)**

(i) && (ii) %

(iii) >= (iv) ++

Ans. The operators are arranged in order of higher to lower precedence.

(iv) ++ (ii) % (iii) >= (i) &&

Q.26 What is meant by precedence of operators? **ICSE 2013**

Ans. Refer to text on page 4-5 (Operator precedence/Hierarchy of operator).

Q.27 What will be the result stored in x after evaluating the following expression? **ICSE 2012**

```
int x=4;
x+=(x++)+(++x)+x;
```

Ans.

```
int x = 4;
x + = (x++) + (++x) + x;     [∴ left to right]
    = 4 + (4 + 6 + 6)
    = 4 + 16 = 20
```

Q.28 What are the value of x and y when the following statements are executed? **ICSE 2012**

```
int a=63, b=36;
boolean x=(a>b)?true:false;
int y=(a<b)?a:b;
```

Ans. The value of x = true, and

The value of y = 36

Q.29 If the value of basic = 1500, what will be the value of tax after the following statement is executed? **ICSE 2019**

```
tax = basic > 1200 ? 200 : 100;
```

Ans. tax = 200

Q.30 What is the result stored in x, after evaluating the following expression.

```
int x = 5;
    x =x++*2+3*––x;
```

Ans. The value of x is

x = x++ * 2 + 3 * ––x;

We know the value of x = 5,

So, = 5 * 2 + 3 * 5

= 10 + 15

= 25

Hence, x = 25

Q.31 What is the use and syntax of a ternary operator?

Ans. Ternary operator deals with three operands. It is also called conditional assignment statement because the value assigned to a variable depends upon the logical expression. The common use of ternary operator is in checking the condition.

Syntax

```
Variable = (test expression)?
Value 1: Value 2
```

Q.32 If a = 5, b = 9 calculate the value of

a+= a++ − ++b+a;

Ans. a+ = a++ − ++b + a (∵ left to right)

= a + (a++ − ++b + a)

= 5 + (5 − 10 + 6)

= 5 + 1= 6

The value of a after execution will be 6.

Q.33 What is the result produced by 2 – 10 * 3 + 100/11? Show the steps. **ICSE SQP 2017**

Ans. The result produced by 2- 10*3+100/11 are as follows:

= 2 − 30 + 9

= − 28 + 9

= − 19

Q.34 What is an operator? Name any two types of operators used in Java. **ICSE 2020**

Ans. An operator is a symbol that performs an operation on one or more operands. Two types of operators in Java are:

1. **Arithmetic Operators** Used for mathematical calculations (e.g., +, -, *, /, %).
2. **Assignment Operators** Used to assign values to variables (e.g., =, +=, -=, *=, /=, %=).

Q.35 Evaluate the following expressions, if the values of the variables are $a = 2$, $b = 3$ and $c = 9$

(i) $a - (b++) * (--c)$

(ii) $a * (++b) \% c$

Ans. (i) $2 - 3 \times 8 = 2 - 24 = -22$

(ii) $2 * 4 \% 9 = 8 \% 9 = 8$

Q.36 Evaluate the given expression when the value of a=2 and b=3 **ICSE SQP 2025**

```
b* = a + + − + + b + + + a;
System.out.println ("a= "+a);
System.out.println ("b= "+b);
```

Ans. 4, 6

Q.37 Evaluate the expression when the value of x = 2 **ICSE SQP 2024**

x = x ++ + ++ x + x

Ans. x=x++ + ++x + x

= 2 + 4 + 4 = 6 + 4 =10

Q.38 Evaluate the expression when x is 4

```
x + = x + + * + + x % 2;
```

Ans.

```
x+ = x++ * ++x %2;
x = 4 + 4 * 6 % 2
x = 4 + 4 * 0
x = 4 + 0
x = 4
```

Q.39 Write the memory capacity (storage size) of short and float data type in bytes. **ICSE 2019**

Ans. Short - 2 bytes

Float - 4 bytes

Q.40 Give one example each of primitive data type and composite data type. **ICSE 2012**

Ans. Primitive data type : char

Composite data type : class

Q.41 Assign the value of pie (i.e. 3.142) to a variable with requisite data type.

Ans. double pie = 3.142;

Here, for pie (3.142) the suitable data type is double because it can hold 64-bit floating point.

Q.42 What are the default values of the primitive data type int and float? **ICSE 2015**

Ans. Default value of primitive data type **int**=0

Default value of primitive data type **float**=0.0f

Q.43 Write the value of n after execution. **ICSE 2023**

```
char ch = 'd':
int n = ch + 5;
```

Ans. 105

Q.44 Classify the following as primitive or non-primitive data types: **ICSE 2018**

(i) char (ii) arrays

(iii) int (iv) classes

Ans. Primitive data types-(i) char (iii) int

Non-primitive data types-(ii) arrays (iv) classes

Q.45 List the variables from those given below that are composite data types

(i) `static int x;`

(ii) `arr [i] = 10;`

(iii) `obj.display( );`

(iv) `boolean b;`

(v) `private char chr;`

(vi) `String str;` **ICSE 2014**

Ans. Composite data types are as:

(i) arr[i] = 10;

(ii) obj.display( );

(vi) String str;

Q.46 Arrange the following primitive data types in an ascending order of their size: **ICSE 2019**

(i) char (ii) byte (iii) double (iv) int

Ans. byte, char, int, double

Q.47 Write an equivalent Java syntax for the following expression.

$$a = \frac{0.05 - 2y^3}{x - y}$$

ICSE 2007

Ans. $a = \frac{0.05 - 2y^3}{x - y}$

We can write this statement in Java like,

```
a = (0.05-2*y*y*y)/(x-y);
```

Q.48 Write a Java expression for the following **ICSE 2017**

$$ax^5 + bx^3 + c$$

Ans. Java expression for $ax^5 + bx^3 + c$

$= a * x * x * x * x * x + b * x * x * x + c$

Q.49 Write Java expression for **ICSE 2024**

$$\frac{|a + b|}{\sqrt{a^2 + b^2}}$$

Ans. The Java expression for:

```
Math.abs(a+b)/Math.sqrt(a*a+b*b);
```

Q.50 Evaluate the expression when x is 4 **ICSE 2024**

```
x + = x + + * + + x % 2;
```

Ans.

```
x+ = x++ * ++x %2;
x = 4 + 4 * 6 % 2
x = 4 + 4 * 0
x = 4 + 0
x = 4
```

Q.51 Write the Java expression for $(p + q)^2$. **ICSE SQP 2024**

Ans. `Math.pow ((p+q), 2)`

Q.52 Evaluate the expression when the value of x = 2

x = x ++ + ++ x + x

Ans. x=x++ + ++x + x

= 2 + 4 + 4 = 6 + 4 =10

Q.53 Write the Java expression for $\sqrt[3]{x} + \sqrt{y}$ **ICSE SQP 2025**

Ans. Math.cbrt(x) + Math.sqrt(y)

Q.54 Write the Java expression for $(a+b)^x$. **ICSE 2023**

Ans. `Math.pow((a + b),x);`

Q.55 Write Java expression for $|x^2 + xy|$. **ICSE SQP 2023**

Ans. `Math.abs (Math.pow (x, 2) + x * y);`

Q.56 Write a Java expression for the following **ICSE 2019**

$$|x^2 + 2xy|$$

Ans. `Math.abs(Math.pow(x, 2) + 2 * x * y);`

Q.57 Write a Java expression for the following

$$\frac{\sqrt{3x + x^2}}{a + b}$$ **ICSE 2018**

Ans. Java expression for $y = \frac{\sqrt{3x+x^2}}{a+b}$

```
y= (Math.sqrt(3*x+x*x))/(a + b);
```

Q.58 Write an expression in Java for $\cos x + \sqrt{a^2 + b^2}$. **ICSE SQP 2017**

Ans. `Math.cos (x) + Math.sqrt(Math.pow (a,2) + Math.pow (b,2));`

Q.59 Write down Java expression for **ICSE 2016**

$$T = \sqrt{A^2 + B^2 + C^2}$$

Ans. Java expression for $T = \sqrt{A^2 + B^2 + C^2}$ is

```
T = Math.sqrt ((Math.pow (A,2)) +
(Math.pow (B,2)) + (Math.pow (C,2)));
```

Q.60 Write the Java expression for $\frac{a^2 + b^2}{2ab}$ **ICSE 2015**

Ans. Java expression for $\frac{a^2 + b^2}{2ab}$

```
y = (a*a + b*b)/(2*a*b);
```

Q.61 Write the java expression to find the product of square root of *P* and the square root of *Q* using the methods of Math class. **ICSE 2025**

Ans. Math.sqrt(p)*Math.sqrt(Q)

Q.62 Evaluate the expression when the value of x = 4: **ICSE 2023**

```
x *= --x + x++ + x
```

Ans. The given expression is evaluated as follows:

x *= --x + x++ + x (x = 4)
x *= 3 + x++ + x (x = 3)
x *= 3 + 3 + x (x = 4)
x *= 3 + 3 + 4 (x = 4)
x *= 10 (x = 4)
x = x * 10 (x = 4)
x = 4 * 10
x = 40

Q.63 Evaluate the expression

```
Z+=a+++--b+++a+--b;
```

where a = 10, b = 5, z = 10 **ICSE SQP 2023**

Ans. Initially, a=10,b=5,Z=10.

Evaluating Z+=a+++--b+++a+--b:

1. a++ uses a=10, then a becomes 11.
2. --b decrements b to 4, uses 4.
3. ++a increments a to 12, uses 12.
4. --b decrements b to 3, uses 3.

So, Z=Z+(10+4+12+3)=10+29=39.

The final value of Z is 39.

Q.64 Write a statement in Java for $\sqrt{\frac{(a+b)^3}{|a-b|}}$ **ICSE SQP 2020**

Ans.
```
double result = Math.sqrt(Math.pow(a + b, 3) /
Math.abs(a - b));
```

Q.65 What is the value of m after evaluating the following expression **ICSE SQP 2020**

```
m-=9%++n+++n/2;
```

when int m = 10, n = 6

Ans. Initially, m=10 and n=6.

Evaluating m-=9%++n++n/2:

1. **++n** n becomes 7.
2. **9 % 7** evaluates to 2.
3. **++n** n becomes 8.
4. **8 / 2** evaluates to 4.

So, the expression becomes m-=2+4, which is m-=6.

Finally, m=m-6=10-6=4.

The value of m after evaluation is 4.

Q.66 Write a Java expression for the following $\sqrt{b^2 - 4ac}$ **ICSE 2020**

Ans. Math.sqrt(b * b - 4 * a * c)

Q.67 Evaluate the following if the value of x=7, y=5

```
x+=x+++x+++y
```

Ans. Given x=7 and y=5.

Evaluating x+=x+++x+++y:

1. **x++** Uses the current value of x (which is 7), then increments x to 8.
2. The expression now effectively is x+=7+x+++y. Here, x is currently 8.
3. **++y** Increments y to 6, and uses the new value 6.
4. The expression becomes x+=7+8+6.
5. 7+8+6=21.
6. x+=21 means x=x+21.
7. Since the current value of x is 8, x=8+21=29.

The final value of x is 29.

Q.68 Rewrite the following program segment using logical operators **ICSE 2020**

```
if (x > 5)
```

```
if (x > y)
System.out.println(x+y);
```

Ans.
```
if (x > 5 && x > y)
{
    System.out.println(x + y);
}
```

Q.69 Write a Java expression for $ut + \frac{1}{2}ft^2$. **ICSE 2013**

Ans. Expression for $ut + \frac{1}{2}ft^2$ = u * t + (1.0 / 2.0) * f * t * t

Q.70 State the value of n and ch.

```
char c='A';
int n=c+1;
char ch=(char) n;
```
ICSE 2012

Ans. Given, c = 'A'

∴ 'A' = 65

n = c + 1 = 65 + 1 = 66

The value of n = 66

ch = n

The value of ch = B [∵ B = 66]

Q.71 Write the value of n after execution. **ICSE 2023**

```
char ch = 'd':
int n = ch + 5;
```

Ans. 105

Q.72 What is the value stored in variable **res** given below:

```
double res = Math.pow ("345". indexOf('5'), 3);
```
ICSE 2015

Ans.
```
double res = Math.pow("345".indexOf('5'),3);
           = Math.pow(2, 3)
       res = 8.0
```

Q.73 Name the mathematical function which is used to find sine of an angle given in radians. **ICSE 2015**

Ans. `double sin(double angle radian);`

e.g. `double d = Math.sin((Math.PI)/2);`

`d =1.0`

Q.74 Give the output of the following **ICSE 2020**

(i) Math.pow (36,0.5) + Math.cbrt (125)

(ii) Math.ceil (4.2) + Math.floor (7.9)

Ans. (i) 11.0 (ii) 12.0

Q.75 What are the types of casting shown by the following examples? **ICSE 2016**

(i) `char c =(char) 120;`

(ii) `int x = 't';`

Ans. (i) Explicit Type Casting

(ii) Implicit Type Casting

Q.76 What do you mean by type conversion? How is implicit conversion different from explicit conversion? **ICSE 2010**

Or

Explain the terms of type casting.

Ans. Type conversion is changing a value from one data type to another type. Data type conversions are either implicit or explicit, it depends on the data capacities of the data type involved.

Difference between implicit and explicit conversion:

Implicit Conversion	Explicit Conversion
It is automatically type conversion.	It is completely defined within a program.
This method is used when upcasting is required like: int to long.	This method is used when downcasting is required like : double to byte.

Q.77 What are the types of casting shown by the following examples? **ICSE 2013**

(i)
```
double x = 15.2;
    int y = (int)x;
```

(ii)
```
int x  = 12;
long y = x;
```

Ans. (i) Explicit type casting, because here we want to assign x value into y, but x is double type variable and y is int type, so int is unable to hold the variable of double and when we required downcasting.

(ii) Implicit type casting, because we require upcasting here as int type is to be convert into long type.

Q.78 Mention two different styles of expressing a comment in a program.

Ans. In Java, two different styles of expressing a comment in a program:

(i) // for single line comment

(ii) /* comment */ for multiline comment.

Q.79 Name the methods of Scanner class that

(i) is used to input an integer data from the standard input stream.

(ii) is used to input a string data from the standard input stream. **ICSE 2013**

Ans. (i) int nextInt()

(ii) String nextLine()

Q.80 System.out.print("BEST "); **ICSE 2018**

System.out.println("OF LUCK");

Choose the correct option for the output of the above statements

(i) BEST OF LUCK

(ii) BEST
OF LUCK

Ans. The correct option for the output of the given statements

(i) BEST OF LUCK

Q.81 Complete the code below to create an object of Scanner class.

```
Scanner sc = ____ Scanner(____)
```

ICSE 2012

Ans. Scanner sc = new Scanner(System.in);

Q.82 State the package that contains the class: **ICSE 2015**

(i) BufferedReader (ii) Scanner

Ans. (i) **java.io** package contains the class BufferedReader.

(ii) **java.util** package contains the class Scanner.

Q.83 What is the purpose of default in a switch? **ICSE SQP 2017**

Or

Explain, with the help of an example, the purpose of default in a switch statement.

Ans. The purpose of default in a switch statement, is that, if no case value matches the switch expression value, then the default clause is executed.

e.g.
```
int ch=10;
switch(ch)
{
   case1:
     System.out.println("Its one");
     break;
   case2:
     System.out.println("Its two");
     break;
   default:
     System.out.println("Not working");
}
```

Output Not working

Q.84 The following is a segment of program

```
x=1; y=1;
if(n>0)
{
   x=x+1;
   y=y-1;
}
```

What will be the value of x and y, if n assumes a value (i) 1 (ii) 0?

Ans. (i) If, n assume as a value 1

```
x=1; y=1;
if(n>0)
{
   x=x+1;
   y=y-1;
}
```

Then, value of x=2, y=0

(ii) If, n assume as a value 0

```
x=1; y=1;
if(n>0)
{
   x=x+1;
   y=y-1;
}
```

Then, value of x=1 and y=1

Q.85 Explain, with an example, if-else-if construct.

Ans. if-else-if statement is a kind of statement, in which a number of logical conditions are checked for executing various statements.

e.g.
```
int x=30;
if(x==10)
{
   System.out.print("value of x is 10");
}
else if(x==20)
{
   System.out.print("value of x is 20");
}
else if(x==30)
{
   System.out.print("value of x is 30");
}
else
{
   System.out.print("This is else
                              statement");
}
```

Q.86 The following code segment should print "You can go out" if you have done your homework (dh) and cleaned your room(cr). However, the code has errors.

Fix the code so that it compiles and runs correctly. **ICSE SQP 2024**

```
boolean dh=True;
boolean cr=true;
if (dh && cr)
System.out.println("You cannot go out");
else
System.out.println ("You can go out");
```

Ans.
```
boolean dh = true;
boolean cr = true;
if (dh && cr)
{
  System.out.println("You can go out");
}
else
{
  System.out.println("You cannot go out");
}
```

Q.87 Find the errors in the given program segment and rewrite the statements correctly to assign values to an integer array. **ICSE 2014**

```
int a = new int(5);
for(int i=0; i<=5; i++) a[i]=i;
```

Ans. The corrected code is

```
int[] a = new int[5];
for(int i=0; i<5; i++)
{
    a[i] = i;
}
```

Q.88 A student executes the following program segment and gets an error. Identify the statement which has an error, correct the same to get the output as WIN. **ICSE SQP 2025**

```
boolean x = true;
switch(x)
{
  case 1: System.out.println("WIN");
  break;
  case 2: System.out.println ("LOOSE");
}
```

Ans. Statement with error – boolean x = true; To get the required output – int x = 1;

Q.89 How many times will the following loop execute? What value will be returned? **ICSE 2013, ICSE SQP 2024**

```
int x=2, y=50;
do
{
   ++x;
   y -= x++;
}
while(x <= 10);
return y;
```

Ans. Initially, x=2, y=50

x	y	++x	y – = x++ ⇒y = y - x++	x <= 10	return y
2	50	3	y = 50 – 3 = 47 Now, x = 4	4 <= 10	47
4	47	5	y = 47 – 5 = 42 Now, x = 6	6 <= 10	42
6	42	7	y = 42 – 7 = 35 Now, x = 8	8 <= 10	35
8	35	9	y = 35 – 9 = 26 Now, x = 10	10 <= 10	26
10	26	11	y = 26 – 11 = 15 Now, x = 12	12 <= 10 (false)	15

Loop will execute 5 times and return the value of y = 15.

Q.90 What is the final value of ctr where the iteration process given below, executes? **ICSE 2013**

```
int ctr=0;
for(int i=1; i<=5; i++)
for(int j=1; j<=5; j+=2)
++ctr;
```

Ans. The final value of ctr = 15

Q.91 Give the output of the following code and mention how many times the loop will execute? **ICSE 2019**

```
int i;
for (i = 5; i >= 1; i--)
{
    if(i% 2 == 1)
    continue;
    System.out.print(i + '' '');
}
```

Ans. Output 4 2

loop will execute five times.

Q.92 Give the output of the following program segment and also mention the number of times the loop is executed **ICSE 2017**

```
int a,b;
for(a=6, b=4; a<=24; a=a+6)
{
   if(a%b==0)
      break;
}
System.out.println(a);
```

Ans. Output 12

Number of times the loop is executed = 2

Q.93 Analyze the given program segment and answer the following questions

```
for(int i=3; i<=4; i++)
{
   for(int j=2; j<i; j++)
   {
      System.out.print(" ");
   }
   System.out.println("WIN");
}
```

(i) How many times does the inner loop execute?

(ii) Write the output of the program segment. **ICSE 2017**

Ans.(i) The inner loop will execute 3 times.

(ii) **Output**

WIN
WIN

Q.94

```
int i=1;
while(i++<=1)
{
     i++;
     System.out.print(i+" ");
}
System.out.print(i);
```

What will be the output of the following code? **ICSE SQP 2017**

Ans. Output 3 4

Q.95 Analyse the given program segment and answer the following questions **ICSE 2016**

```
for(int m=5; m<=20; m+ =5)
{
   if(m%3= =0)
      break;
   else
      if(m%5==0)
```

```
            System.out.println(m);
        continue;
    }
```

(i) Write the output of the program segment

(ii) How many times does the body of the loop get executed?

Ans. (i) **Output**

5

10

(ii) Three times the body of the loop will be executed.

Q.96 Write the output of the following program code: **ICSE 2015**

```
char ch;
int x = 97;
do
{
   ch = (char)x;
   System.out.print(ch+" ");
   if (x%10==0)
    break;
   --x;
}
while(x<=100);
```

Ans. Output a b c d

Q.97 What is an infinite loop? Write an infinite loop statement. **ICSE 2014, 08**

Ans. Infinite loop is that in which iteration never stops. This is because, condition output is always true, loop continues for an infinite number of times. e.g. entry control loop.

Statement

```
int a=0;
for(a=10; a>0; a++)
{
 System.out.println("The value of a="+a);
}
```

In the above example, the 'for' loop will check condition first and as the initial values of a (i.e. 10) is greater than 0 so it will execute once.

Next time, the loop will increase the value of a by 1 and the condition will again evaluated.

This process will be repeated again and again and the loop will execute infinite times.

Q.98 Analyse the following program segment and determine how many times the loop will be executed and what will be the output of the program segment?

```
int k=1, i=2;
while(++i<6)
{
   k* = i;
}
System.out.println(k);
```

ICSE 2010

Ans. int k=1, i=2

++i < 6	k *= i	k
3 < 6 (True)	$k = k \times i = 1 \times 3 = 3$	3
4 < 6 (True)	$k = 3 \times 4 = 12$	12
5 < 6 (True)	$k = 12 \times 5 = 60$	60

The value of k=60

The loop will be executed 3 times.

Q.99 Analyse the following program segment and determine how many times the body of loop will bẹ executed (show the working). **ICSE 2009**

```
x=5; y=50;
while(x<=y)
{
   y = y/x;
   System.out.println(y);
}
```

Ans.

Value of x and y	(x <= y)	y = y/x;
5 and 50	5 <= 50 (True)	y = 50/5; y = 10
5 and 10	5 <= 10 (True)	y = 10/5; y = 2
5 and 2	5 <= 2 (False)	Exit the loop

Thus, loop will execute 2 times and now value of y = 2.

Q.100 How many times the following loop will gets executed? What is the output of the same? **ICSE SQP 2023**

```
int counter=1;
do
{
 System.out.println(counter);
}
while (counter++<5);
```

Ans. Output

1

2

3

4

Q.101 What is an infinite loop? Give an example. **ICSE 2020**

Ans. An infinite loop is a loop whose condition for termination is never met, causing it to execute indefinitely.

Example

```
while (true)
```

```
{
 System.out.println("This will print
                              forever.");
}
```

Q.102 How many times will the following loop execute? Write the output of the code: **ICSE SQP 2025**

```
int x = 10;
while (true)
{
 System.out.println(x++*2);
 if(x%3==0)
   break;
}
```

Ans. Output

20
22
24

Q.103 Name any two jump statements.

Ans. break, continue

Q.104 Name two jump statements and their use. **ICSE 2010**

Or

Explain the function of each of the following with an example.

(i) break; (ii) continue;

Or

Explain the meaning of break and continue statement.

Ans. Two jump statements :

(i) A **break statement** terminates the current loop and proceeds to the first statement that follows the loop.

e.g.

```
for(int i=2; i<n; i++)
{
  if=(n%1==0)
  System.out.println(n);
  break;
}
```

(ii) A **continue statement** transfers the control to the next iteration leaving all the other statement unexecuted that follows after the continue statement.

e.g.

```
for(int i=1; i<20; i++)
{
  if(i%2==0)
     continue;
  System.out.println(i);
}
```

The above loop will print all the odd numbers.

Q.105 State the type of errors if any in the following statements: **ICSE SQP 2020**

(i) switch (n > 2)

(ii) System.out.println(100/0);

Ans. (i) **Syntax Error** The expression of switch statement must resolve to byte, short, int, char or String. It cannot resolve to a boolean type so this statement will result in a syntax error.

(ii) **Runtime Error/Exception(Division by Zero)** The program will compile successfully but when this line is executed it will result in "division by zero" error as dividing any number by 0 is an invalid division operation.

Q.106 Name the type of errors (syntax, runtime or logical error) in each case given below: **ICSE 2012**

(i) Division by a variable that contains a value of zero.

(ii) Multiplication operator used when the operation should be division.

(iii) Missing semicolon.

Ans. (i) runtime error (ii) logical error

(iii) syntax error

Q.107 Name the type of error (syntax, run time or logical error) in each case given below: **ICSE 2016**

(i) Math.sqrt(36-45) (ii) int a;b;c;

Ans. (i) Runtime error (ii) Syntax error

Q.108 Sam executes the following program segment and the answer displayed is zero irrespective of any non-zero values are given. Name the error. How the program can be modified to get the correct answer? **ICSE SQP 2024**

```
void triangle(double b, double h)
{
 double a;
 a = ½ * b * h;
 System.out.println("Area="+a);
}
```

Ans. In the modified code, 0.5 is used instead of ½ to correctly calculate the area of the triangle.

Q.109 What is the function of catch block in exception handling? Where does it appear in a program? **ICSE 2015**

Ans. The main function of catch block is to handle the exception that is thrown by try block. It catches the exception into the object of same type that is specified in the argument of catch function definition. It is also used to represent the notification and causes during which exception raises. It appears after try block in the program.

Q.110 John was asked to write a Java code to calculate the surface area of a cone, the following code was written by him: **ICSE 2025**

Surface area of cone is $A = \pi r l$

$$l = \sqrt{r^2 + h^2}$$

```
class area
```

```
{
  double area (double r, double h)
  {
     double l, a;
     a=22.0/7*r*l;
     l=Math.sqrt(r*r+h*h);
     return a;
  }
}
```

Specify the type of the error in the above program, correct and write the program to be error free.

Ans.

```
class area
{
   double surfaceArea(double r, double h)
   {
      double l = Math.sqrt(r * r + h * h);
      // Correct slant height calculation
      return Math.PI * r * (r + l);
      // Correct total surface area formula
   }
}
```

Q.111 What are the various types of errors in Java? **ICSE 2019**

Ans. There are 3 types of errors in java

1. Syntax Error
2. Runtime Error
3. Logical Error

TYPE - 5 — 02 Marks

Differentiate

Q.1 Differentiate between base class and derived class. **ICSE 2008**

Ans. Difference between base class and derived class are as follows :

Base Class	Derived Class
A base class facilitates the creation of other class.	Derived classes use the functionality of base class.
It is also known as parent/super class.	It is also known as child/sub class.

Q.2 State the difference between token and identifier. **ICSE 2008**

Ans. Difference between token and identifier are as follows

Token	Identifier
It is the smallest element in a program that is meaningful to the compiler.	These are the names of variable, method, class, package, interface, etc.
These define the structure of the language. e.g. keyword, literal etc.	These are used to uniquely identify them to the compiler. e.g. 123ab, __ salary etc.

Q.3 State one difference between the floating point literals float and double. **ICSE 2014**

Ans. Difference between floating point literals float and double are as follows

Float Literals	Double Literals
The float literal has a limited range to store decimal data item. It can hold 32-bit data.	The double literal has a wider range as compared to float, to store decimal data items. It can hold 64-bit data.

Q.4 State the difference between a boolean literal and character literal. **ICSE 2009**

Ans. Difference between boolean literal and character literal are as follows

Boolean Literal	Character Literal
Boolean literal consists of the keyword true and false.	Character literal is expressed by a single character.
Boolean literal are never enclosed within quotes. e.g. true, false	A character literal constant enclosed within single quotes. e.g. 'A' ,'d', '*', etc.

Q.5 Differentiate between = and = = operators. **ICSE SQP 2020**

Ans. Difference between = and == operator:

= operator	= = operator
It is assignment operator.	It is relational (binary) operator.
It is used to assign a value to any variable. e.g. x = 10;	It compares two object, based on memory reference. e.g. (A = = B)

Q.6 What is the difference between / and % operator? **ICSE 2017, 11**

Ans. Difference between / and % operator are as follows

/ Operator	% Operator
This is a division operator.	This is a modulus operator.
It is used to find the remainder of division of two numbers.	It is used to find the quotient in the division of two numbers.
e.g. int x = 10, y = 5, z; x = x/y; value of z will be 2.	e.g. int x = 10, y = 5, z; z = x%y; value of z will be 0.

Q.7 Differentiate between operator and expression.

Ans. Differences between operator and expression:

Operator	Expression
Operators are special symbols used for mathematical or logical function.	An expression is a statement that can convey a value.
Generally, these are used between two operands. e.g. x + y here + is an operator.	It may be any combination of variables, literals, operators. e.g. a = b + c is an expression.

Q.8 What is the difference between the Scanner class functions next() and nextLine()? **ICSE 2017**

Ans. Differences between the Scanner class functions next() and nextLine() are as follows

next( )	**nextLine( )**
next( ) can read the input only till the space.	nextLine( ) reads input including space between the words.
next( ) only gets up to the next space.	nextLine( ) gets to the line break.

Q.9 Differentiate between if-else-if and switch case statements. **ICSE 2019**

Ans. Differences between if-else-if and switch case statement are as follows

if-else-if	**switch case**
Range of values are checked.	Only one value is compared.
Supports both primitive and composite data types.	Supports only integer (byte, short, int, long), char.
Relational/Logical expressions can be checked.	Only equality can be checked.

Q.10 Differentiate between if and switch statements.

Ans. Difference between if and switch statement are as follows

if Statement	**switch Statement**
It works under the boolean literals.	It works under the integer/character literals.
It uses relational operator for check conditions.	It uses 'case' for check conditions.

Q.11 Differentiate between break and System.exit(0). **ICSE SQP 2020**

Ans. Differences between break and System.exit(0) are as follows

break	**System.exit(0)**
break statement is used to jump out from the loop or switch-case.	System.exit(0) terminates the entire program.
break is a keyword.	System.exit(0) is a method provided by Java standard library.

Q.12 What is the difference between a break statement and a continue statement when they occur in a loop? **ICSE 2013**

Ans. Difference between break and continue statement are as follows

break Statement	**continue Statement**
When break is executed, the statements following break are skipped and cause the loop to be terminated.	When continue statement is executed, the statements following continue are skipped and cause the loop to be continued with the next iteration.

e.g.`for(i=1; i<=5; i++)`
`{if(i%2==0) break;`
`System.out.print(i);`
`}`
	e.g.`for(i=1; i<=5; i++)`
	`{`
	`if(i%2==0) continue;`
	`System.out.print(i);`
	`}`

Output 1	**Output** 1 3 5

Q.13 What is the difference between local variable and instance variable? **ICSE SQP 2017**

Ans. Difference between local variable and instance variable are as follows

Feature	**Local Variable**	**Instance Variable**
Declaration	Inside a method, constructor, or block.	In a class, outside any method, constructor, or block.
Scope/Lifetime	Exists only within the block of declaration.	Exists for the lifetime of the object.

TYPE - 6 02 Marks

Rewrite/Convert the Code

Q.1 Rewrite the following code using the if-else statement. **ICSE 2023**

```
int m=400;
double ch=(m>300) ? (m/10.0)*2:(m/20.0)-2:
```

Ans.

```
int m = 400;
if (m > 300)
    double ch = (m / 10.0) * 2;
else
    double ch = (m / 20.0) - 2;
```

Q.2 Rewrite the following program segment using if-else statements instead of the ternary operator. **ICSE 2014**

```
String
grade=(mark>=90)?"A":(mark>=80)?"B":"C";
```

Ans. Program segment using if-else statements

```
if(mark>=90)
{
    String grade="A";
}
else
{
    if(mark>=80)
    {
        String grade="B";
    }
    else
    {
        String grade="C";
    }
}
```

Q.3 Rewrite the following program segment using the if-else statement. **ICSE 2013**

```
comm=(sale>15000) ? sale*5/100:0;
```

Ans. Program segment using the if-else statement

```
if(sale>15000)
{
    comm=(sale*5)/100;
}
else
{
    comm=0;
}
```

Q.4 Rewrite the following using ternary operators **ICSE SQP 2023**

```
if( x > y)
    c= 'A';
else
    c = 'a';
```

Ans. c = (x > y)? 'A' : 'a';

Q.5 Rewrite the following condition without using logical operators. **ICSE SQP 2020**

```
if( a>b || a>c) .
System.out.println(a);
```

Ans. Condition without using logical operators:

```
if (a > b)
    System.out.println(a);
else if (a > c)
    System.out.println(a);
```

Q.6 Rewrite the following using ternary operator **ICSE 2018**

```
if (bill >10000 )
   discount = bill * 10.0/100;
else
   discount = bill * 5.0/100;
```

Ans. Using ternary operator

```
discount =  bill >10000? (bill*10.0/100):
(bill*5.0/100);
```

Q.7 Rewrite the following using ternary operator **ICSE 2016**

```
if (x% 2 = = 0)
   System.out.print("EVEN");
else
   System.out.print("ODD");
```

Ans. Using ternary operator

```
System.out.println ((x%2 = = 0)? "EVEN":
"ODD")
```

Q.8 Rewrite the following using ternary operator **ICSE 2007**

```
if(income<=10000)
   tax=0;
else
   tax=12;
```

Ans. tax=income < = 10000 ? 0 : 12;

Q.9 Rewrite the following code using single if statement. **ICSE SQP 2025**

```
if (code= = 'g')
  System.out.println ("GREEN");
else if (code=='G')
  System.out.println ("GREEN ");
```

Ans.

```
if (code = = 'g'||code = = 'G')
    System.out.println("GREEN");
```

Q.10 Rewrite the following while loop using for loop **ICSE SQP 2023**

```
int x = 5;
while ( x < = 5)
{
    x++;
}
System.out.println(x);
```

Ans.

```
int x;
for(x = 5; x <= 5; x++);
System.out.println(x);
```

Q.11 Rewrite the following loop using for loop. **ICSE SQP 2020**

```
while (true)
System.out.print("*");
```

Ans.

```
for (;;)
{
    System.out.print("*");
}
```

Q.12 Rewrite the following *do while* program segment using for **ICSE 2024**

```
x = 10;  y = 20;
    do
    {
        x + +;
        y + +;
    } while (x < = 20);
    System.out.println(x * y) ;
```

Ans.

```
int x = 10;
int y = 20;
for (; x <= 20; x++, y++)
{
}
System.out.println(x * y);
```

Q.13 Rewrite the following program segment using while instead of for statement **ICSE 2012**

```
int f=1, i;
for(i=1; i<=5; i++)
{
   f*=i;
   System.out.println(f);
}
```

Ans.
```
int f=1, i;
while(i<=5)
{
    f*=i;
    System.out.println(f);
    i++;
}
```

Q.14 Rewrite the following using ternary operator. **ICSE 2020**
```
if(n1 > n2)
 r=true;
else
 r=false;
```
Ans. boolean r = (n1 > n2) ? true : false;

Q.15 Convert the given loop into exit controlled loop. **ICSE 2025**
```
int a,b;
for (a=10,b=1; a>=1;a- =2)
{
  b+ =a;
  b+ +;
}
System.out.print(b);
```
Ans.
```
int a, b;
a = 10;
b = 1;
do
{
  b = b + a;
  b++;
  a -= 2;
} while (a > = 1);
System.out.println(b);
```

Q.16 Convert the following if else if construct into switch case **ICSE 2020**
```
if (ch =='c' || ch=='C')
System.out.print("COMPUTER");
else if (ch=='h' || ch=='H')
System.out.print("HINDI");
else
System.out.print("PHYSICAL EDUCATION");
```
Ans.
```
switch (ch)
{
    case 'c':
    case 'C':
        System.out.print("COMPUTER");
        break;
    case 'h':
    case 'H':
        System.out.print("HINDI");
        break;
    default:
        System.out.print("PHYSICAL EDUCATION");
}
```

Q.17 Convert the following if else if construct into switch case **ICSE 2018**
```
if (var == 1)
{
   System.out.println("good");
}
else if (var == 2)
{
   System.out.println("better");
}
else if (var == 3)
{
   System.out.println("best");
}
else
{
   System.out.println("invalid");
}
```
Ans.
```
switch (var)
{
    case 1:
        System.out.println("good");
        break;
    case 2:
        System.out.println("better");
        break;
    case 3:
        System.out.println("best");
        break;
    default:
        System.out.println("invalid");
        break;
}
```

Q.18 Convert the following do … while loop to for loop **ICSE 2023**
```
int x=10;
do
{x– –;
System.out.print(x);
}while (x>=1):
```
Ans.
```
int x;
for(x=10; x >= 1; x--)
System.out.println(x);
```

Q.19 Convert the following while loop of the corresponding for loop **ICSE 2016**
```
int m = 5, n = 10;
while(n>=1)
{
   System.out.println(m*n);
   n - - ;
}
```
Ans.
```
int m= 5;
for (int n= 10; n>= 1; n--)
{
   System.out.println (m * n);
}
```

Q.20 Convert the following segment into equivalent for loop **ICSE 2008**

```
int i=0;
while(i<=20)
{
   System.out.print(i+ " ");
   i++;
}
```

Ans. Program in for loop

```
for(int i=0; i<=20; i++)
{
   System.out.print(i+ " ");
```

Q.21 Convert the following segment into an equivalent do-while loop **ICSE 2009**

```
int x, c;
for(x=10, c=20; c>=10; c=c-2)
x++;
```

Ans. do-while loop segment

```
int x, c;
x=10; c=20;
do
{
    x++;
    c = c-2;
}
while(c >= 10);
```

TYPE - 7 — 02 Marks

Output Based Questions

Q.1 What will be the output of the following code?

```
int k = 5, j = 9;
k+=k++ - ++j+k;
System.out.println("k ="+k);
System.out.println("j ="+j);
```

ICSE 2011

Ans. k + = (k++) − (++j) + k;

= k + (k++ − ++j + k); [∴ left to right]

= 5 + (5 − 10 + 6);

k = 6

Hence, k = 6, j = 10

Q.2 Find the output of the following program segment, when

(i) val= 500

(ii) val=1600

```
int val, sum, n = 550;
sum = n +val>1750?400:200;
System.out.println(sum);
```

Ans. (i) When, val = 500, n = 550

Sum = n+val > 1750 ? 400 : 200;

= 550 + 500 > 1750 ? 400 : 200;

= 1050 > 1750 ? 400 : 200;

Sum = 200

(ii) When, val = 1600, n = 550

Sum = n + val > 1750 ? 400 : 200;

= 550 + 1600 > 1750 ? 400 : 200;

= 2150 > 1750 ? 400 : 200;

Sum = 400

Q.3 What will be the output for the following program segment?

```
int a=0, b=30,c=40;
a=--b + c + ++b;
System.out.println("a ="+ a);
```

Ans. int a = 0, b = 30, c = 40;

a = −−b + c + ++b (∵ left to right)

= 29 + 40 + 30 = 99

Q.4 What will be the output of the following, if x = 5 initially?

(i) 5*++x;

(ii) 5*x++;

Ans. Given, x = 5

(i) 5 * ++x;
5 * 6 = 30

(ii) 5 * x++;
5 * 5 = 25

Q.5 If m = 5 and n = 2, output the values of m and n after execution in (i) and (ii)

(i) m −= n;

(ii) $n = m + \frac{m}{n}$;

Ans. Given, m = 5, n = 2

(i) m−= n; m = m − n = 5 − 2 ⇒ m = 3

(ii) $n = m + \frac{m}{n} = 5 + \frac{5}{2} = 5 + 2$

n = 7

Hence, m = 3, n = 7

Q.6 What is the output of the following?

```
char c='A';
short m=26;
int n=c+m;
System.out.println(n);
```

Ans. char c = 'A' (∴ We know 'A' = 65)

short m = 26

int n = c + m = 65 + 26 = 91

Output 91

Q.7 Write the output **ICSE 2017**

```
char ch='F';
int m=ch;
m=m+5;
System.out.println(m+" "+ch);
```

Ans. When ch = F [∵ F = 70]

m = ch

m = 70

m = m + 5 = 70 + 5 = 75

Output = 75F

Q.8 Give the output of the following expression **ICSE 2016**

a+ = a ++ + ++ a + -- a +a -- ; when a =7

Ans. When a = 7

a+ = a++ ++ +a + -- a + a --

= a+[(a++] + (++a) + (--a) + (a—)]

= 7 + [7 + 9 + 8 + 8]

= 7 + 32 = 39

Q.9 Give the output of the following. **ICSE 2019**

```
Math.sqrt(Math.max (9, 16));
```

Ans. 4.0

Q.10 What will be the output of the following code? **ICSE SQP 2017**

```
float x = 7.87;
System.out.println(Math.ceil(x));
System.out.println(Math.floor(x));
```

Ans. Output 8.0

7.0

Q.11 Give the output of the following Math functions: **ICSE 2016**

(i) Math.ceil(4.2)

(ii) Math.abs(-4)

Ans. Output

(i) 5 (ii) 4

Q.12 Give the output of the following: **ICSE 2018**

(i) Math.floor (-4.7)

(ii) Math.ceil(3.4) + Math.pow(2, 3)

Ans. Output

(i) – 5.0 (ii) 12.0

Q.13 Predict output of the following **ICSE SQP 2020**

(i) Math.pow(25, 0.5)+Math.ceil(4.2)

(ii) Math.round (14.7) + Math.floor (7.9)

Ans. (i) 10.0

(ii) 22.0

Q.14 Write the output for the following **ICSE 2018**

```
System.out.println("Incredible"+"\n" +"world");
```

Ans. Output

Incredible
world

Q.15 What is the output of the following **ICSE SQP 2020**

```
String a ="Java is programming language
\n developed by \t\'James Gosling\'";
System.out.println(a);
```

Ans. Java is programming language
developed by "James Gosling"

Q.16 Write the output of the following statement:

```
System.out.println("A picture is worth
\t\"A thousand words.\" ");
```

ICSE 2020

Ans. A picture is worth "A thousand words."

Q.17 What will be the output of the following code? **ICSE SQP 2017**

```
int a = 0;
if(a>0 && a <20)
    a++;
else a-- ;
    System.out.println(a);
```

Ans. Output – 1

Q.18 What will be the output of the following code? **ICSE SQP 2017**

```
int a=5, b=2, c;
if (a>b || a ! = b)
c = ++a+--b;
System.out.print(c+" "+a+" "+b);
```

Ans. Output 7 6 1

Q.19 Give the output of the following code fragment **ICSE 2009**

when (i) opn = 'b' (ii) opn = 'x'

(iii) opn = 'a'

```
switch(opn)
{
   case 'a':
      System.out.println("Platform
                           Independent");
      break;
   case 'b':
      System.out.println("Object
                           Oriented");
   case 'c':
      System.out.println("Robust and
                           Secure");
      break;
   default:
      System.out.println("Wrong Input");
}
```

Ans (i) opn='b'

When opn = 'b' it reach on case 'b'. Then print the value:

Object Oriented

Robust and Secure

(ii) opn='x'

When opn = 'x' it check all case but no one is equivalent to x, so it reach in default segment and print the value :

Wrong Input

(iii) opn='a'

When opn = 'a' it found case 'a'. Then enter in that case and print value:

Platform Independent

Q.20 Give the output of the following program segment. **ICSE 2023**

```
int n = 4279; int d;
while(n>0)
{d=n%10;
    System.out.println(d);
    n=n/100;
}
```

Ans. 92

Q.21 Give the output of the following code and mention how many times the loop will execute? **ICSE 2019**

```
int i;
for (i = 5; i >= 1; i--)
{
    if(i% 2 == 1)
    continue;
    System.out.print(i + '' '');
}
```

Ans. **Output** 4 2

loop will execute five times.

Q.22 Give the output of the following program segment and also mention, how many times the loop is executed? **ICSE 2018**

```
int i;
for ( i = 5 ; i > 10; i ++ )
System.out.println( i );
System.out.println( i * 4 );
```

Ans. **Output**

20

0 time the loop will be executed.

Q.23 Give the output of the following program segment and also mention the number of times the loop is executed **ICSE 2017**

```
int a,b;
for(a=6, b=4; a<=24; a=a+6)
{
    if(a%b==0)
        break;
}
System.out.println(a);
```

Ans. **Output** 12

Number of times the loop is executed = 2

Q.24

```
int i=1;
while(i++<=1)
{
    i++;
    System.out.print(i+" ");
}
System.out.print(i);
```

What will be the output of the following code? **ICSE SQP 2017**

Ans. **Output** 3 4

Q.25 Write the output of the following program code: **ICSE 2015**

```
char ch;
int x = 97;
do
{
   ch = (char)x;
   System.out.print(ch+" ");
   if (x%10==0)
    break;
   --x;
}
while(x<=100);
```

Ans. **Output** a b c d

Q.26 What will be the output of the following code? **ICSE 2010**

(i)
```
int m = 2;
int n = 15;
for(int i=1;i<5; i++)
  m++;
--n;
System.out.println("m ="+m);
System.out.println("n ="+n);
```

(ii)
```
char x='A'
int m;
m = (x=='a'?'A':'a');
System.out.println("m ="+m);
```

Ans (i) m = 6, n = 14 (ii) m = 97

Q.27 Give the output of the following program segment. How many times is the loop executed? **ICSE 2024**

```
for (x = 10; x > 20; x + +)
System.out.println (x);
System.out.println (x * 2);
```

Ans. Output of the program will be 20.

The loop is not executed at all.

So, the loop is executed 0 times.

Q.28 How many times will the following loop execute? What value will be returned?

```
int x=2;
int y=50;
do
{
 ++x;
 y-=x++;
}
while(x<=10);
return y;
```

Ans. The loop executed 5 times.

The final value of y returned by the program will be 15.

Q.29 How many times will the following loop execute? Write the output of the code:

```
int x = 10;
while (true)
```

```
{
  System.out.println (x++*2);
  if (x%3==0)
  break;
}
```

Ans. Loop is executed two times

20

22

Q.30 Give the output of the following program segment and mention how many times the loop will execute? **ICSE 2020**

```
int k;
for (k = 5; k < = 20; k + = 7)
if (k%6==0)
continue;
System.out.println(k);
```

Ans. Output

5

19

TYPE - 8 — 15 Marks

Long Answer Type Questions

Q.1 Write a program to accept a number and check and display whether it is a **Niven** number or not.

(Niven number is that number which is divisible by its sum of digits).

Example

Consider the number 126.

Sum of its digits is 1+ 2 + 6 = 9 and 126 is divisible by 9.

Ans.

```
import java. io.*;
public class Niven
{
    public static void main(String args[])
                                    throws IOException
    {
        BufferedReader br = new BufferedReader(new
        InputStreamReader(System.in));
        System.out.println("Enter any number");
        int num=Integer.parseInt(br.readLine());
        int t=num,sum = 0,f;
        while(t>0)
        {
            f=t%10;
            sum=sum+f;
            t=t/10;
        }
        if(num%sum = = 0)
            System.out.println("Entered number is
                                    a Niven number");
        else
            System.out.println("Entered number is
                                    not a Niven number");
    }
}
```

Q.2 Write a program to input a number and check and print whether it is a **Pronic** number or not. (Pronic number is the number which is the product of two consecutive integers) **ICSE 2018**

Examples : 12 = 3 × 4
20 = 4 × 5
42 = 6 × 7

Ans.

```
import java.util.*;
class PronicNumber
{
  public static void main (String args[])
  {
    Scanner sc = new Scanner(System.in);
    System.out.print("Enter a number:");
    int n=sc.nextInt();
    int flag = 0;
    for(int i=0; i<n; i++)
    {
      if(i*(i+1)==n)
      {
        flag = 1;
        break;
      }
    }
    if (flag==1)
    System.out.println (n+"is a Pronic
                                Number.");
    else
    System.out.println (n+"is not a
                            Pronic Number.");
  }
}
```

Q.3 Using if/else statement, write a program to perform following operations **ICSE SQP 2020**

(i) To print the value of Z, where $Z = \frac{x^3 + 0.5x}{Y}$, where x ranges from – 10 to 10 with an increment of 2 and Y remains constant at 5.5.

(ii) To print the Floyds triangle with N rows

Example: If N = 5,

Output

```
1
2  3
4  5  6
7  8  9  10
11 12 13 14 15
```

Ans.

```
import java.util.Scanner;
public class OperationsProgram
{
    public static void main(String[] args)
```

```
        {
            Scanner sc = new Scanner(System.in);
            System.out.println("Choose operation:");
            System.out.println("1. Calculate Z =
                                (x³ + 0.5x) / y");
            System.out.println("2. Print Floyd's
                                    Triangle");
            int choice = sc.nextInt();
            if (choice == 1)
             {
                double y = 5.5;
                for (int x = -10; x <= 10; x += 2)
                {
                    double z = (Math.pow(x, 3) +
                                    0.5 * x) / y;
                    System.out.printf("x = %d,
                            Z = %.2f\n", x, z);
                }
            }
            else if (choice == 2)
            {
                System.out.print("Enter number
                                of rows (N): ");
                int n = sc.nextInt();
                int num = 1;
                for (int i = 1; i <= n; i++)
                {
                    for (int j = 1; j <= i; j++)
                    {
                      System.out.print(num + " ");
                      num++;
                    }
                    System.out.println();
                }
            }
            else
            {
              System.out.println("Invalid
                                    choice.");
            }
        }
    }
```

Q.4 Using the if-else statement, write a program for the following:

(a) To print the Floyd's triangle [Given below]

1
2 3
4 5 6
7 8 9 10
11 12 13 14 15

(b) To display the following pattern

I
I C
I C S
I C S E

For an incorrect option, an appropriate error message should be displayed.

Ans.
```
import java.util.Scanner;
public class PatternProgram
{
    public static void main(String[] args)
    {
        Scanner sc = new Scanner(System.in);
        System.out.println("Choose an operation:");
        System.out.println("1. Print Floyd's
                                        Triangle");
        System.out.println("2. Display ICSE Pattern");
        int choice = sc.nextInt();
        if (choice == 1)
        {
            System.out.print("Enter number of rows: ");
            int rows = sc.nextInt();
            int num = 1;
            for (int i = 1; i <= rows; i++)
            {
                for (int j = 1; j <= i; j++)
                {
                    System.out.print(num + " ");
                    num++;
                }
                System.out.println();
            }
        }
        else if (choice == 2)
        {
            String word = "ICSE";
            for (int i = 1; i <= word.length(); i++)
            {
                for (int j = 0; j < i; j++)
                {
                    System.out.print(word.charAt(j)
                                            + " ");
                }
                System.out.println();
            }
        }
        else
        {
          System.out.println("Invalid choice.
                Please select either 1 or 2.");
        }
    }
}
```

Q.5 Write a program to calculate the sum of all the prime numbers between the range of 1 and 100.

ICSE SQP 2017

Ans.
```
import java.io. *;
class abc
{
    public static boolean checkPrime(int a)
    {
```

```
        for(int b=2; b<=a/2; b++)
        if(a%b==0) //a divisor of 'a' has been
              found except for 1 and 'a' itself
        return false;
        return true; //no divisor of 'a' was
                  found except 1 and 'a' itself
    }
    public static void main(String arg[])
    {
        int sum=0;
        for(int i=1; i<=100; i++)
        if(checkPrime(i)==true)
        sum+=i;
        System.out.println(sum);
    }
}
```

Q.6 Write a program to perform following operations as per users choice

(i) To print the value of $c=a^2+2ab$, where a varies from 1.0 to 20.0 with increment of 2.0 and b=3.0 is a constant.

(ii) To display the following pattern using for loop:

A
A B
A B C
A B C D
A B C D E

Display proper message for an invalid choice.

ICSE 2020

Ans.

```
import java.util.Scanner;
public class ChoiceBasedOperations
{
    public static void main(String[] args)
    {
        Scanner sc = new Scanner(System.in);
        System.out.println("Choose an operation:");
        System.out.println("1. Calculate c = a² + 2ab");
        System.out.println("2. Display pattern using
                                        for loop");
        int choice = sc.nextInt();
        if (choice == 1)
        {
            double b = 3.0;
            for (double a = 1.0; a <= 20.0; a += 2.0)
            {
                double c = (a * a) + (2 * a * b);
                System.out.printf("a = %.1f, c =
                                    %.2f\n", a, c);
            }
        }
        else if (choice == 2)
        {
            for (int i = 1; i <= 5; i++)
            {
                for (char ch = 'A'; ch < 'A' + i; ch++)
                {
                    System.out.print(ch);
                }
                System.out.println();
            }
        }
        else
        {
            System.out.println("Invalid choice.
                            Please select 1 or 2.");
        }
    }
}
```

Q.7 Write two separate programs to generate the following patterns using iteration (loop) statements:

ICSE 2015

(a)
```
*
* #
* # *
* # * #
* # * # *
```

(b)
```
5 4 3 2 1
5 4 3 2
5 4 3
5 4
5
```

Ans. (a)

```
public class KboatPattern
{
public static void main(String[] args)
{
    for (int i = 1; i <= 5; i++)
    {
        for (int j = 1; j <= i; j++)
        {
            if (j % 2 == 0)
                System.out.print("# ");
            else
                System.out.print("* ");
        }
        System.out.println();
    }
}
}
```

(b)

```
public class KboatPattern
{
public static void main(String[] args)
{
    for (int i = 1; i <= 5; i++)
    {
        for (int j = 5; j >= i; j--)
        {
            System.out.print(j + " ");
        }
        System.out.println();
    }
}
}
```

Q.8 Write a program to display the pattern as per user's choice.

Pattern 1	Pattern 2
ABCDE	B
ABCD	LL
ABC	UUU
AB	EEEE
A	

Ans.
```
import java.util.Scanner;
public class PatternChoice
{
    public static void main(String[] args)
    {
        Scanner sc = new Scanner(System.in);
        System.out.println("Choose a pattern to
                                        display:");
        System.out.println("1. Pattern 1");
        System.out.println("2. Pattern 2");
        int choice = sc.nextInt();
        if (choice == 1)
        {
            // Pattern 1: ABCDE, ABCD, ..., A
            for (int i = 5; i >= 1; i--)
            {
                for (char ch = 'A'; ch < 'A' + i;ch++)
                 {
                    System.out.print(ch);
                }
                System.out.println();
            }
        }
        else if (choice == 2)
        {
            // Pattern 2: B, LL, UUU, EEEE
            char[] patternChars = {'B', 'L', 'U', 'E'};
            for (int i = 0; i < patternChars.length; i++)
            {
                for (int j = 0; j <= i; j++)
                {
                    System.out.print(patternChars[i]);
                }
                System.out.println();
            }
        }
        else
        {
            System.out.println("Invalid choice.
                        Please enter 1 or 2.");
        }
    }
}
```

Q.9 Using if else statement write a program to do the following

(a) To generate and print Letters from A to Z and their Unicode

Letters	Unicode
A	65
B	66
.	.
.	.
.	.
Z	90

(b) Display the following pattern using iteration (looping) statement:

1
1 2
1 2 3
1 2 3 4
1 2 3 4 5

Ans.
```
import java.util.Scanner;
public class UnicodeAndPattern
{
    public static void main(String[] args)
    {
        Scanner sc = new Scanner(System.in);
        System.out.println("Choose an option:");
        System.out.println("1. Print Letters A to Z
                                   with Unicode");
        System.out.println("2. Display Number Pattern");
        int choice = sc.nextInt();
        if (choice == 1)
        {
            // Option (a): Print Letters A-Z
                                     and Unicode
            System.out.println("Letter\tUnicode");
            for (char ch = 'A'; ch <= 'Z'; ch++)
            {
                System.out.println(ch + "\t" + (int)
                                              ch);
            }
        }
        else if (choice == 2)
        {
            // Option (b): Print number pattern
            for (int i = 1; i <= 5; i++)
            {
                for (int j = 1; j <= i; j++)
                {
                    System.out.print(j + " ");
                }
                System.out.println();
            }
        }
        else
        {
            // Invalid input
            System.out.println("Invalid choice.
                           Please select 1 or 2.");
        }
    }
}
```

02

CLASS AS THE BASIS OF ALL COMPUTATION

Introduction to Objects and Classes

Classes

A class is a user-defined data type that serves as a blueprint for creating objects. It defines both the structure (attributes) and behavior (methods) of an object.

Syntax
```
class ClassName
{
    // Attributes (fields)
    dataType variableName;
    // Methods (functions)
    void methodName()
    {
        // Code
    }
}
```

Objects

An object is an instance of a class that represents a real-world entity. It encapsulates both data and behavior, making it a fundamental part of object-oriented programming.

Syntax `ClassName obj = new ClassName();  // Creating an object`

Objects State and Behavior

In object-oriented programming, objects represent real-world entities and consist of two key aspects: State and Behavior.

State (Variables, Attributes, Features)

The state of an object refers to its data, which is stored in variables (also called attributes or features). It defines the characteristics of the object.

Example A Car object with attributes like:

- color = "Red"
- model = "Tesla Model S"
- speed = 120 km/h

Behavior (Methods, Operations, Messages)

The behavior of an object is defined by the actions it can perform, implemented as methods. These methods allow interaction with the object's state.

Example A Car object may have methods like:

- start() → Turns on the engine
- stop() → Stops the car
- accelerate() → Increases speed

Classes as Abstractions for Sets of Objects

In programming, abstraction is the concept of hiding complex details and exposing only the essential parts. It helps in simplifying the system by focusing on what an object does rather than how it does it.

Classes act as blueprints or templates to create objects, defining the properties (attributes) and behaviors (methods) shared by all instances of that class.

For example, an "Animal" class can define attributes like name and age and methods like eat(). Objects like Dog, Cat, and Lion can be created from this class, each with unique attributes and behaviors.

Class as an Object Factory

A class acts as an object factory, enabling the creation of multiple instances (objects) with the same structure but different values.

For example, a "Student" class can define attributes like name, age, and rollNumber. Using this class, multiple student objects can be created, each representing a unique student with different values.

Constructors play a crucial role in object creation by initializing objects with specific values when they are created.

Objects as Instances of a Class

An object is an instance of class or a class type variable that holds individual copy of data. An object can access all fields and methods of class. The data type of an object is the class itself.

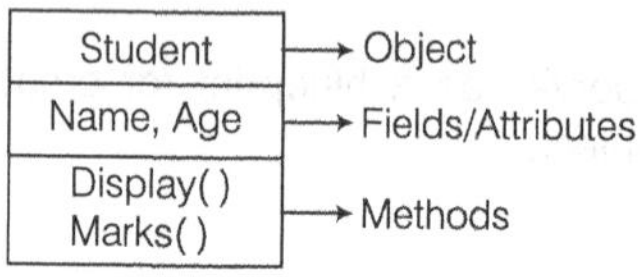

Creating Objects of a Class

An object is created from a class. In Java, the 'new' keyword is used to create a new object. There are three steps to create an object of a class:

Declaration An object is declared with an object name as class type.

Instantiation The 'new' keyword is used to create the object.

Initialization The new keyword is followed by a call to a constructor. This call initializes the new object (i.e. to set the initial value of instance variable).

e.g.

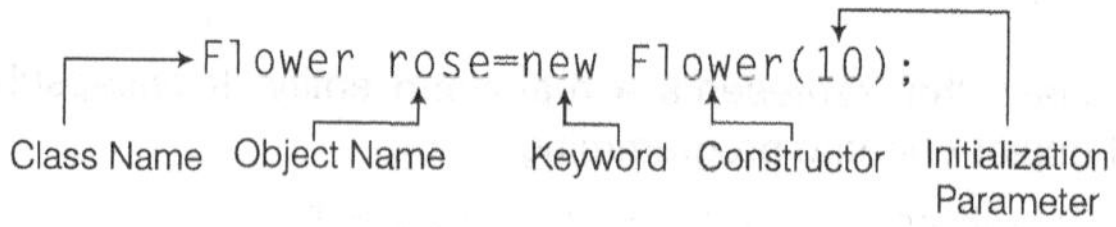

Data Types

It refers to the type of data that can be stored in a variable. Sometimes, Java is called a **strongly typed language** because when you declare a variable, you must specify the variable type. The Java language is rich in its data types. Data types in Java are classified into two types:

Primitive Data Types

These are the data types defined by the language itself. A primitive data type can have only one value at a time and is the simplest built in form of data within Java. Java supports eight primitive data types, they are as follows :

Type	Size	Range	Default Value	Example
byte	8-bit	–128 to +127	0	byte x = 90;
short	16-bit	–32,768 to +32,767	0	short s = 20000;
int	32-bit	–2,147,483,648 to +2,147,483,647	0	int a = 50000;
long	64-bit	-2^{63} to $+2^{63}-1$	0L	int a = 100000L;
float	32-bit	–3.4e-38 to +3.4e+38	0.0f	float fl = 234.5f;
double	64-bit	–1.7e-308 to +1.7e+308	0.0d	double d = 123.4d;
boolean	1-bit	True/False	False	Boolean one = true;
char	16-bit	0 to 65,535	'\u0000' or 0	char letter = 'n';

Non-Primitive Data Types (Composite Data Types)

Non-primitive data types in Java are built using primitive types,also known as reference types because they store references (memory addresses) to the actual data, rather than the data itself.

There are five types of non-primitive data types in Java, which are as follows:

- **Class** A blueprint for creating objects. It defines the structure (attributes/fields) and behavior (methods) that objects of that class will possess.
- **Object** A specific instance of a class. It's a concrete realization of the class blueprint, with its own unique data values for the attributes.
- **Interface** A contract that specifies a set of methods that a class must implement. Interfaces define what a class should do, not how it should do it.
- **String** A sequence of characters. Strings are immutable, meaning their values cannot be changed after creation.
- **Array** A collection of elements of the same data type (primitive or non-primitive). Elements are accessed using their index (position).

Difference between Primitive and Non-Primitive Data Types

Primitive Data Type	Non-Primitive Data Type
Primitive types are pre-defined in Java.	Non-primitive types are created by the programmer and is not defined by Java.
A primitive type always has a value.	Non-primitive types can be null.
A primitive type starts with a lowercase letter.	Non-primitive types start with an uppercase letter.
The size of a primitive type depends on the data type.	Non-primitive types have all the same size.
Examples of primitive data type are int, char, float, etc.	Examples of non-primitive data type are array, class, interface, etc.

Variable Declarations for Both Data Types

The Java programming language defines three principal kinds of variables: instance variables, class (or static) variables, and local variables.

1. **Instance Variables** These non-static variables are bound to individual object instances. Each object maintains its own distinct copy, representing its unique state. Access is *via* `objectReference.variableName`.
2. **Class (Static) Variables** Declared with the static modifier, these belong to the class itself. A single copy is shared among all objects. Access is *via* `ClassName.variableName`.
3. **Local Variables** These variables are declared within methods, constructors, or blocks. They exist only within that scope and must be explicitly initialized. Access is *via* `variableName`.

Access Modifiers in Java

Access modifiers (or visibility modifiers) in Java define how accessible classes, methods, variables, and constructors are from other parts of a program. They help enforce encapsulation and maintain code security.

Example
```
class Animal {
    public void method1() { ... }   // Accessible everywhere
    private void method2() { ... }  // Accessible only within this class
}
```

Types of Access Modifiers

Modifier	Scope of Access
public	Visible from anywhere in the program.
private	Visible only within the class where it's declared.
protected	Visible within the same package and in subclasses, even in other packages.
(default)	No modifier – accessible only within the same package.

Note *Getter methods are usually public, but their access modifier should not be changed if they override superclass methods.*

Access modifiers are essential when working with **Java packages** and **object-oriented design** principles like **inheritance** and **encapsulation**.

EXAM ORIENTED QUESTIONS

TYPE - 1 01 Mark

Multiple Choice Questions

Q.1 The blueprint that defines the variables and the methods common to all of a certain kind is termed as **ICSE 2022 (Sem I)**

(a) class (b) object (c) package (d) method

Q.2

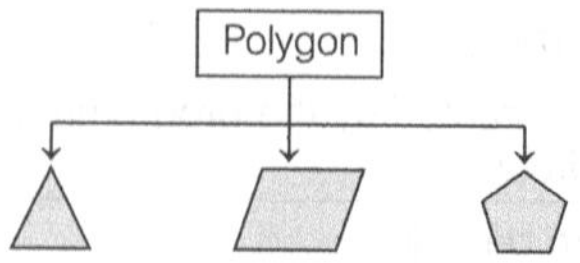

Consider the above picture and choose the correct statement from the following **ICSE 2024**

(a) Polygon is the object and the pictures are classes
(b) Both polygon and the pictures are classes
(c) Polygon is the class and the pictures are objects
(d) Both polygon and the pictures are objects

Q.3 The .... is called an instance of a class **ICSE SQP 2022 (Sem I)**

(a) Object (b) Attributes
(c) State (d) None

Q.4

Based on the image above, which of the following statements is TRUE?

(a) Car is a class, and car1, car2, car3 are its instances (objects).
(b) drive() and brake() are member variables that define the state of the class.
(c) Attributes like color, model, and speed are behaviors of the object.
(d) Constructors are used to destroy objects created from the class.

Q.5 The correct statement to create an object named mango of class fruit **ICSE 2024**

(a) `Fruit Mango = new fruit();`
(b) `fruit mango = new fruit();`
(c) `Mango fruit = new Mango();`
(d) `fruit mango = new mango();`

Q.6

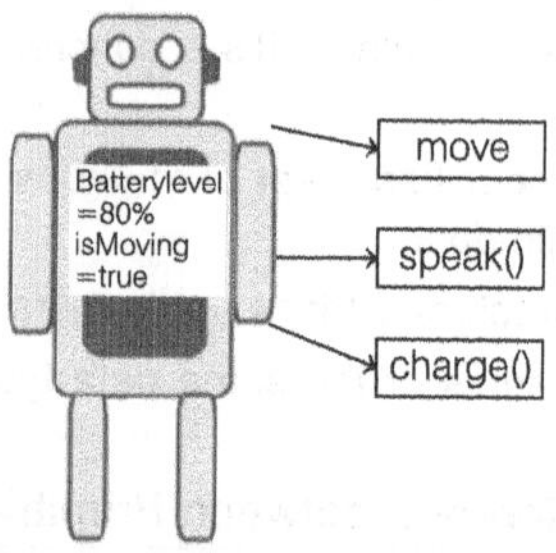

In the image, the labels batteryLevel and isMoving represent the robot's:

(a) Behaviour (b) Actions
(c) State (d) Class name

Q.7 Which of the following is true for the given object creation statement?

`Game cricket = new Game ();`

(a) Game is an object of cricket class
(b) New keyword creates object Game
(c) Game is a class and cricket is an object
(d) Game and cricket are objects

Q.8 The keyword to create an object of a class is .... **ICSE 2022 (Sem I)**

(a) create (b) new
(c) New (d) NEW

Q.9 Which of the following keyword is used to create an instance of a class? **ICSE SQP 2022 (Sem I)**

(a) new (b) public
(c) class (d) None of these

Q.10 The number of bits occupied by the value 'a' are **ICSE 2023**

(a) 1 bit (b) 2 bits (c) 4 bits (d) 16 bits

Q.11 A data type which contains integer as well as fractional part and occupies 32 bits space is **ICSE 2022 (Sem I)**

(a) float (b) char (c) double (d) byte

Q.12 The number of bytes occupied by char data type is .... byte/s. **ICSE SQP 2022 (Sem I)**

(a) 4 (b) 8 (c) 2 (d) None

Q.13

Which of the following best describes the difference between the two boxes in the image?

(a) Both are primitive types
(b) age is composite and Student is primitive
(c) age is a primitive data type, Student is a composite data type
(d) Both are objects

Q.14 A variable that is bounded to the object itself is called as **ICSE SQP 2022 (Sem I)**
(a) Instance variable (b) class variable
(c) Local variable (d) Argument variable

Q.15 Variable that is declared with in the body of a method is termed as **ICSE SQP 2022 (Sem I)**
(a) Instance variable (b) class variable
(c) Local variable (d) Argument variable

Q.16 The keyword to make a variable as a class variable **ICSE SQP 2022 (Sem I)**
(a) static (b) Static (c) final

Q.17 Read the following text, and choose the correct answer.

A class encapsulate Data Members that contains the information necessary to represent the class and Member methods that perform operations on the data member.

What does a class encapsulate? **ICSE SQP 2024**
(a) Information and operation
(b) Data members and Member methods
(c) Data members and information
(d) Member methods and operation

Q.18 Method which is a part of a class rather than an instance of the class is termed as: **ICSE 2023**
(a) Static method (b) Non Static method
(c) Wrapper class (d) String method

Answers

1. (a) 2. (c) 3. (a) 4. (a) 5. (b)
6. (c) 7. (c) 8. (b) 9. (a) 10. (d)
11. (a) 12. (c) 13. (c) 14. (a) 15. (c)
16. (a) 17. (b) 18. (a)

TYPE - 2 01 Mark

Assertion-Reason Type Questions

Directions (Q. Nos. 1-5) The following questions are Assertion-Reason based questions. Choose the answer based on the code given below
(a) Both Assertion (A) and Reason (R) are true and Reason (R) is a correct explanation of Assertion (A).
(b) Both Assertion (A) and Reason (R) are true and Reason (R) is not a correct explanation of Assertion (A).
(c) Assertion (A) is true and Reason (R) is false.
(d) Assertion (A) is false and Reason (R) is true.

Q.1 Assertion (A) Static method can access static and instance variables.

Reason (R) Static variable can be accessed only by static method. **ICSE 2024**

Q.2 Assertion (A) The new keyword is used to define the structure of a class.

Reason (R) The new keyword allocates memory for an object and calls its constructor.

Q.3 Assertion (A) Primitive data types are passed by value to methods.

Reason (R) When you pass a primitive value to a method, a copy of the value is created and used within the method.

Q.4 Assertion (A) Non-primitive data types store the actual data.

Reason (R) Non-primitive data types store references (memory addresses) to where the data is located.

Q.5 Assertion (A) Local variables must be declared before they are used.

Reason (R) Java requires explicit initialization of local variables to prevent unpredictable behavior.

Answers

1. (d) 2. (d) 3. (a) 4. (d) 5. (a)

TYPE - 3 01 Mark

Odd One Out

Q.1 Find the odd one out
(a) Data members (b) Methods
(c) Properties (d) Characteristic

Q.2 Find the odd one out:
(a) Object (b) Class
(c) Method (d) Loop

Q.3 Find the odd one out:
(a) Polymorphism (b) Encapsulation
(c) Debugging (d) Abstraction

Q.4 Find the odd one out:
(a) new (b) class
(c) object (d) for

Q.5 Find the odd one out:
(a) Constructor (b) Method
(c) Attribute (d) Compiler

Answers

1. (d) 2. (d) 3. (c) 4. (d) 5. (d)

TYPE - 4 02 Marks

Short Answer Type Questions

Q.1 Write a Java statement to create an object "mp4" of class "digital". **ICSE 2013**

Ans Class name is "digital" and object name is "mp4"

```
digital mp4 = new digital();
```

Q.2 Explain the term object using an example.

Ans Object is an instance of a class. The relationship is such that many objects can be created by using only one class.

Each object has its own data but its underlying structure (i.e. the type of data it stores, its behaviour) is defined by the class.

e.g. Class Book, in which objects are created

```
Book buk=new Book("The short books");
Book lbuk=new Book("Long books");
Book opt=new Book("Objective type");
Book All=new Book("All in one");
```

Q.3 What does the following mean? **ICSE 2008**

```
Employee staff = new Employee();
```

Ans In given statement, Employee is a class and it creates a object whose name is staff.

Q.4 Why is class called a factory of objects? **ICSE 2009**

Ans Class is called a factory of objects, because the class contains a collection of objects and all the attributes to create an object.

Q.5 Why is an object called an instance of a class? **ICSE 2017, 10**

Ans An object is an instance of class or a class type variable that holds individual copy of data. An object can access all fields and methods of class. The data type of an object is the class itself.

Q.6 Why is class known as composite data type? **ICSE 2009**

Ans A class is known as composite data type because it binds both member variables and functions as a single identity.

Composite data type holds reference of any variable, it is assigned with the help of reference. e.g. A class abc has two value *x* and *y* and the value of these variable cannot be assigned directly. They can be assigned with the help of reference

```
abc  obj1;    //Creating an object of abc class
obj1.x = 5;  //Referencing the variables
obj1.y = 10;
```

Thus a class is a composite data type because it requires a reference to use its attributes.

Q.7 (a) Write a Java statement to declare a class named Book with instance variables title and author of type String.

(b) Define an object myBook of the Book class and assign "Treasure Island" as the title and "R. L. Stevenson" as the author using dot notation.

Ans. (a)

```
class Book
{
  String title;
  String author;
}
```

(b)

```
Book myBook = new Book();
myBook.title = "Treasure Island";
myBook.author = "R. L. Stevenson";
```

Q.8 State the two kinds of data types.

Ans Data types are used within type system, which means to identify the type of data and associated operations for handling it.

There are two types of data type:

(i) **Primitive Data Types** byte, float, char, boolean, int.

(ii) **Composite Data Types** class, array, interface.

Q.9 Classify the following as primitive or non-primitive datatypes **ICSE 2018**

(i) char (ii) arrays
(iii) int (iv) classes

Ans **Primitive datatypes**

(i) char (iii) int

Non-primitive datatypes

(ii) arrays (iv) classes

Q.10 Arrange the following primitive data types in an ascending order of their size: **ICSE 2015**

(i) char (ii) byte
(iii) double (iv) int

Ans Ascending order of primitive data types with their size

byte < char < int < double

Q.11 Which of the following are primitive data types? **ICSE 2020**

(i) double (ii) String
(iii) char (iv) Integer

Ans. Primitive data types – double, char and Integer

Q.12 State the number of bytes occupied by char and int data types. **ICSE 2017**

Ans Number of bytes occupied by
char → 2-bytes

Number of bytes occupied by
int → 4-bytes

Q.13 Observe the code below and answer the following questions:

```
class Student
```

```
{
  int rollNo;
  String name;
  void show()
  {
    System.out.println(rollNo + " - " + name);
  }
}
```

(a) What type of data is name — primitive or non-primitive?

(b) Is show() an attribute or a behaviour of the class?

Ans. (a) name is of type String, which is a non-primitive data type in Java.

(b) show() is a behaviour of the class, as it is a method that defines what action the object can perform.

Q.14 Define a variable.

Ans A variable provides us with named storage that our programs can manipulate. Each variable in Java has a specific type, which determines the size and layout of the variable's memory; range of values that can be stored within memory and the set of operations that can be applied to the variable.

Q.15 Explain instance variable. Give an example. **ICSE 2008**

Or

Define instance variable. Give an example of the same. **ICSE 2007**

Ans Instance variables are any variables, without "static" field modifier, that are defined within the class body and outside any class's methods body. It can be declared in class level before or after use. For numbers, the default value is 0 and for boolean, it is false.

e.g.
```
class Book
{
   int sub;
    //instance variable
   int price;
    //instance variable
}
```

Q.16 Consider the following program and answer the questions given below **ICSE SQP 2023**

```
class sample
{
    int a,b;
    sample(int x,int y)
    {
          a=x;b=y;
    }
    void calculate()
    {
          int z;
          z= a+b;
          System.out.println(z);
    }
}
```

(i) Name the global variables.

(ii) What are the method variables?

Ans (i) a and b

(ii) x, y, z

Q.17 In the program given below, state the name and the value of the **ICSE 2012**

(i) method argument or argument variable.

(ii) class variable.

(iii) local variable.

(iv) instance variable.

```
class myClass
{
   static int x=7;
   int y=2;
   public static void main(String args[])
   {
      myClass obj=new myClass();
      System.out.println(x);
      obj.sampleMethod(5);
      int a=6;
      System.out.println(a);
   }
   void sampleMethod(int x)
   {
      System.out.println(x);
      System.out.println(y);
   }
}
```

Ans (i) method argument or argument variable= x

(ii) class variable = x

(iii) local variable = a

(iv) instance variable = y

Q.18 Name the keyword which is used to resolve the conflict between method parameter and instance variables/fields. **ICSE 2015**

Ans. When a method parameter has the same name as an instance variable, within the method, the parameter name takes precedence.

To access the instance variable, you must use the this keyword. this refers to the current object of the class.

```
public class Car
{
    String model; // Instance variable
    public void setModel(String model)
    { // Parameter with same name
        this.model = model; // this.model
         refers to the instance variable
           // model refers to the parameter
    }
}
```

In the setModel method, this.model refers to the Car object's model instance variable, while just model refers to the method's model parameter.

Q.19 Mention any two attributes required for class declaration.

Ans Two attributes required for class declaration

(i) Modifiers such as public, private.

(ii) The class name with the initial letter capitalised by convention.

TYPE - 5 — 2 Marks

Differentiate

Q.1 Write a difference between Class and Object **ICSE 2020**

Ans. Difference between Class and Object are as follows

	Class	Object
Definition	A class is a blueprint or template for creating objects.	An object is an instance of a class, created based on the class template.
Memory Allocation	A class itself does not consume memory until objects are created.	An object occupies memory as it stores data and has a specific state.
Structure	A class defines attributes (variables) and methods (functions).	An object holds actual values for attributes and can invoke methods.
Example	The Car class defines properties like brand, color, and methods like start().	An object like car1 represents a specific car with a brand "Toyota" and color "Red".
Reusability	A class can be used as a blueprint to create multiple objects.	Each object is independent and holds its own unique state.

Q.2 Write some differences between primitive data types and composite data types. **ICSE 2016**

Ans Differences between primitive data types and composite data types.

Primitive Data Type	Composite Data Type
Primitive types are pre-defined in Java.	Composite types are created by the programmer and is not defined by Java.
A primitive type always has a value.	Composite types can be null.
A primitive type starts with a lowercase letter.	Composite types start with an uppercase letter.
The size of a primitive type depends on the data type.	Composite types have all the same size.
Examples of primitive data type are int, char, float, etc.	Examples of composite data type are array, class, interface, etc.

Q.3 What is the difference between local variable and instance variable? **ICSE SQP 2017**

Ans Differences between local variable and instance variable are as follows

Feature	Local Variable	Instance Variable
Declaration	Inside a method, constructor, or block	Inside a class, but outside any method
Scope	Limited to the method, constructor, or block	Belongs to the object; accessible throughout
Lifetime	Exists during method/block execution only	Exists as long as the object exists
Default Value	No default value; must be initialized	Has s default value (0, 0.0, false, null)
Access	Only within the declaring method/block	Accessible by all methods of the class

TYPE - 6 — 15 Marks

Long Answer Type Questions

Q.1 Write a class with name employee and Basic as its data member, to find the gross pay of an employee for the following allowances and deduction. Use meaningful variables.

Dearness Allowance = 25% of Basic Pay

House Rent Allowance = 15% of Basic Pay

Provident Fund = 8.33% of Basic Pay

Net Pay = Basic Pay + Dearness Allowance + House Rent Allowance

Gross Pay = Net Pay – Provident Fund

Ans

```
class employee
{
    private int Basic;
    void salary(int Basic, String name)
            //Enter basic salary and name
    {
        double DA, HR, PF, NP, GP;
        DA=(25.0/100) * Basic;
        HR=(15.0/100) * Basic;
        PF=(8.33/100) * Basic;
        NP=Basic + DA + HR;
        GP=NP - PF;
        System.out.println("Gross Pay" +GP);
    }
}
```

Q.2 Defined a class called **ParkingLot** with the following description: **ICSE 2015**

Instance variables/data members	
int vno	To store the vehicle number
int hours	To store the number of hours the vehicle is parked in the parking lot
double bill	To store the bill amount

Member methods	
void input()	To input and store the vno and hours.
void calculate()	To compute the parking charge at the rate of ` 3 for the first hour or part thereof and ` 1.50 for each additional hour or part thereof.
void display()	To display the detail.

Write a main method to create an object of the class and call the above methods.

Ans.
```
import java.util.Scanner;
public class ParkingLot
{
    int vno;
    int hours;
    double bill;
    void input()
    {
        Scanner sc = new Scanner(System.in);
        System.out.print("Enter vehicle number: ");
        vno = sc.nextInt();
        System.out.print("Enter parking hours: ");
        hours = sc.nextInt();
    }
    void calculate()
    {
        if (hours <= 1)
        {
            bill = 3.0;
        } else {
            bill = 3.0 + (hours - 1) * 1.50;
        }
    }
    void display()
    {
        System.out.println("Vehicle Number: " + vno);
        System.out.println("Parking Hours: "
                                        + hours);
        System.out.println("Total Bill: Rs. "
                                        + bill);
    }
    public static void main(String[] args)
    {
        ParkingLot pl = new ParkingLot();
        pl.input();
        pl.calculate();
        pl.display();
    }
}
```

Q.3 Design a class **RailwayTicket** with following description: **ICSE 2018**

Instance variables/data members

String name	:	To store the name of the customer
String coach	:	To store the type of coach customer wants to travel
long mobno	:	To store customer's mobile number
int amt	:	To store basic amount of ticket
int totalamt	:	To store the amount to be paid after updating the original amount

Member methods

void accept () — To take input for name, coach, mobile number and amount.

void update() — To update the amount as per the coach selected (extra amount to be added in the amount as follows)

Type of Coaches	Amount
First_AC	700
Second_AC	500
Third_AC	250
Sleeper	None

void display() — To display all details of a customer such as name, coach, total amount and mobile number.

Write a main method to create an object of the class and call the above member methods.

Ans.
```
import java.util.Scanner;
public class RailwayTicket
{
  String name;
  String coach;
  long mobno;
  int amt;
  int totalamt;
  void accept()
  {
    Scanner sc = new Scanner(System.in);
    System.out.print("Enter customer name: ");
        name = sc.nextLine();
        System.out.print("Enter coach type
   (First_AC, Second_AC, Third_AC, sleeper): ");
        coach = sc.nextLine();
        System.out.print("Enter mobile number: ");
        mobno = sc.nextLong();
        System.out.print("Enter basic ticket
                                    amount: ");
        amt = sc.nextInt();
  }
  void update()
  {
      switch (coach)
      {
          case "First_AC":
              totalamt = amt + 700;
              break;
          case "Second_AC":
              totalamt = amt + 500;
              break;
```

```
            case "Third_AC":
                totalamt = amt + 250;
                break;
            case "sleeper":
                totalamt = amt;
                  // No extra charge
                break;
            default:
                System.out.println("Invalid
                                        coach type!");
                totalamt = amt;
                  // Or handle the error as needed
        }
    }
    void display()
    {
        System.out.println("Customer Name: "
                                            + name);
        System.out.println("Coach Type: " + coach);
        System.out.println("Total Amount: "
                                        + totalamt);
        System.out.println("Mobile Number: "
                                            + mobno);
    }
    public static void main(String[] args)
    {
        RailwayTicket rt = new RailwayTicket();
        rt.accept();
        rt.update();
        rt.display();
    }
}
```

Q.4 DTDC a courier company charges for the courier based on the weight of the parcel. Define a class with the following specifications: **ICSE 2024**

Class name	Courier
Member variables	
name	name of the customer
weight	weight of the parcel in kilograms
address	address of the recipient
bill	amount to be paid
type	'D'-domestic, 'I'-international
Member methods:	
void accept( )	to accept the details using the methods of the Scanner class only.
void calculate( )	to calculate the bill as per the following criteria: Weight in Kgs — Rate per Kg First 5 Kgs — Rs. 800 Next 5 Kgs — Rs. 700 Above 10 Kgs — Rs. 500 An additional amount of Rs. 1500 is charged if the type of the courier is I (International)
void print( )	To print the details
void main( )	to create and object of the class and invoke the methods

Ans.
```
import java.util.Scanner;
class Courier
{
  String name;
  double weight;
  String address;
  double bill;
  char type;
  void accept()
  {
    Scanner scanner = new
                         Scanner(System.in);
    System.out.println
                ("Enter customer name:");
    name = scanner.nextLine();
    System.out.println
            ("Enter weight of the parcel
                       in kilograms:");
    weight = scanner.nextDouble();
    scanner.nextLine();
            // Consume newline character
    System.out.println("Enter address of
                          the recipient:");
    address = scanner.nextLine();
    System.out.println("Enter type of
          courier (D for domestic, I for
                       international):");
    type = scanner.nextLine().charAt(0);
  }
  void calculate()
  {
    if (weight <= 5)
    {
      bill = weight * 800;
    }
    else if (weight <= 10)
    {
      bill = 5 * 800 + (weight - 5) * 700;
    }
    else
    {
      bill = 5 * 800 + 5 * 700 +
                     (weight - 10) * 500;
    }
    if (type == 'I')
    {
      bill += 1500;
    }
  }
```

```java
    void print()
    {
      System.out.println("\nCustomer
                              Name: " + name);
      System.out.println("Weight
                              of the parcel: "
                          + weight + " kgs");
      System.out.println("Address
                              of the recipient:
                                  " + address);
      System.out.println("Type of
                          courier: " + type);
      System.out.println("Bill Amount:
                              Rs. " + bill);
    }
    public static void main(String[] args)
    {
      Courier courier = new Courier();
      courier.accept();
      courier.calculate();
      courier.print();
    }
}
```

Q.5 Define a class to accept a number from user and check if it is an EvenPal number or not. (The number is said to be EvenPal number when number is palindrome number (a number is palindrome if it is equal to its reverse) and sum of its digits is an even number.) **ICSE 2024**

Example 121 is a palindrome number

Sum of the digits 1+2+1=4 which is an even number

Ans.

```java
import java.util.Scanner;
public class EvenPalNumberChecker
{
  // Function to check if a number is
                                palindrome
  public static boolean
                  isPalindrome(int num)
  {
    int reversedNum = 0;
    int originalNum = num;
    while (num != 0)
    {
      int digit = num % 10;
      reversedNum = reversedNum *
                              10 + digit;
      num /= 10;
    }
    return originalNum == reversedNum;
  }
  // Function to calculate sum of digits
  public static int sumOfDigits(int num)
  {
    int sum = 0;
    while (num != 0)
    {
      sum += num % 10;
      num /= 10;
    }
    return sum;
  }
  // Main method
  public static void main(String[] args)
  {
    Scanner scanner = new
                      Scanner(System.in);
    // Accepting the number from the user
    System.out.print("Enter a number: ");
    int number = scanner.nextInt();
    // Checking if it's a palindrome
                and sum of digits is even
    if (isPalindrome(number) &&
            sumOfDigits(number) % 2 == 0)
    {
      System.out.println(number + " is
                    an EvenPal number.");
    }
    else
    {
      System.out.println(number + " is
                not an EvenPal number.");
    }
    scanner.close();
  }
}
```

Q.6 Define a class to accept the gmail id and check for its validity. **ICSE 2024**

A gmail id is valid only if it has:

→ @
→ .(dot)
→ gmail
→ com

Example icse2024@gmail.com is a valid gmail id.

Ans.

```java
import java.util.Scanner;
public class GmailValidator
{
  private String gmailId;
  public GmailValidator(String gmailId)
  {
    this.gmailId = gmailId;
  }
```

```java
public boolean isValid()
{
  // Checking if the gmailId
      contains '@', '.', and 'gmail.com'
  if (gmailId.contains("@")
          && gmailId.contains (".") &&
        gmailId.endsWith("gmail.com"))
  {
    int atIndex = gmailId.indexOf("@");
    int dotIndex = gmailId.indexOf
                          (".", atIndex);
    // Checking if '.' comes after '@'
    if (dotIndex > atIndex)
    {
      return true;
    }
  }
  return false;
}
public static void main(String[] args)
{
  Scanner scanner = new
                      Scanner(System.in);
  System.out.println("Enter your
                           Gmail ID:");
  String gmailId = scanner.nextLine();
  GmailValidator validator = new
                 GmailValidator(gmailId);
  if (validator.isValid())
  {
    System.out.println(gmailId + " is a
                       valid gmail id.");
  }
  else
  {
    System.out.println(gmailId + "
           is not a valid gmail id.");
  }
  scanner.close();
}
}
```

Q.7 Define a class with the following specifications
Understanding/Application **ICSE SQP 2025**

Class name	Bank
Member variables	
double p	stores the principal amount
double n	stores the time period in years
double r	stores the rate of interest
double a	stores the amount
Member methods	
void accept ()	input values for p and n using Scanner class methods only.
void calculate ()	calculate the amount based on the following conditions:

Time in (Years)	Rate %
Upto ½	9
> ½ to 1 year	10
> 1 to 3 years	11
> 3 years	12

$$a = p\left(1 + \frac{r}{100}\right)^n$$

void display ()	display the details in the given format. Principal Time Rate Amount XXX XXX XXX XXX

Write the main method to create an object and call the above methods.

Ans.

```java
import java.util.*;
class Bank
{
  double p, n, r, a;
  Scanner ob = new Scanner(System.in);
  void accept()
  {
    System.out.println("Enter principal");
    p = ob.nextDouble();
    System.out.println("Enter number
                              of years");
    n = ob.nextDouble();
  }
  void calculate()
  {
    if (n <= 0.5)
      r = 9;
    else if (n > 0.5 && n < 1)
      r = 10;
    else if (n >= 1 && n <= 3)
      r = 11;
      a = p * Math.pow(1 + r / 100, n);
  }
  void display()
  {
    System.out.println("Principal"
          + "\t" + "Rate" + "\t" + "Time"
                  + "\t" + "Amount");
    System.out.println(p + "\t" + r +
                 "\t" + n + "\t" + a);
  }
  public static void main(String[] args)
  {
    Bank b = new Bank();
    b.accept();
    b.calculate();
```

```
        b.display();
    }
}
```

Q.8 Define a class to accept a number and check whether it is a SUPERSPY number or not. A number is called SUPERSPY if the sum of the digits equals the number of the digits. **ICSE SQP 2025**

Example1:

Input: 1021

Output: SUPERSPY number

[SUM OF THE DIGITS = 1+ 0 + 2 + 1= 4,

NUMBER OF DIGITS = 4]

Example2:

Input: 125

Output: Not an SUPERSPY number [1+2+5 is not equal to 3]

Understanding/Application

Ans.

```
class Superspy
{
  int n;
  Superspy(int x)
  {
    n = x;
  }
  boolean isSuperspy()
  {
    int d, s = 0, c = 0;
    int temp = n;  // Use a temporary variable
                      to keep the original value of n
    while (temp > 0)
    {
      d = temp % 10;
      s = s + d;
      c++;
      temp = temp / 10;
    }
    return s == c;
  }
  public static void main(String[] args)
  {
    Superspy spy = new Superspy(123);
    if (spy.isSuperspy())
    {
      System.out.println("The number is a
                                  superspy number.");
    }
    else
    {
      System.out.println("The number is not a
                                  superspy number.");
    }
  }
}
```

Q.9 Define a class called with the following specifications **ICSE SQP 2024**

Class name	Eshop
Member variables	
String name	name of the item purchased
double price	Price of the item purchased
Member methods	
void accept()	Accept the name and the price of the item using the methods of Scanner class.
void calculate()	To calculate the net amount to be paid by a customer, based on the following criteria:
	Price / **Discount**
	1000-25000 / 5.0%
	25001-57000 / 7.5%
	57001-100000 / 10.0%
	More than 100000 / 15.0%
void display()	To display the name of the item and the net amount to be paid.

Write the main method to create an object and call the above methods.

Ans

```
import java.util.Scanner;
class Eshop
{
  String name;
  double price;
  void accept()
  {
    Scanner scanner = new Scanner(System.in);
    System.out.print("Enter the name of
                              the item purchased: ");
    name = scanner.nextLine();
    System.out.print("Enter the price of the
                                  item purchased: ");
    price = scanner.nextDouble();
  }
  void calculate()
  {
    double discount = 0.0;
    if (price >= 1000 && price <= 25000)
    {
      discount = 0.05;
    }
    else if (price > 25000 && price <= 57000)
    {
      discount = 0.075;
    }
    else if (price > 57000 && price <= 100000)
    {
      discount = 0.1;
    }
```

```
        else if (price > 100000)
        {
          discount = 0.15;
        }
        double netAmount = price - (price * discount);
        System.out.println("Net amount to be paid: "
                                        + netAmount);
    }
    void display()
    {
        System.out.println("Name of the item
                              purchased: " + name);
    }
    public static void main(String[] args)
    {
        Eshop eshop = new Eshop();
        eshop.accept();
        eshop.calculate();
        eshop.display();
    }
}
```

Q.10 Define a class taximeter having the following description.

Data members instance variables	
int taxino	to store taxi number
String name	to store passenger's name
int km	to store number of kilometers travelled
Member functions	
taximeter()	constructor to initialize taxino to 0, name to " " and b to 0.
input()	to store taxino, name, km
calculate()	to calculate bill for a customer according to given conditions

kilometers travelled(km)	Rate/km
≤ 1 km	Rs 25
1 < km ≤ 6	Rs 10
6 < km ≤ 12	Rs 15
12 < km ≤ 18	Rs 20
> 18 km	Rs 25

display()	To display the details in the following format

Taxino	Name	Kilometres travelled	Bill amount
–	–	–	–

Create an object in the main method and call all the above methods in it. **ICSE SQP 2017**

Ans.
```
import java.util.Scanner;
class Taximeter
{
    int taxino;
    String name;
    int km;
    double bill;
    // Constructor
    Taximeter()
    {
        taxino = 0;
        name = "";
        km = 0;
        bill = 0;
    }
    // Method to take input
    void input()
    {
        Scanner sc = new
                    Scanner(System.in);
        System.out.print("Enter taxi
                              number: ");
        taxino = sc.nextInt();
        sc.nextLine(); // Consume newline
        System.out.print("Enter passenger
                                name: ");
        name = sc.nextLine();
        System.out.print("Enter
              kilometres travelled: ");
        km = sc.nextInt();
    }
    // Method to calculate bill
    void calculate()
    {
        if (km <= 1)
        {
            bill = km * 25;
        } else if (km <= 6) {
            bill = km * 10;
        } else if (km <= 12) {
            bill = km * 15;
        } else if (km <= 18) {
            bill = km * 20;
        } else {
            bill = km * 25;
        }
    }
    // Method to display the output

    void display()
    {
        System.out.println("Taxino
        \tName\tKilometres Travelled\tBill
                                  Amount");
```

```
        System.out.println(taxino + "\t"
            + name + "\t" + km + "\t\t\tRs
                                    " + bill);
    }
    // Main method
    public static void main(String[] args)
    {
        Taximeter t = new Taximeter();
        t.input();
        t.calculate();
        t.display();
    }
}
```

Q.11 Anshul transport company charges for the parcels of its customers as per the following specifications given below.

Class name	**Atransport**	
Member variables		
String name	to store the name of the customer	
int w	to store the weight of the parcel in Kg	
int charge	to store the charge of the parcel	
Member functions		
void accept()	to accept the name of the customer, weight of the parcel from the user (using Scanner class)	
void calculate()	to calculate the charge as per the weight of the parcel as per the following criteria.	
	Weight in Kg	**Charge per Kg**
	Upto 10 Kgs	Rs. 25 per Kg
	Next 20 Kgs	Rs 20 per Kg
	Above 30 Kgs	Rs. 10 per Kg
A surcharge of 5% is charged on the bill.		
void print()	to print the name of the customer, weight of the parcel, total bill inclusive of surchargbe in a tabular form in the following format	
	Name Weight Bill amount	

Define a class with the above-mentioned specifications, create the main method, create an object and invoke the member methods.

ICSE SQP 2020

Ans.
```
import java.util.Scanner;
class Atransport
{
    String name;
    int w;
    int charge;
    void accept()
    {
        Scanner sc = new Scanner(System.in);
        System.out.print("Enter customer
                                    name: ");
        name = sc.nextLine();
        System.out.print("Enter weight
                          of parcel in Kg: ");
        w = sc.nextInt();
        sc.close();
    }
    void calculate()
    {
        int remainingWeight = w;
        charge = 0;
        if (remainingWeight > 30)
        {
            charge += (remainingWeight -
                                30) * 10;
            remainingWeight = 30;
        }
        if (remainingWeight > 10)
        {
            charge += (remainingWeight -
                                10) * 20;
            remainingWeight = 10;
        }
        if (remainingWeight > 0)
        {
            charge += remainingWeight * 25;
        }
        // 5% surcharge
        charge += Math.round(charge *
                                    0.05);
    }
    void print()
    {
        System.out.println("\nName
                   \tWeight\tBill amount");
        System.out.println("----
                   \t------\t-----------");
        System.out.println(name +
                "\t" + w + "\t" + charge);
    }
    public static void main(String[] args)
    {
        Atransport obj = new Atransport();
        obj.accept();
        obj.calculate();
        obj.print();
    }
}
```

Q.12 Define a class with the following specifications

Class name	employee
Member variables	
eno	employee number
ename	name of the employee
age	age of the employee
basic	basic salary

Declare the variables using appropriate data types		
void accept()	accept the details using scanner class	
void calculate()	to calculate the net salary as per the given specifications	
	net = basic + hra + da – pf	
	hra = 18.5% of basic	
	da = 17.45% of basic	
	pf = 8.10% of basic	
	if the age of the employee is above 50 he/she	
void print	to print the details as per the following format	
	eno ename age basic net	
void main()	to create an object of the class and invoke the methods	

ICSE SQP 2023

Ans.
```
import java.util.Scanner;
class Employee
{
    int eno;
    String ename;
    int age;
    double basic;
    double net;
    public void accept()
    {
        Scanner in = new
                    Scanner(System.in);
        System.out.print("Employee
                        number: ");
        eno = Integer.parseInt
                    (in.nextLine());
        System.out.print("Employee name: ");
        ename = in.nextLine();
        System.out.print("Age: ");
        age = Integer.parseInt
                    (in.nextLine());
        System.out.print("Basic salary: ");
        basic = Double.parseDouble
                    (in.nextLine());
    }
    public void calculate()
    {
        double hra = 0.185 * basic;
        double da = 0.1745 * basic;
        double pf = 0.0810 * basic;
        net = basic + hra + da - pf;
        if (age > 50)
        {
            net += 5000;
        }
    }
    public void print()
    {
        System.out.println
          ("eno\tename\tage\tbasic\tnet");
        System.out.println(eno + "\t" +
         ename + "\t" + age + "\t" + basic
                        + "\t" + net);
    }
    public static void main(String[] args)
    {
        Employee obj = new Employee();
        obj.accept();
        obj.calculate();
        obj.print();
    }
}
```

Q.13 Design a class with the following specifications:

Class name	Student	
Member variables		
name	name of student	
age	age of student	
mks	marks obtained	
stream	stream allocated	
(Declare the variables using appropriate data types)		
Member methods		
void accept()	Accept name, age and marks using methods of Scanner class.	
void allocation()	Allocate the stream as per following criteria:	
	mks	**stream**
	>= 300	Science and Computer
	>= 200 and < 300	Commerce and Computer
	>= 75 and < 200	Arts and Animation
	< 75	Try Again
void print()	Display student name, age, mks and stream allocated.	

Call all the above methods in main method using an object.

Ans.
```
import java.util.Scanner;
public class Student
{
    private String name;
    private int age;
    private double mks;
    private String stream;
    public void accept()
    {
        Scanner in = new Scanner
                            (System.in);
        System.out.print("Enter student
                              name: ");
        name = in.nextLine();
        System.out.print("Enter age: ");
        age = in.nextInt();
        System.out.print("Enter marks: ");
        mks = in.nextDouble();
    }
    public void allocation()
    {
        if (mks < 75)
            stream = "Try again";
        else if (mks < 200)
            stream = "Arts and Animation";
        else if (mks < 300)
            stream = "Commerce and Computer";
        else
            stream = "Science and Computer";
    }
    public void print()
    {
        System.out.println("Name: " + name);
        System.out.println("Age: " + age);
        System.out.println("Marks: " + mks);
        System.out.println("Stream
                  allocated: " + stream);
    }
    public static void main(String args[])
    {
        Student obj = new Student();
        obj.accept();
        obj.allocation();
        obj.print();
    }
}
```

Q.14 Define a class named Cloud Storage with the following specifications **ICSE 2025**

Member variables	
int acno	stores the user's account number,
int space	stores the amount of storage space in GB purchased by the user.
double bill	stores the total price to be paid by the user.
Member Methods	
void accept()	prompts the user to input their account number and storage space using Scanner class methods only.
void calculate()	calculates the bill total price based on the storage space purchased using the pricing table provided: Storage range — Price per GB (Rs) First 15 GB — 15 Next 15 GB — 13 Above 30 GB — 11
void display()	displays the account number, storage space and bill to be paid.

Write a main method to create an object of the class and invoke the methods of the class with respect to the object.

Ans.
```
import java.util.Scanner;
class CloudStorage
{
    // Member Variables
    int acno;
    int space; // in GB
    double bill;
    // Method to accept user input
    void accept()
    {
        Scanner sc = new
                     Scanner(System.in);
        System.out.print("Enter account
                              number: ");
        acno = sc.nextInt();
        System.out.print("Enter storage
              space purchased (in GB): ");
        space = sc.nextInt();
        sc.close();
    }
    // Method to calculate bill
    void calculate()
    {
        int remaining = space;
        bill = 0;
        if (remaining > 30)
```

```java
        {
            bill += (remaining - 30) * 11;
            remaining = 30;
        }
        if (remaining > 15)
        {
            bill += (remaining - 15) * 13;
            remaining = 15;
        }
        if (remaining > 0)
        {
            bill += remaining * 15;
        }
    }
    // Method to display results
    void display()
    {
        System.out.println("\nAccount No:"
                                    + acno);
        System.out.println("Storage Space
                          (GB): " + space);
        System.out.println("Total Bill
                          (Rs): " + bill);
    }
    // Main method to test the class
    public static void main(String[] args)
    {
        CloudStorage cs = new
                              CloudStorage();
        cs.accept();
        cs.calculate();
        cs.display();
    }
}
```

Q.15 Define a class to accept a number. Check if the sum of the largest digit and the smallest digit is an even number or an odd number. Print appropriate messages.

Sample Input:	6425	3748
Largest digit:	6	8
Smallest digit:	2	3

Sample Output: Sum is even Sum is odd

Ans.

```java
import java.util.Scanner;
class DigitSumCheck
{
    int num;
    // Method to accept input
    void accept()
    {
        Scanner sc = new
                      Scanner(System.in);
        System.out.print("Enter a number: ");
        num = sc.nextInt();
        sc.close();
    }
    // Method to find largest and
        smallest digit and check the sum
    void checkSumEvenOdd()
    {
        int temp = num;
        int largest = 0;
        int smallest = 9;
        while (temp > 0)
        {
            int digit = temp % 10;
            if (digit > largest)
            {
                largest = digit;
            }
            if (digit < smallest)
            {
                smallest = digit;
            }
            temp /= 10;
        }
        int sum = largest + smallest;
        System.out.println("Largest
                  digit: " + largest);
        System.out.println("Smallest
                  digit: " + smallest);
        if (sum % 2 == 0)
        {
            System.out.println("Sum is
                                even");
        } else {
            System.out.println("Sum is
                                 odd");
        }
    }
    // Main method
    public static void main(String[] args)
    {
        DigitSumCheck obj = new
                          DigitSumCheck();
        obj.accept();
        obj.checkSumEvenOdd();
    }
}
```

03

USER-DEFINED METHODS

Method

A Java method (function) is a collection of statements that are grouped together to perform a coherent task or any particular operation.

```
public static void main(String[] args)
{ .........
  .........
}
```

It is main method in Java, which is always called by the JVM at starting.

Declaration of a Method

To declare a method in Java, required components are

(i) **Modifier** public, private, protected, etc.

(ii) **Return type** int, float, void (if method does not return a value), etc.

(iii) **Method name** depends on user.

(iv) **Parameter list in parenthesis** proceeded by their data type.

(v) **Method body** The method code enclosed by curly braces.

(vi) **Method Signature** Every method has method signature. It is a part of the method declaration. It includes the method name and parameter list.

e.g. Access modifier | Return type | Method name | Parameters

```
public void add(int a, int b)
{
    //method body
}
```

Method Prototype

It is the first line of the method definition that tells the program about the type of the value returned by the method and number and type of arguments.

With the help of prototype, a compiler can compare each use of the method with the prototype to determine whether the function is invoked properly.

Types of Method (Function)

In Java, we have two different types of methods. These are as follows:

Instance Method

It is **non-static method** which is defined in a class and only accessible through the object of the class.

Syntax <<objectname>>.<<methodname>>;

Instance methods are classified into two ways:

(i) **Accessor Methods** (pure method) Used to read instance variable. e.g. 'get' method.

(ii) **Mutator Methods** (impure method) Used to not only read but also modify the data. e.g. 'set' method.

Class Method

Class method **(static method)** is a method that can be called and executed without creating an object. In general, static methods are used to create instance methods.

Syntax `class.classMethod(parameter lists);`

Need of Method

A function is a block of code that performs a particular task. Sometimes, we need to write a particular block of code for more than once in our program. This may lead to bugs and irritation for the programmer. To prevent programs from these problems, functions are needed.

Modular Programming

It is the process of subdividing a computer program into separate subprograms or methods. These subprograms or methods are called **modules**. These modules have their own functions within the class.

Calling/Invoking an Object's Method

We can use an object reference to invoke an object's method. We append the method's simple name to the object reference, with an intervening dot operator(.).

Syntax `objectReference.methodName();`

Note *Object creation has already discussed in Chapter 2.*

Instance Function

Instance functions are the group of codes that performs a particular task. There are two types of instance functions in Java

(i) **Pure functions** define a relationship between input and output. A pure function does not depend on any state beyond its local scope. It does not modify arguments, since it is used only for input/output. Operations like square root, sine and cosine are pure functions.

(ii) **Impure functions** are those functions, which modify their behaviour based on external state.

It is also called **modifier function** that can cause a change of state in the object.

e.g. `printf(), random()`

Pure and impure are mainly used to access or set the value for the private member of the class in the main method.

Use of static Data Member with static Function

static Keyword

It becomes important when we want to define a class member that will be used independently at class level. When a class member is declared 'static', it can be accessed without creating any object of its class.

Note *When function name comes without static keyword, that means this function will be non-static.*

Java static Data Member

Data members or fields of a Java class declared static are called **class members**. There exists exactly only one copy of static field or class member, no matter how many objects of the class are finally created.

Java static Method (Function)

It is used to implement class behaviours that are not affected by the state of any instance. Java static methods have many restrictions over themselves:

- They can only call **static** method within from them.
- Java **static** methods can only access **static** data members.
- Java **static** methods cannot refer **this** and **super**.

e.g.
```
class StaticMethod
{
  int instVar=10;
  static int staticVar=20;
  public static void staticmethod()
  {
    System.out.println(instVar);
      // Here, an error will occur as it is a non static variable.
    System.out.println(staticVar);
```

```
        StaticMethod sm=new StaticMethod();
        System.out.println(sm.instVar);
    }
}
public class StaticMethodDemo
{
    public static void main(String[] args)
    {
        StaticMethod.staticmethod();
    }
}
```

Ways of Invoke/Calling Functions

In Java, we can call functions through two ways. These are, call by value and call by reference. The main objective of passing arguments to functions is message passing.

Call by Value

Call by value or **pass by value** in Java means passing a copy of the value, which is to be passed. Primitive types are passed through call by value.

e.g.
```
int a=34;
public void math(int num)
math(a);
```

a	num	memory
34	34	

Call by Reference

Call by reference or **pass by reference** in Java means the passing reference itself. Reference types are passed through call by reference.

e.g.
```
Student S1 = new Student();
Student S2 = new Student();
        S2.copy(S1);          ← Call by reference
void copy(Student S)
{
    _
    _  } body of the copy function
    _
}
```

Actual Parameter and Formal Parameter

In relation to function calling, parameters are two types

(i) Actual parameter (ii) Formal parameter

Actual parameters are situated in caller method and **formal parameters** are written in called funciton.

e.g.
```
class Addition                 ← Formal Parameter: int a, int b
{
    int sum ( int a, int b )
    {
        return a + b;
    }
    public static void main ()
    {
        Addition ad = new Addition ();
        int x = 10, y = 20;     ← Actual Parameter: x, y
        int z = sum ( x, y );
        System.out.print('Output' + z);
    }
}
```

Returning from a Function

It does not only terminate the function's execution but also passes the control back to the calling function.

Return Statement

On executing the return statement, it immediately transfers the control back to the calling function. There is no restriction on the number of return statements that may be present in a function.

Returning Values

The functions which are not declared as void or declared as any data type, return a value. A function can return only a single value.

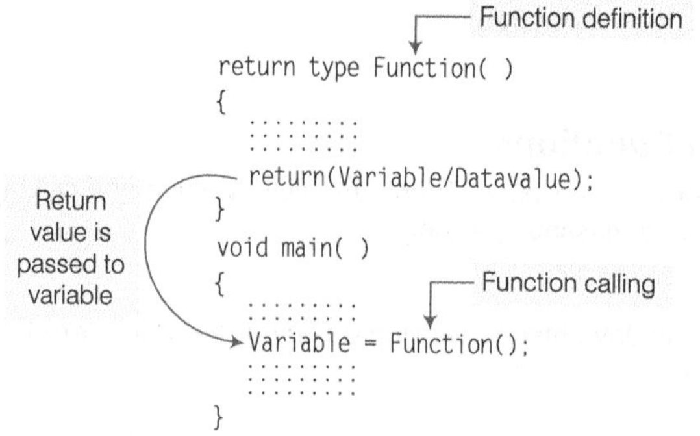

Function Overloading (Polymorphism)

If two or more methods in a class have the same name but different parameters, it is known as **method overloading**. Method overloading can be done by changing number of arguments or by changing the data type of arguments. There are two ways of method overloading

By Changing Data Type of Arguments

e.g.
```
class Calculate
{
    void sum(int a, int b)        //method 1
    {
        System.out.println("sum is " +(a+b));
    }
    void sum(double a, float b)   //method 2
    {
        System.out.println("sum is " +(a+b));
    }
    public static void main(String[] args)
    {
        Calculate cal=new Calculate();
        cal.sum(8,5);      //method 1 is called
        cal.sum(4.6, 3.8F);   //method 2 is called
    }
}
```

By Changing Number of Arguments

e.g.
```
class Area
{
    void find(int l, int b)        //method 1
    {
        System.out.println("Area is " +(l * b));
    }
    void find(int l, int b, int h) //method 2
    {
        System.out.println("Area is " +(l*b*h));
    }
    public static void main(String[] args)
    {
        Area ar = new Area();
        ar.find(8, 5);
            //method 1 is called
        ar.find(4, 6, 2);
            //method 2 is called
    }
}
```

EXAM ORIENTED QUESTIONS

TYPE - 1   01 Mark

Multiple Choice Questions

Q.1 The keyword which indicates that the method returns no value. **ICSE 2022 (Sem I)**
(a) public (b) static (c) void (d) abstract

Q.2 Method which is a part of a class rather than an instance of the class is termed as **ICSE 2023**
(a) static method (b) non-static method
(c) wrapper class (d) string method

Q.3 A method needs to be called with help of an object. **ICSE 2022 (Sem I)**
(a) void (b) class (c) non-static (d) static

Q.4 An object Student is created, and the program tries calling a non-static method showDetails() without creating an object. What will happen?
(a) Program runs normally
(b) Compile-time error
(c) Object will be created automatically
(d) showDetails() will be skipped

Q.5 A method which does not modify the value of variables is termed as **ICSE 2023**
(a) impure method (b) pure method
(c) primitive method (d) user defined method

Q.6

Student thinks which one is an "impure method"?
(a) add() because it adds numbers
(b) showMessage() because it prints output
(c) Both are pure
(d) Both are impure

Q.7 Method which reverses a given number is **ICSE 2024**
(a) Impure method (b) Pure method
(c) Constructor (d) Destructor

Q.8. Parameters used in the method call statement are **ICSE 2022 (Sem I)**
(a) actual parameters (b) informal parameters
(c) formal parameters (d) void parameters

Q.9 The number of values that a method can return is **ICSE 2023**
(a) 1 (b) 2 (c) 3 (d) 4

Q.10 Write a method prototype name check() which takes an integer argument and returns a char **ICSE 2023**
(a) char check () (b) void check (int x)
(c) check (int x) (d) char check (int x)

Q.11 Method prototype for the method compute which accepts two integer arguments and returns true/false. **ICSE SQP 2025**
(a) void compute (int a, int b)
(b) boolean compute (int a, int b)
(c) Boolean compute (int a,b)
(d) int compute (int a, int b)

Q.12 Invoking a method by passing the objects of a class is termed as **ICSE 2024, ICSE SQP 2022 (Sem I)**
(a) call by value (b) call by reference
(c) call by method

Q.13

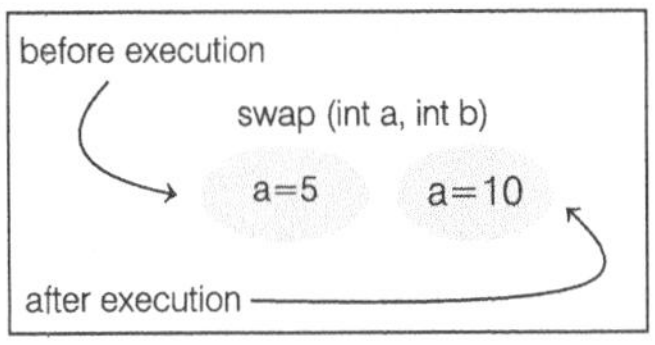

Why do the original values not change after the method call?
(a) Java uses call by reference
(b) Java always returns the modified values
(c) Java uses call by value, and changes are made to copies
(d) Swap method must be static

Q.14 What is this technique called?

```
class calculator:
add (int a, int b)
add (int a, int b, int c)
```

(a) Method overriding (b) Method hiding
(c) Method overloading (d) Inheritance

Q.15 Which of the following pairs of methods will cause a compile-time error due to incorrect method overloading? **ICSE 2025**
(a) void test(int a , int b) and void test (double a, double b)
(b) void test (int a, double b) and void test(double a, int b)
(c) void test (int a, double b) and void test (int a)
(d) void test (int a) and int test (int a)

Answers

1. (c) 2. (a) 3. (c) 4. (b) 5. (b)
6. (b) 7. (b) 8. (a) 9. (a) 10. (d)
11. (b) 12. (b) 13. (c) 14. (c) 15. (d)

TYPE - 2 01 Mark

Assertion-Reason Type Questions

Directions (Q. Nos. 1-6) The following questions are Assertion-Reason based questions. Choose the answer based on the code given below

(a) Both Assertion (A) and Reason (R) are true and Reason (R) is a correct explanation of Assertion (A).
(b) Both Assertion (A) and Reason (R) are true and Reason (R) is not a correct explanation of Assertion (A).
(c) Assertion (A) is true and Reason (R) is false.
(d) Assertion (A) is false and Reason (R) is true.

Q.1 Assertion (A) A method declared with a void return type does not return any value.

Reason (R) void is a keyword indicating that the method's execution does not produce a result that needs to be returned to the caller.

Q.2 Assertion (A) A static method can be called directly using the class name.

Reason (R) Static methods belong to the class itself, not to specific instances of the

Q.3 Assertion (A) A pure method can modify the state of objects passed to it as arguments.

Reason (R) Pure methods do not have side effects and do not depend on external state.

Q.4 Assertion (A) An argument is a value that is passed to a method when it is called. **ICSE SQP 2025**

Reason (R) Variables which are declared in a method prototype to receive values are called actual parameters.

Q.5 Assertion (A) call by value is known as pure method

Reason (R) The original value of variable does not changes as operation is performed on copied values. **ICSE SQP 2024**

Q.6 Assertion (A) Method overloading enhances code reusability.

Reason (R) Overloading allows multiple methods with the same name but different parameters, reducing the need for distinct names for similar operations.

Answers

1. (a) 2. (a) 3. (a) 4. (c) 5. (b)
6. (a)

TYPE - 3 01 Mark

Odd One Out

Q.1 Identify the odd one out with respect to method types in Java.
(a) Static Methods
(b) Pure Methods
(c) Parameterized Methods
(d) Non-Static Methods

Q.2 Which among the following is the odd one out regarding method components?
(a) Return Type (b) Parameters
(c) Method Name (d) Constructor

Q.3 Select the odd one out in the context of method invocation in Java.
(a) objectName.methodName()
(b) ClassName.methodName()
(c) returnType.methodName()
(d) obj.methodName(arguments)

Q.4 Identify the odd one out related to how methods behave.
(a) Method Overloading (b) Call by Value
(c) Pure Method (d) Impure Method

Q.5 Choose the odd one out based on method invocation styles.
(a) Call by Reference (b) Call by Value
(c) Method Overloading (d) Actual Parameters

Answers

1. (c) 2. (d) 3. (c) 4. (a) 5. (c)

TYPE - 4 02 Marks

Short Answer Type Questions

Q.1 Write two advantages of using functions in a program. **ICSE 2010**

Ans. There are two advantages of using functions in a program:
(i) Functions make code reusable.
(ii) Functions improve modularity and facilitate easy debugging.

Q.2 Write the prototype of a function search which takes two arguments a string and a character and returns an integer value. **ICSE SQP 2020**

Ans `int search(String str, char ch);`

Q.3 Write the prototype of a function check which takes an integer as an argument and returns a character. **ICSE 2018**

Ans `public char check(int x)`

Q.4 Write a function prototype of the following
A function PosChar which takes a string argument and a character argument and returns an integer value. **ICSE 2016**

Ans `int PosChar (String s, char c)`

Q.5 Give the prototype of a function search which receives a sentence sentnc and a word wrd and returns 1 or 0. **ICSE 2011**

Ans `int search(String sentnc, String wrd)`

Q.6 Give the prototype of a function check which receives a character ch and an integer n and returns true or false. **ICSE 2010**

Ans The prototype of a function check
`boolean check(char ch, int n)`

Q.7 Write a function prototype of the following:
A function **PosChar** which takes a string argument and a character argument and returns an integer value.

Ans. int PosChar (String s, char c)

Q.8 When there are multiple definitions with the same function name, what make them different from each other? **ICSE 2009**

Ans. The function signature makes multiple definitions with the same function name and make different to each other by differentiate their (number and types) parameters. This helps the compiler to recognise, which function is to be executed.

Q.9 What is the role of keyword void in declaring functions? **ICSE 2014, 07**

Ans The keyword void indicates that the function would not return any value.

Q.10 If a function contains several return statements, how many of them will be executed? **ICSE 2007**

Ans In any call of function, only one return statement can be executed at a time.

Q.11 What are the two ways of invoking functions? **ICSE 2018, 11**

Ans. In Java, two ways to invoke a function are
(i) Call by value (ii) Call by reference
If the function is static, it can be invoked by using the class name.
If the function is non-static, it can be invoked by using object.

Q.12 (i) What is call by value?
(ii) How are the following passed
(a) Primitive Types?
(b) Reference Types? **ICSE 2005**

Ans. (i) Call by value is that when a copy of the variable is passed to the function as an argument. Any change to the copy in the function will not change the original variables' value. It is used to primitive data type passing only, in Java.
(ii) (a) Primitive types, are passed through call by value.
(b) Reference types, are passed through call by reference.

Q.13 Consider and give the following programs:

```
class CallByValue
{
  void modify(int n)
  {
    n = n + 5;
  }
  public static void main(String[] args)
  {
    int x = 10;
    CallByValue obj = new CallByValue();
    obj.modify(x);
    System.out.println("After method call,
                                    x = " + x);
  }
}
```

Ans. Output
After method call, x = 10

Q.14 Consider and give the following programs:

```
class PureImpureDemo
{
  int x = 10;
  int pureMethod(int a, int b)
  {
    return a + b;
      // no change to instance variables
  }
  void impureMethod(int val)
  {
    x += val;
      // changes instance variable
  }
  public static void main(String[] args)
  {
    PureImpureDemo obj = new
                         PureImpureDemo();
    System.out.println("Pure: "
                  + obj.pureMethod(5, 3));
    obj.impureMethod(5);
    System.out.println("Impure, x = "
                              + obj.x);
  }
}
```

Ans. Pure: 8
Impure, x = 15

Q.15 Write the prototype of a function check which takes an integer as an argument and returns a character.

Ans. The prototype of function which takes an integer as an argument and returns a character: public char check (int x)

Q.16 Consider the following code and answer the questions that follow **ICSE 2009**

```
class academic
{
  int x, y;
  void access()
  {
    int a, b;
    academic student = new academic();
    System.out.println("object created");
  }
}
```

(i) What is the object name of class academic?

(ii) Name the instance variable used in the program.

(iii) Write the local variable used in the program.

(iv) Give the type of function used and its name.

Ans The output of the given code will be

(i) Object name → student

(ii) Instance variable used in the program → x and y

(iii) Local variable used in the program → a and b

(iv) Type of function → instance (impure type)

Name of function → access( )

Q.17 What are the values of a and b after the following function is executed, if the values passed are 30 and 50? **ICSE 2015**

```
void paws(int a, int b)
{
  a = a + b;
  b = a - b;
  a = a - b;
  System.out.println(a+","+b);
}
```

Ans. Output 50, 30

Q.18 Explain function overloading with an example. **ICSE 2006**

Ans Function overloading is the process of defining functions/methods with the same function names but with different numbers and types of parameters. i.e. function name is the same but function signature (numbers and types of parameters) is different.

e.g.

```
class Display
{
    public void disp(char c)
    {
       System.out.println(c);
    }
    public void disp(char c, int num)
  {
    System.out.println(c+ "" + num);
    }
}
class Sample
{
  public static void main(string args [])
  {
    Display ob = new Display();
    ob.disp('a');
    ob.disp('a', 10);
  }
}
```

Output

a

a 10

Q.19 Consider and give the following programs:

```
class OverloadDemo
{
  void display(int a)
  {
    System.out.println("One parameter: "
                                        + a);
  }
  void display(int a, int b)
  {
    System.out.println("Two parameters:"
                              + a + ", " + b);
  }
  public static void main(String[] args)
  {
    OverloadDemo obj = new OverloadDemo();
    obj.display(5);
    obj.display(10, 20);
  }
}
```

Ans. Output

One parameter: 5

Two parameters: 10, 20

TYPE - 5 02 Marks

Differentiate

Q.1 Static Member Function and Non-Static Member Function

Ans.

	Static Member Function	Non-Static Member Function
Access	Can be accessed using the class name and scope resolution operator (::) or through an object of the class.	Must be accessed through an object of the class.
Implicit this pointer	Does not have a this pointer.	Has an implicit this pointer that refers to the object the function is called on.

Q.2 Static and Non-static

Ans.

Static	Non-static
These variable are preceded by static keyword.	These variable should not be preceded by static keyword.
Memory for static variable is created only one in the program at the time of loading of class.	Memory for non-static variable is created at the time of create an object of class.

Q.3 Pure Function and Impure Function

Ans.

Pure Function	Impure Function
Pure function does not change the state of the object.	Impure function changes the state of the object by modifying instance variables.
Example of pure function is get function.	Example of impure function is set function.

Q.4 Call by Value and Call by Reference

Ans.

Call by Value	Call by Reference
It works with primitive data type.	It works with non-primitive data type.
The original value of variable remains unchanged.	The original value of variable changes.
Operation is performed on duplicate value of variables.	Operation is performed on original values of variables.

Q.5 Actual Parameter and Formal Parameter

Ans.

Actual Parameter	Formal Parameter
It is used when method is called.	It appears in the definition of a method.
e.g. `int a=5;` `int b=4;` `sum(a,b);` `//actual`	e.g. `int a=5;` `int b=4;` `public sum(int c,int d); //formal`

TYPE - 6 (15 Marks)

Long Answer Type Questions

Q.1 Define a class to overload the function print as follows **ICSE 2023**

void print ()	To print the following format 1 1 1 1 2 2 2 2 3 3 3 3 4 4 4 4 5 5 5 5
void print (int n)	To check whether the number is a lead number. A lead number is the one whose sum of even digits are equal to sum of odd digits. e.g. 3669 odd digits sum = 3 + 9 = 12 even digits sum = 6 + 6 = 12 3669 is a lead number.

Ans.

```
public class Example
{
  public void print()
  {
    for (int i = 1; i <= 5; i++)
    {
      for (int j = 1; j <= 4; j++)
      {
        System.out.print(i + " ");
      }
      System.out.println();
    }
  }
  public void print(int n)
  {
    int oddSum = 0;
    int evenSum = 0;
    while(n!=0)
    {
      int digit = n % 10;
      if (digit % 2 == 0)
      {
        evenSum += digit;
      }
      else
      {
        oddSum += digit;
      }
      n /= 10;
    }
    if (oddSum == evenSum)
    {
      System.out.println(n + " is a lead
                                  number");
    }
    else
    {
      System.out.println(n + " is not a
                             lead number");
    }
  }
  public static void main (String[] args)
  {
    Example ex = new Example ();
    ex.print();
    ex.print(123456);
    // prints "123456 is not a lead number"
    ex.print(3669);
    // prints "3669 is a lead number"
  }
}
```

Q.2 Define a class to overload the method print as follows **ICSE SQP 2023**

void print ()	to print the format 1 2 3 4 5 6 7 8 9 10
boolean print (int n)	to check whether the number is a Dudeney number, a number is dudeney if the cube of the sum of the digits is equal to the number itself. e.g. $512=(5+1+2)^3=(8)^3=512$
void print (int a, char ch)	if ch = s or S print the square of the number else if ch = c or C print the cube of the number.

Ans.

```
import java.util.Scanner;
class Overload
{
    public void print ()
    {
        int k = 1;
        for (int i = 1; i <= 4; i++)
        {
            for (int j = 1; j <= i; j++)
                System.out.print(k++ + " ");
            System.out.println();
        }
    }
    public boolean print (int n)
    {
        int sum = 0;
        for (int i = n; i != 0; i /= 10)
        sum += i % 10;
        int cube = (int) Math.pow (sum, 3);
        if (n == cube)
            return true;
        return false;
    }
    public void print(int a, char ch)
    {
        if (ch == 'S' || ch == 's')
            System.out.println("Square
                                 ="+(a*a));
        else if (ch == 'C' || ch == 'c')
            System.out.println("Cube
                                 ="+(a*a*a));
    }
    public static void main (String [] args)
    {
        Scanner in = new Scanner (System.in);
        System.out.print("Enter a number: ");
        int n = Integer.parseInt
                        (in.nextLine());
        System.out.print("Enter character
                        'c' or 's' ");
        char c = in.next().charAt(0);
        Overload obj = new Overload ();
        obj.print();
        boolean r=obj.print(n);
        System.out.println(r);
        obj.print(n,c);
    }
}
```

Q.3 Design a class to overload a function Sum () as follows

(i) **int Sum (int A, int B)** with two integer arguments (A and B) calculate and return sum of all the even numbers in the range of A and B.

Sample input: $A = 4$ and $B = 16$

Sample output: sum = 4 + 6 + 8 + 10 + 12 + 14 + 16

(ii) **double Sum (double N)** with one double arguments (N) calculate and return the product of the following series:

$sum = 1.0 \times 1.2 \times 1.4 \times \ldots\ldots\ldots \times N$

(iii) **int Sum (int N)** with one integer argument (N) calculate and return sum of only odd digits of the number N.

Sample input : $N = 43961$

Sample output : sum = 3 + 9 + 1 = 13

Write the main method to create an object and invoke the above methods. **ICSE SQP 2020**

Ans.

```
public class SumOverload
{
    public int Sum(int A, int B)
    {
        int sum = 0;
        for (int i = A; i <= B; i++)
        {
            if (i % 2 == 0)
            sum += i;
        }
        return sum;
    }
    public double Sum(double N)
    {
        double p = 1.0;
        for (double i = 1.0; i <= N; i += 0.2)
            p *= i;
        return p;
    }
    public int Sum(int N)
    {
        int sum = 0;
        while (N != 0)
        {
            int d = N % 10;
            if (d % 2 != 0)
                sum += d;
            N /= 10;
        }
        return sum;
    }
    public static void main(String args[])
    {
```

```
        SumOverload obj = new SumOverload();
        int evenSum = obj.Sum(4, 16);
        System.out.println("Even sum from 4
                    to 16 = " + evenSum);
        double seriesProduct = obj.Sum(2.0);
        System.out.println("Series
                Product =" + seriesProduct);
        int oddDigitSum = obj.Sum(43961);
        System.out.println("Odd Digits
                    Sum =" + oddDigitSum);
    }
}
```

Q.4 Design a class to overload a function volume() as follows **ICSE 2018**

(i) **double volume (double R)** with radius (R) as an argument, returns the volume of sphere using the formula.

$$V = 4/3 \times 22/7 \times R^3$$

(ii) **double volume (double H, double R)** with height(H) and Radius(R) as the arguments, returns the volume of a cylinder using the formula.

$$V = 22/7 \times R^2 \times H$$

(iii) **double volume (double L, double B, double H)** with length(L), breadth(B) and Height(H) as the arguments, returns the volume of a cuboid using the formula.

$$V = L \times B \times H$$

Ans.

```
class OverloadFunction
{
    double volume (double R)
    {
        double V;
        V=(4.0/3.0)*(22.0/7.0)*R*R*R;
        return V;
    }
    double volume (double H,double R)
    {
        double V= (22.0/7.0)*R*R*H;
        return V;
    }
    double volume (double L, double B,
                        double H)
    {
        double V=L*B*H;
        return V;
    }
    public static void main (String[]args)
    {
        OverloadFunction ofn=new
                    OverloadFunction();
        System.out.println("Sphere
                volume="+ofn.volume(5));
        System.out.println("Cylinder
                volume="+ofn.volume(5, 4));
        System.out.println("Cuboid
                volume="+ofn.volume(3, 4, 5));
    }
}
```

Q.5 Design a class to overload a function SumSeries() as follows **ICSE 2016**

(a) **void SumSeries(int n, double x)** with one integer argument and one double argument to find and display the sum of the series given below:

$$s = \frac{x}{1} - \frac{x}{2} + \frac{x}{3} - \frac{x}{4} + \frac{x}{5} \ldots \ldots \ldots \text{ to n terms}$$

(b) **void SumSeries()** To find and display the sum of the following series

$$s = 1 + (1 \times 2) + (1 \times 2 \times 3) + \ldots \ldots \ldots + (1 \times 2 \times 3 \times 4 \ldots \ldots \ldots \ldots \ldots \times 20)$$

Ans.

```
public class Overload
{
  void sumSeries(int n, double x)
  {
    double sum = 0;
    for (int i = 1; i <= n; i++)
    {
      double t = x / i;
      if (i % 2 == 0)
        sum -= t;
      else
        sum += t;
    }
    System.out.println("Sum = " + sum);
  }
  void sumSeries()
  {
    long sum = 0, term = 1;
    for (int i = 1; i <= 20; i++)
    {
      term *= i;
        sum += term;
    }
    System.out.println("Sum=" + sum);
  }
}
```

Q.6 Design a class to overload a function area( ) as follows **ICSE 2014**

(i) **double area (double a, double b, double c)** with three double arguments, returns the area of a scalene triangle using the formula

Area = $\sqrt{s(s-a)(s-b)(s-c)}$

where $s = (a + b + c) / 2$

(ii) **double area (int a, int b, int height)** with three integer arguments, returns the area of a trapezium using the formula

area = 1/2 * height (a + b)

(iii) **double area (double diagonal1, double diagonal2)** with two double arguments, returns the area of a rhombus using the formula

area = 1/2 * (diagonal1 * diagonal2)

Ans.

```
class Overloadfunction
{
    double area(double a, double b,
                                double c)
    {
        double s, r;
        s=(a + b + c)/2;
        r=s*(s - a)*(s - b)*(s - c);
        double ar=Math.sqrt(r);
        return ar;
    }
    double area(int a, int b, int height)
    {
        double ar=(height * (a + b))/2;
        return ar;
    }
    double area(double diagonal1, double
                                diagonal2)
    {
        double ar=(diagonal1 * diagonal2)/2;
        return ar;
    }
    public static void main(String[] args)
    {
        Overloadfunction ofn=new
                        Overloadfunction();
        ofn.area(2.5, 3.2, 1.2);
        ofn.area(10, 20, 5);
        ofn.area(20, 30);
    }
}
```

Q.7 Design a class to overload a function series() as follows **ICSE 2013**

(i) **double series (double n)** with one double argument and returns the sum of the series.

$$sum = \frac{1}{1} + \frac{1}{2} + \frac{1}{3} + \ldots + \frac{1}{n}$$

(ii) **double series (double a, double n)** with two double arguments and returns the sum of the series.

$$sum = \frac{1}{a^2} + \frac{4}{a^5} + \frac{7}{a^8} + \frac{10}{a^{11}} + \ldots + n \text{ terms}$$

Ans.

```
public class Series
{
  double series (double n)
  {
    double sum = 0;
    for (int i = 1; i <= n; i++)
    {
      double term = 1.0 / i;
      sum += term;
    }
    return sum;
  }
  double series (double a, double n)
  {
    double sum = 0;
    int x = 1;
    for (int i = 1; i <= n; i++)
    {
      int e = x + 1;
      double term = x / Math.pow(a, e);
      sum += term;
      x += 3;
    }
    return sum;
  }
  public static void main(String args[])
  {
    Series obj = new Series();
    System.out.println("First series sum
                    = " + obj.series(5));
    System.out.println("Second series sum
                = " + obj.series(3, 8));
  }
}
```

Q.8 Design a class to overload a function polygon() as follows

(i) **void polygon(int n, char ch)** with one integer argument and one character type argument that draws a filled square of side n using the character stored in ch.

(ii) **void polygon(int x, int y)** two integer arguments that draws filled rectangle of length x and breadth y, using the symbol '@'.

(iii) **void polygon()** with no argument that draws a filled triangle shown below. **ICSE 2012**

```
*
* *
* * *
```

Ans.

```
class Poly
{
    public static void polygon(int n, char ch)
    {
        System.out.println("Overloaded
                                method 1");
        for(int i = 1; i <= n; i++)
        {
            printChar(ch, n);
```

```
            System.out.println();
        }
    }
    public static void polygon(int n,
                                int y)
    {
        System.out.println("Overloaded
                                method 2");
        for(int i = 1; i <= n; i++)
        {
            printChar('@', y);
            System.out.println();
        }
    }
    public static void polygon()
    {
        System.out.println("Overloaded
                                method 3");
        for(int i = 1; i <= 3; i++)
        {
            printChar('*', i);
            System.out.println();
        }
    }
    public static void printChar(char ch,
                                int n)
    {
        for(int i=1; i <= n; i++)
            System.out.print(ch);
    }
    public static void main(String[] args)
                        throws IOException
    {
        Poly ss=new Poly();
        ss.polygon(2, 'O');
        ss.polygon(2, 5);
        ss.polygon();
    }
}
```

Q.9 Write a class with the name volume using function overloading that computes the volume of a cube, a sphere and a cuboid.

Formula

Volume of a cube (vc) = s*s*s

Volume of a sphere (vs) = 4/3* pi* r* r*r (where pi = 3.14 or 22/7)

Volume of a cuboid (vcd) = l*b*h **ICSE 2008**

Ans.
```
class vol
{
  void volume(int s)
  {
    int vc = s * s * s;
    System.out.println("The Volume of
                        a Cube is " + vc);
  }
  void volume(double r)
  {
    double vs = (4.0 / 3.0) * 3.14159 *
     r * r * r; // Using Math.PI for better
                                precision
    System.out.println("The Volume of
                        Sphere is " + vs);
  }
  void volume(int l, int b, int h)
  {
    int vcd = l * b * h;
    System.out.println("The Volume of a
                        Cuboid is " + vcd);
  }
  public static void main(String[] args)
  {
    vol v = new vol();
    v.volume(5);
      // Volume of a cube with side 5
    v.volume(3.5);
      // Volume of a sphere with radius 3.5
    v.volume(10, 5, 2);
      // Volume of a cuboid with length
                10, breadth 5, height 2
  }
}
```

Q.10 Define a class to overload the method display() as follows: **ICSE SQP 2025**

void display()	To print the following format using nested loop. 1 2 1 2 1 1 2 1 2 1 1 2 1 2 1
void display (int n, int m)	To print the quotient of the division of m and n if m is greater than n otherwise print the sum of twice n and thrice m.
double display (double a, double b, double c)	To print the value of z where $z = p \times q, p = \frac{a+b}{c}$, $q = a+b+c$

Ans.
```
class Overload
{
 // Method to display a pattern of 1s
                                and 2s
  void display()
 {
  int r, c;
  for (r = 1; r <= 3; r++)
  {
    for (c = 1; c <= 5; c++)
    {
      if (c % 2 == 0)
        // Fixed condition to check for
                            even numbers
        System.out.print(2);
```

```
        else
          System.out.print(1);
      }
      System.out.println();
    }
  }
  // Method to display result based on
                          comparison of m and n
  void display(int m, int n)
  {
    if (m > n)
      System.out.println(m / n);
    else
      System.out.println(2 * n + 3 * m);
  }
  // Method to perform calculations
                           with double values
  void display(double a, double b, double c)
  {
    double z, p, q;
    p = (a + b) / c;
    q = a + b + c;
    z = p * q; // Corrected multiplication
    System.out.println(z);
  }
  // Main method to run the program
  public static void main(String[] args)
  {
    Overload obj = new Overload();
    obj.display();
      // Calls method with no arguments
    obj.display(10, 5);
      // Calls method with int arguments
    obj.display(5.0, 3.0, 2.0);
      // Calls method with double arguments
  }
}
```

Q.11 Define a class to overload the method perform as follows: **ISC 2024**

`double perform (double r, double h)`	to calculate the return the value of Curved surface area of cone CSA = $\pi rl \quad l = \sqrt{r^2 + h^2}$
`void perform (int r, int c)`	Use NESTED FOR LOOP to generate the following format r = 4, c = 5 output—1 2 3 4 5 1 2 3 4 5 1 2 3 4 5 1 2 3 4 5
`void perform (int m, int n, char ch)`	to print the quotient of the division of m and n, if ch is Q else print the remainder of the division of m and n if ch is R

Ans.
```
public class OverloadedMethods
{
  // Method to calculate and
              return the curved surface area
                                   of a cone
  double perform(double r, double h)
  {
    double CSA = Math.PI * r *
                     Math.sqrt(r*r + h*h);
    return CSA;
  }
  // Method to print a nested
                         format of numbers
  void perform(int r, int c)
  {
    for (int i = 1; i <= r; i++)
    {
      for (int j = 1; j <= c; j++)
      {
        System.out.print(j);
      }
      System.out.println();
    }
  }
  // Method to print quotient or
                                 remainder
          based on the character provided
  void perform(int m, int n,char ch)
  {
    if (ch == 'Q')
    {
      System.out.println("Quotient:
                             " + (m / n));
    }
    else if (ch == 'R')
    {
      System.out.println("Remainder:
                             " + (m % n));
    }
    else
    {
      System.out.println
            ("Invalid character provided.");
    }
  }
  // Main method to test the class
  public static void main(String[] args)
  {
    OverloadedMethods obj = new
                     OverloadedMethods();
    // Testing perform(double r, double h)
    double r = 3.0;
```

```
        double h = 4.0;
        System.out.println("Curved Surface
                        Area of Cone: " +
                        obj.perform(r, h));
        // Testing perform(int r, int c)
        int rows = 4;
        int columns = 5;
        System.out.println("Nested
                        Format of Numbers:");
        obj.perform(rows, columns);
        // Testing perform(int m, int n,char ch)
        int m = 10;
        int n = 3;
        char ch = 'Q';
        obj.perform(m, n, ch);
                        // Should print quotient
        ch = 'R';
        obj.perform(m, n, ch);
                        // Should print remainder
    }
}
```

Q.12 Design a class to overload a function **series ( )** as follows: **ICSE 2019**

(a) **void series (int x, int n)** To display the sum of the series given below:

$x^1 + x^2 + x^3 + ...x^n$ terms

(b) **void series (int p)** To display the following series:

0, 7, 26, 63 .... *p* terms

(c) **void series ( )** To display the sum of the series given below: $\frac{1}{2} + \frac{1}{3} + \frac{1}{4} .... \frac{1}{10}$

Ans.
```
import java.util.Scanner;
public class OverloadSeries
{
  // Series with x1 + x2 + ... + xn
  void series(int x, int n)
  {
    long sum = 0;
    for (int i = 1; i <= n; i++)
    {
      sum += Math.pow(x, i);
    }
    System.out.println("Sum = " + sum);
  }
  // Series with i3 - 1
  void series(int p)
  {
    for (int i = 1; i <= p; i++)
    {
      int term = (int)(Math.pow(i, 3) - 1);
      System.out.print(term + " ");
    }
    System.out.println();
  }
  // Series 1/2 + 1/3 + ... + 1/10
  void series()
  {
    double sum = 0.0;
    for (int i = 2; i <= 10; i++)
    {
      sum += 1.0 / i;
    }
    System.out.println("Sum = " + sum);
  }
  public static void main(String[] args)
  {
    Scanner sc = new Scanner(System.in);
    OverloadSeries obj = new
                        OverloadSeries();
    System.out.println("Calling
                        series():");
    obj.series();  // No arguments
    System.out.print("\nEnter a number (p)
                        for series(p): ");
    int p = sc.nextInt();
    obj.series(p); // One argument
    System.out.print("\nEnter base (x): ");
    int x = sc.nextInt();
    System.out.print("Enter exponent
                        limit (n): ");
    int n = sc.nextInt();
    obj.series(x, n);  // Two arguments
    sc.close();
  }
}
```

Q.13 Design a class to overload a method Number() as follows **ICSE 2020**

(i) **void Number (int num, int d)** to count and display the frequency of a digit in a number.

Example

num = 2565685

d = 5

Frequency of digit 5 = 3

(ii) **void Number (int n1)** To find and display the sum of even digits of a number.

Example

n1 = 29865

Sum of even digits = 16

Write a main method to create an object and invoke the above methods.

Ans.
```
public class SumOverload
{
  // Sum of even numbers between A and B
  public int Sum(int A, int B)
  {
    int sum = 0;
    for (int i = A; i <= B; i++)
    {
      if (i % 2 == 0)
      sum += i;
    }
    return sum;
  }
  // Product of a series with step 0.2
                              from 1.0 to N
  public double Sum(double N)
  {
    double p = 1.0;
    for (double i = 1.0; i <= N; i += 0.2)
      p *= i;
    return p;
  }
  // Sum of odd digits in a number
  public int Sum(int N)
  {
    int sum = 0;
    while (N != 0)
    {
      int d = N % 10;
      if (d % 2 != 0)
        sum += d;
      N /= 10;
    }
    return sum;
  }
  public static void main(String args[])
  {
    KboatSumOverload obj = new SumOverload();
    int evenSum = obj.Sum(4, 16);
    System.out.println("Even sum from 4
                      to 16 = " + evenSum);
    double seriesProduct = obj.Sum(2.0);
    System.out.println("Series Product = "
                          + seriesProduct);
    int oddDigitSum = obj.Sum(43961);
    System.out.println("Odd Digits Sum = "
                            + oddDigitSum);
  }
}
```

Q.14 Define a class to overload the method display as follows **ICSE SQP 2024**

void display()	To print the following format using nested loop 1 1 2 1 2 3 1 2 3 4 1 2 3 4 5
void display(int n)	To print the square root of each digit of the given number
Example	n = 4329 Output 3.0 1.414213562 1.732050808 2.0

Ans.
```
import java.util.Scanner;
class MethodOverload
{
  public void display()
  {
    for (int i = 1; i <= 5; i++)
    {
      for (int j = 1; j <= i; j++)
      {
        System.out.print(j + " ");
      }
      System.out.println();
    }
  }
  public void display(int n)
  {
    String numberString = Integer.toString(n);
    for (int i = 0; i < numberString.length(); i++)
    {
      int digit = Character.getNumericValue
                    (numberString.charAt(i));
      double squareRoot = Math.sqrt(digit);
      System.out.println(squareRoot);
    }
  }
  public static void main(String[] args)
  {
    MethodOverload obj = new MethodOverload();
    System.out.println("Using display() method:");
    obj.display();
    System.out.println("Using display(int n)
                                  method:");
    Scanner scanner = new Scanner(System.in);
    System.out.print("Enter a number: ");
    int number = scanner.nextInt();
    obj.display(number);
  }
}
```

Q.15 Define a class to overload the method print( ) as follows: **ICSE 2025**

void print( )	To print the given format using nested loops. @#@#@ @#@#@ @#@#@ @#@#@
double print(double a, double b)	To display the sum of numbers between a and b with difference of 0.5 eg. if a = 1.0, 6 = 4.0 output is: 1.0 + 1.5 + 2.0 + 2.5 + ... + 4.0
int print(char ch1, char ch2)	compare the two characters and return the ASC|| code of the largest character,

Ans.

```
import java.util.Scanner;
class Printer
{
    public void print()
    {
        for (int i = 0; i < 5; i++)
        {
            for (int j = 0; j < 5; j++)
            {
                System.out.print("@");
            }
            System.out.println();
        }
    }
    public void print(double a, double b)
    {
        if (a > b)
        {
            double temp = a;
            a = b;
            b = temp;
        }
        for (double i = a; i <= b; i += 0.5)
        {
            System.out.print(i);
            if (i + 0.5 <= b)
            {
                System.out.print(" + ");
            }
        }
        System.out.println();
    }
    public int print(char ch1, char ch2)
    {

        if (ch1 > ch2)
        {
            return (int) ch1;
        } else {
            return (int) ch2;
        }
    }
    public static void main(String[] args)
    {
        Scanner scanner = new Scanner(System.in);
        Printer printer = new Printer();
        System.out.println("Calling print() with no
                                        arguments:");
        printer.print();
        System.out.println();
        System.out.println("Calling print(double a,
                                        double b):");
        System.out.print("Enter the value of a: ");
        double a = scanner.nextDouble();
        System.out.print("Enter the value of b: ");
        double b = scanner.nextDouble();
        printer.print(a, b);
        System.out.println();
        System.out.println("Calling print(char
                                    ch1, char ch2):");
        System.out.print("Enter the first character: ");
        char char1 = scanner.next().charAt(0);
        System.out.print("Enter the second character: ");
        char char2 = scanner.next().charAt(0);
        int largestASCII = printer.print(char1, char2);
        System.out.println("ASCII code of the
                largest character: " + largestASCII);
        scanner.close();
    }
}
```

CONSTRUCTORS

A constructor is a special method in a class that is automatically invoked when an object is created. It is used to initialize object attributes and set up necessary configurations.

Characteristics of Constructors

- **Automatic Invocation** A constructor is called automatically when an object is created.
- **No Return Type** Constructors do not have a return type, not even void.
- **Same Name as Class** The constructor's name must match the class name exactly.
- **Can Call Another Constructor** A constructor can call another constructor of the same class using this().

Types of Constructors

1. Default Constructor

A default constructor is a constructor that does not accept any parameters. It is automatically provided by Java if no other constructors are defined. Its role is to initialize objects with default values for their fields.

e.g.
```
public class Smart
{
  public Smart()
  {
    System.out.println("Default constructor ");
  }
  public static void main(String[] args)
  {
    Smart sc=new Smart();
  }
}
```

2. Parameterized Constructor

A parameterized constructor takes parameters to initialize an object with specific values at creation, providing more control over its state. It is defined explicitly and is not provided by default.

e.g.
```
public class Smart
{
  private String name;
  public Smart(String str)
  {
    this.name=str;
    System.out.println("The parameterised constructor" +str);
  }
  public static void main(String args[])
  {
    Smart sc=new Smart("Aaliya");
  }
}
```

Uses of Constructor

The uses of constructor are as follows:

(i) Constructors are used to initialize the instances of classes.

(ii) You can use a constructor to create new objects often with parameters specifying the initial state about the object.

Constructor Overloading

Constructor overloading is the way of having more than one constructors, which do different-different tasks. In other words, constructor overloading in Java allows to have more than one constructor inside one class. The number of parameters can be same but it can have different data types.

e.g.
```
public class Smart
{
  public Smart()
  {
    //statement
  }
  public Smart(int i)
  {
    //statement
  }
  public Smart(String str)
  {
    //statement
  }
  public static void main(String args[])
  {
    Smart s=New Smart();
    Smart ss=New Smart(10);
    Smart st=New Smart("java");
  }
}
```

Using this( ) with a Constructor

The this( ) can be used to invoke another constructor in the same class. Also, this constructor can be used to implement local chaining of constructors in a class.

The this( ) call in a constructor invokes an other constructor with the corresponding parameter list within the same class. This approach, is better if you have many constructor in the class and want to reuse the constructor.

e.g.
```
class Student
{
  int id;
  String name;
  Student()
  {
    System.out.println("default constructor");
  }
  Student(int id, String name)
  {
    this();
    this.id=id;
    this.name=name;
  }
  void display()
```

```
        {
          System.out.println(id + " " +name);
        }
        public static void main(String args[])
        {
          Student e1=new Student(111, "Karan");
          Student e2=new Student(222, "Arjun");
          e1.display();
          e2.display();
        }
      }
```

Output

default constructor
default constructor
111 Karan
222 Arjun

Difference between Constructor and Method

Constructor		Method	
(i)	It should not have any return type.	(i)	It should have return type.
(ii)	It will be called automatically whenever object is created.	(ii)	It should be called explicitly either with object reference or class reference.
(iii)	Constructor must be class name.	(iii)	Method can be any user defined name.
(iv)	The Java compiler provides a default constructor, if we do not have any constructor.	(iv)	Method is not provided by compiler in any case.

EXAM ORIENTED QUESTIONS

TYPE - 1   01 Mark

Multiple Choice Questions

Q.1 Which of the following statements is true about constructors in Java?
(a) Constructors have a return type, which is usually void.
(b) Constructors have the same name as the class.
(c) A class can have only one constructor.
(d) Constructors are automatically called when an object is declared but not instantiated.

Q.2 If the name of the class is "Yellow", what can be the possible name for its constructors? **ICSE 2024**
(a) yellow
(b) YELLOW
(c) Yell
(d) Yellow

Q.3 The method with the same name as of the class and which does not have a return data type is called as **ICSE SQP 2022 (Sem I)**
(a) Constructor
(b) Function
(c) Method

Q.4 Observing the two code snippets, which of the following statements about constructors is best supported?

```
public class Dog
{
 public Dog()
 {
  System.out.println("Woof!");
 }
}
```

```
public class Cat
{
 public int Cat()
 {// Note the return type
  System.out.println("Meow!");
  return 0;
 }
}
```

(a) Constructors must always have a void return type.
(b) The name of a constructor can be different from the class name if it has a return type.
(c) Snippet B demonstrates a valid constructor with an integer return type.
(d) Constructors do not have a return type, as seen in Snippet A.

Q.5 What is the purpose of a constructor in Java?
(a) To define the methods that an object can perform.
(b) To allocate memory for the object.
(c) To initialize the object's instance variables.
(d) To declare the class name.

Q.6 If a class does not explicitly define any constructors, what happens?
(a) A compilation error occurs.
(b) The program runs but no objects of that class can be created.
(c) Java automatically provides a default no-argument constructor.
(d) The instance variables of the objects are not initialized.

Q.7 Which of the following is NOT a valid characteristic of a constructor in Java?
(a) It can have access modifiers like public, private, protected, or default.
(b) It can be overloaded (have multiple constructors with different parameter lists).
(c) It can be declared as static.
(d) It is called using the new keyword followed by the constructor call.

Q.8 A method with the same name as of the class and with arguments and no return data type is termed as **ICSE SQP 2023**
(a) parameterized constructor
(b) default constructor
(c) non-parameterized constructor
(d) wrapper class method

Q.9 The concept of having more than one constructor with different types of parameters. **ICSE 2022 (Sem I)**
(a) Copy constructor (b) Method overloading
(c) Constructor overloading (d) Overloaded methods

Q.10 Constructor overloading follows which principle of Object Oriented programming? **ICSE SQP 2024**
(a) Inheritance (b) Polymorphism
(c) Abstraction (d) Encapsulation

Q.11 Which keyword is used to call one constructor from another constructor within the same class in Java?
(a) this (b) super (c) new (d) instanceof

Q.12 Consider the following Java code snippet:

```
class MyClass
{
  int x;
  public MyClass(int a)
  {
    x = a;
  }
}
public class Main
```

```
{
  public static void main(String[] args)
  {
    MyClass obj = new MyClass();
    System.out.println(obj.x);
  }
}
```

What will be the output of this code?

(a) 0

(b) The code will not compile because there is no no-argument constructor in MyClass.

(c) A runtime error will occur.

(d) Some garbage value.

Answers

1. (b) 2. (d) 3. (a) 4. (d) 5. (c)
6. (c) 7. (c) 8. (a) 9. (c) 10. (b)
11. (a) 12. (b)

TYPE - 2 01 Mark

Assertion-Reason Type Questions

Directions (Q. Nos. 1-6) The following questions are Assertion-Reason based questions. Choose the answer based on the code given below

(a) Both Assertion (A) and Reason (R) are true and Reason (R) is a correct explanation of Assertion (A).

(b) Both Assertion (A) and Reason (R) are true and Reason (R) is not a correct explanation of Assertion (A).

(c) Assertion (A) is true and Reason (R) is false.

(d) Assertion (A) is false and Reason (R) is true.

Q.1 Assertion(A) Constructors have a return type of void.

Reason(R) They are used to initialize objects, not return values.

Q.2 Assertion (A) A constructor's name must be different from the class name.

Reason(R) This helps distinguish it from regular methods.

Q.3 Assertion (A) Constructors in Java have a return type of void.

Reason (R) Constructors serve the purpose of initializing objects and setting their initial state; they do not return a specific value.

Q.4 Assertion (A) Within a Java class, one constructor can invoke another constructor of the same class.

Reason (R) This capability promotes code reusability by allowing common initialization logic to be shared between multiple constructors, leading to more concise and maintainable code.

Q.5 Assertion (A) If you don't define any constructors, Java provides a default constructor.

Reason (R) This ensures that objects can always be created.

Q.6 Assertion (A) Parameterized constructors offer more control over object initialization than default constructors.

Reason (R) They allow you to set specific values for object attributes upon creation.

Answers

1. (d) 2. (d) 3. (d) 4. (a) 5. (a)
6. (a)

TYPE - 3 01 Mark

Odd One Out

Q.1 Choose the odd one out:

(a) Automatic Invocation

(b) No Return Type

(c) Different Name than Class

(d) Can Call Another Constructor

Q.2 Choose the odd one out:

(a) Default Constructor

(b) Parameterized Constructor

(c) Static Constructor

(d) No-Argument Constructor

Q.3 Choose the odd one out

(a) Initializes object attributes

(b) Sets up necessary configurations

(c) Returns a value

(d) Is automatically invoked

Q.4 Choose the odd one out

(a) With no parameters

(b) With parameters

(c) With a void return type

(d) Using this() to call another constructor

Q.5 Choose the odd one out

(a) It takes parameters.

(b) It is automatically provided.

(c) It initializes objects with default values.

(d) It has no parameters.

Q.6 Choose the odd one out

(a) Takes parameters

(b) Initializes objects with specific values

(c) Is automatically provided by Java

(d) Provides control over object state

Q.7 Choose the odd one out
(a) Same as the class name
(b) Can be any valid identifier
(c) Must match the class name exactly
(d) Used for automatic invocation

Answers

1. (c) 2. (c) 3. (c) 4. (c) 5. (a)
6. (c) 7. (b)

TYPE - 4 02 Marks

Short Answer Type Questions

Q.1 What is constructor? When is it invoked? **ICSE 2014**

Ans Constructor in Java is a block of code, which is executed at the time of object creation. It has the same name as the name of the class to which it belongs. It never returns a value.

Q.2 State two features of a constructor. **ICSE 2018, 10**

Or Write two characteristics of a constructor.

Ans There are two features of a constructor
(i) A constructor does not have any return type
(ii) A constructor automatically called whenever object is created.

Q.3 Why do we need a constructor as a class member?

Ans A constructor is like a method with no return type. We need a constructor as a class type to create objects and to initialise value for an instance variable.

Q.4 What is a default constructor?

Ans The default constructor automatically initializes all instance variables to zero. When we do not explicitly define a constructor for a class, then Java creates a default constructor for that class.

Q.5 What is parameterised constructor? **ICSE 2016**

Ans **Parameterised constructors** are required to pass parameters on creation of objects. Unlike default constructor which does not have any parameters, it is however possible to have one or more parameters in a constructor.

Sample (int a, int b) is a parameterised constructor in which Sample is a class name and a, b are arguments.

Q.6 Name the two types of constructor. **ICSE 2015**

Ans Two types of constructor are
(i) Default constructor
(ii) Parameterised constructor

Q.7 Create a class with one integer instance variable. Initialize the variable using
(i) default constructor
(ii) parameterized constructor **ICSE 2012**

Ans (i)
```
class Books
{
    int que;
    public Books() //default constructor
    {
      System.out.println("Computer
                             Application");
      que=0;
    }
    public static void main(String[] args)
    {
      Books bs=new Books();
      System.out.println("Question="
                                +bs.que);
    }
}
```

Output Computer Application
Question = 0

(ii)
```
class Books1
{
    int que1;
    public Books1(int que1)
            //parameterised constructor
    {
      this.que1 = que1;
    }
    public static void main(String[]
                                  args)
    {
      Books1 bs1 = new Books1(40);
      System.out.println("Questions
                          =" +bs1.que1);
    }
}
```

Output Questions = 40

Q.8 Consider the following program segment and answer the questions below: **ICSE SQP 2025**

```
class calculate
{
  int a; double b;
  calculate()
  {
    a=0;
    b=0.0;
  }
    calculate(int x, double y)
    {
      a=x;
      b=y;
    }
    void sum()
    {
      System.out.println(a*b);
    }
}
```

Name the type of constructors used in the above program segment?

Ans. Default constructor, Parameterized Constructor

Q.9 Explain the concept of constructor overloading with an example. **ICSE 2020, 2017, ICSE SQP 2016, 2011**

Or What is constructor overloading. **ICSE SQP 2020**

Ans Constructor overloading is the concept to make constructor with same name of class and using different signature. A class can have more than one constructors.

Example of constructor overloading

```
class Age
{
    int age; //variable declaration
    public Age()
            //Constructor 1
    {
      age = -1;
    }
    public Age(int age) //Constructor 2
    {
      this.age = age;
    }
    public static void main(String[] args)
    {
      Age a1 = new Age();
                  //Calling constructor 1
      Age a2 = new Age(20);
                  //Calling constructor 2
    }
}
```

Q.10 Enter any two variables through constructor parameters and write a program to swap and print the values.

Ans.

```
class point
{
    int x, y;    //instance variables
    public point(int a, int b)
            // parameterised constructor
    {
      this.x = a;
      this.y = b;
    }
    public void swap()
    {
      int temp = x;
      x = y;
      y = temp;
    }
    public void display()
    {
      System.out.println("Point = ("+x+",
                                    "+y+")");
    }
    public static void main(String[] args)
    {
      point p = new point(3, 4);
      p.display(); //value before swapping
      p.swap();
      p.display();
                  //value after swapping
    }
}
```

Output Point = (3, 4)

Point = (4, 3)

Q.11 Consider and give the output of the following program **ICSE 2025**

```
class report
{
  int a,b;
  report()
  {
    a=10;
    b=15;
  }
  report(int x, int y)
  {
    a=x;
    b=y;
  }
  void print()
  {
    System.out.println(a*b);
  }
  static void main()
  {
    report r = new report();
    r.print();
    report p = new report(4, 5);
    p.print();
  }
}
```

Ans. Output

150

20

Q.12 Consider the given program and answer the questions given below: **ICSE 2024**

```
class temp
{
 int a;
 temp()
 {
     a=10;
 }
 temp(int z)
 {
     a=z;
 }
```

```
    void print()
    {
        System.out.println(a);
    }
    void main()
      {
        temp t = new temp();
        temp x = new temp(30);
        t.print();
        x.print();
      }
}
```

(a) What concept of OOPs is depicted in the above program with two constructors?

(b) What is the output of the method main()?

Ans. (a) The concept of Constructor Overloading (Polymorphism) is depicted in the program.

(b) Output of the main() method:

10

30

TYPE - 5 — 02 Marks

Differentiate

Q.1 What is the difference between a constructor function and a member function of a class? **ICSE SQP 2017**

Or

Give a difference between a constructor and a method. **ICSE 2013**

Or

State the difference between constructor and method.

Ans. Difference between constructor and method (function) are as follows

Constructor	Method (Function)
It has no return type.	It has a return type.
Constructor name should be same as the class name.	Method name can be any valid identifier.
Constructor is automatically called upon object creation.	Method are invoked explicitly.

Q.2 Differentiate between a default constructor and a parameterized constructor.

Ans. Difference between default constructor and parameterized constructor

Default Constructor	Parameterized Constructor
Takes no arguments (no parameters).	Takes one or more arguments (parameters).
Initializes object with default values for instance variables.	Initializes object with specific values provided as arguments.
Automatically provided by the compiler if no other constructor is defined.	Must be explicitly defined by the programmer.
Called when an object is created without any arguments.	Called when an object is created with arguments.
Instance variables are initialized with their default values (e.g., 0 for integers, null for objects, false for booleans).	Instance variables are initialized with the values passed as arguments.

Q.3 Explain the difference between constructor overloading and method overloading.

Ans. Difference between constructor overloading and method overloading

Constructor Overloading	Method Overloading
Defining multiple constructors in the same class, each with a different signature (parameter list).	Defining multiple methods in the same class, each with a different signature (parameter list).
To allow creating objects of the same class in different ways, with different initializations. Provides flexibility in object creation.	To perform similar operations on different types or numbers of arguments. Makes the class more versatile.
Automatically invoked during object creation using the new keyword. The specific constructor called depends on the arguments provided.	Explicitly called by name. The specific method called depends on the arguments provided.
Constructors do not have a return type (not even void).	Methods have a return type (which can be void).

TYPE - 6 — 15 Marks

Long Answer Type Questions

Q.1 Define a class Student described as below

Data members/instance variables

name, age, m1, m2, m3 (marks in 3 subjects), maximum, average

Member methods

(i) A parameterized constructor to initialize the data numbers.

(ii) To accept the details of a student.

(iii) To compute the average and the maximum out of three marks.

(iv) To display the name, age, marks in three subjects, maximum and average.

Write a main method to create an object of a class and call the above member methods.

ICSE 2010

Ans
```java
import java.io.*;
import java.util.Scanner;
class Student
{
  String name;
  int age;
  int m1, m2, m3;
  double average;
  int maximum;
  public void acceptDetails() throws
                                IOException
  {
    Scanner br = new Scanner(System.in);
    System.out.print("Enter name : ");
    name = br.nextLine();
    System.out.print("Enter age : ");
    age = Integer.parseInt(br.nextLine());
    System.out.print("Enter marks1 : ");
    m1 = Integer.parseInt(br.nextLine());
    System.out.print("Enter marks2 : ");
    m2 = Integer.parseInt(br.nextLine());
    System.out.print("Enter marks3 : ");
    m3 = Integer.parseInt(br.nextLine());
  }
  public void compute()
  {
    average = (m1 + m2 + m3) / 3.0;
    maximum = Math.max(m1, Math.max(m2,
                                m3));
  }
  public void display()
  {
    System.out.println("Name = " + name);
    System.out.println("Age = " + age);
    System.out.println("Marks1 = " + m1);
    System.out.println("Marks2 = " + m2);
    System.out.println("Marks3 = " + m3);
    System.out.println("Maximum = "
                          + maximum);
    System.out.println("Average = "
                          + average);
  }
  public static void main(String[] args)
                    throws IOException
  {
    Student student = new Student();
    student.acceptDetails();
    student.compute();
    student.display();
  }
}
```

Q.2 A private cab service company provides service within the city at the following rates: **ICSE 2020**

	AC CAR	NON AC CAR
UPTO 5 KM	₹ 150/-	₹ 120/-
BEYOND 5 KM	₹ 10/- PER KM	₹ 08/- PER KM

Design a class CabService with the following description:

Member variables/data members:	
String carType	to store the type of car (AC or NON AC)
double km	to store the kilometer travelled
double bill	to calculate and store the bill amount
Member methods:	
CabService()	default constructor to initialize data members. String data members to "" and double data members to 0.0.
void accept()	to accept carType and km (using Scanner class only).
void calculate()	to calculate the bill as per the rules given above.
void display()	to display the bill as per the following format CAR TYPE: KILOMETER TRAVELLED: TOTAL BILL:

Create an object of the class in the main() method and invoke the member methods.

Ans.
```java
import java.util.Scanner;
class CabService
{
  String carType;
  double km;
  double bill;
  public CabService()
  {
    carType = "";
    km = 0.0;
    bill = 0.0;
  }
  public void accept()
  {
    Scanner in = new Scanner(System.in);
    System.out.print("Car type
                        (AC/Non-AC): ");
    carType = in.nextLine().toUpperCase();
    System.out.print("Distance travelled
                              (in km): ");
    km = Double.parseDouble(in.nextLine());
  }
  public void calculate()
  {
    if(km <= 5)
```

```
{
  if(carType.startsWith("AC"))
  {
    carType = "AC CAR";
    bill = 150.0;
  }
  else if(carType.startsWith("NON"))
  {
    carType = "NON AC CAR";
    bill = 120.0;
  }
  else
  {
    System.out.println("Invalid car
                        type entered.");
    bill = -1; // Indicate an error
  }
}
else
{
  if(carType.startsWith("AC"))
  {
    carType = "AC CAR";
    bill = 150.0 + (km - 5) * 10;
  }
  else if(carType.startsWith("NON"))
  {
    bill = 120.0 + (km - 5) * 8;
    carType = "NON AC CAR";
  }
  else
  {
    System.out.println("Invalid car
                        type entered.");
    bill = -1; // Indicate an error
  }
}
}
public void display()
{
  System.out.println("------------");
  System.out.println("CAR TYPE: "
                        + carType);
  System.out.println("KILOMETER
                 TRAVELLED: " + km);
  System.out.println("TOTAL BILL: "
                           + bill);
  System.out.println("------------");
}
public static void main(String[] args)
{
  CabService obj = new CabService();
  obj.accept();
  obj.calculate();
  if(obj.bill != -1)
  {
    obj.display();
  }
}
}
```

Q.3 Design a class name ShowRoom with the following description: **ICSE 2019**

Instance variables / Data members:	
String name	To store the name of the customer
long mobno	To store the mobile number of the customer
double cost	To store the cost of the items purchased
double dis	To store the discount amount
double amount	To store the amount to be paid after discount
Member methods:	
ShowRoom()	default constructor to initialize data members
void input()	To input customer name, mobile number, cost
void calculate()	To calculate discount on the cost of purchased items, based on following criteria

Cost	Discount (in percentage)
Less than or equal to ₹10000	5%
More than ₹10000 and less than or equal to ₹20000	10%
More than ₹20000 and less than or equal to ₹35000	15%
More than ₹35000	20%

void display()	To display customer name, mobile number, amount to be paid after discount.

Write a main method to create an object of the class and call the above member methods.

Ans.
```
import java.util.Scanner;
public class ShowRoom
{
  private String name;
  private long mobno;
  private double cost;
  private double dis;
  private double amount;
  public ShowRoom()
  {
    name = "";
    mobno = 0;
    cost = 0.0;
    dis = 0.0;
    amount = 0.0;
  }
  public void input()
```

```
  {
    Scanner in = new Scanner(System.in);
    System.out.print("Enter customer name: ");
    name = in.nextLine();
    System.out.print("Enter customer
                                  mobile no: ");
    mobno = in.nextLong();
    System.out.print("Enter cost: ");
    cost = in.nextDouble();
  }
  public void calculate()
  {
    int disPercent = 0;
    if (cost <= 10000)
      disPercent = 5;
    else if (cost <= 20000)
      disPercent = 10;
    else if (cost <= 35000)
      disPercent = 15;
    else
      disPercent = 20;
    dis = cost * disPercent / 100.0;
    amount = cost - dis;
  }
  public void display()
  {
    System.out.println("Customer Name: "
                                     + name);
    System.out.println("Mobile Number: "
                                     + mobno);
    System.out.println("Amout after
                      discount: " + amount);
  }
  public static void main(String args[])
  {
    ShowRoom obj = new ShowRoom();
    obj.input();
    obj.calculate();
    obj.display();
  }
}
```

Q.4 Define a class named BookFair with the following description:

Instance variables/Data members:	
String Bname	stores the name of the book
double price	stores the price of the book
Member methods:	
BookFair()	Default constructor to initialize data members
void Input()	To input and store the name and the price of the book.
void calculate()	To calculate the price after discount. Discount is calculated based on the following criteria.

Price	Discount
Less than or equal to ₹1000	2% of price
More than ₹1000 and less than or equal to ₹3000	10% of price
More than ₹3000	15% of price

void display()	To display the name and price of the book after discount.

Write a main method to create an object of the class and call the above member methods.

Ans.
```
import java.util.Scanner;
public class BookFair
{
  private String bname;
  private double price;
  public BookFair()
  {
    bname = "";
    price = 0.0;
  }
  public void input()
  {
    Scanner in = new Scanner(System.in);
    System.out.print("Enter name of the
                                       book: ");
    bname = in.nextLine();
    System.out.print("Enter price of the
                                       book: ");
    price = in.nextDouble();
  }
  public void calculate()
  {
    double disc;
    if (price <= 1000)
      disc = price * 0.02;
    else if (price <= 3000)
      disc = price * 0.1;
    else
      disc = price * 0.15;
    price -= disc;
  }
  public void display()
  {
    System.out.println("Book Name: "
                                   + bname);
    System.out.println("Price after
                      discount: " + price);
  }
  public static void main(String args[])
  {
    BookFair obj = new BookFair();
    obj.input();
    obj.calculate();
    obj.display();
  }
}
```

05

LIBRARY CLASSES

Java provides pre-made library classes (also called **standard** or **built-in classes**) to help programmers. These classes are organized into **packages**.

Packages

Java packages group classes to ensure unique names and prevent conflicts. Examples include java.lang (automatically included), java.util, java.io, etc. Packages allow you to use their classes in your programs.

Java packages group related classes. You can import and reuse these classes in your programs as needed. A package is a container for related classes, some of which are accessible for use.

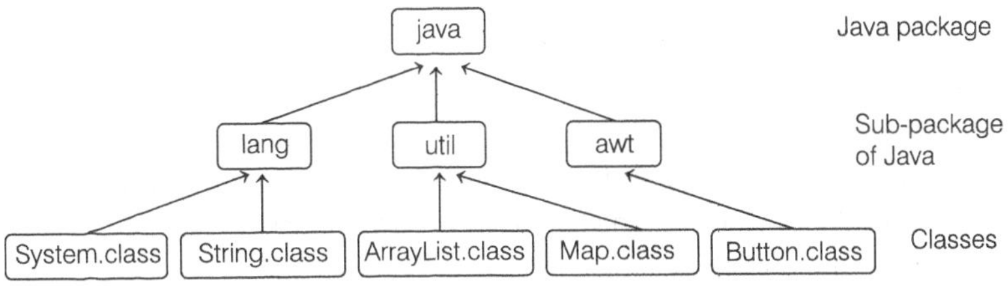

Introduction to Wrapper Classes

Wrapper classes in Java provide an object representation for primitive data types such as **int**, **double**, and **char**. Each primitive type has a corresponding wrapper class. These wrapper classes are part of the java.lang package, so they are available by default and do not require explicit import.

Data Type	Wrapper Class
byte	Byte
short	Short
int	Integer
long	Long
float	Float
double	Double
char	Character
boolean	Boolean

Need for Wrapper Classes

Primitive data types do not have built-in methods and cannot be used in collections like ArrayList, which store only objects. Wrapper classes solve this by converting primitive values into objects, enabling method use and easy data conversion between strings and numbers.

Import Statements

These statements in Java, allow to refer those classes, which are declared in other packages to be accessed without referring to the full package name.

Syntax `import package_name.classname;`

e.g. the package java.util contains many useful classes, such as ArrayList, then instead of referring to java.util.ArrayList wherever the ArrayList class is being used, you can just refer it by ArrayList.

Such as:
```
import java.util.ArrayList;
..............
..............
ArrayList ArrayList1=new ArrayList();
```

Methods of Wrapper Classes and Their Usage

Wrapper classes provide built-in methods to perform operations on numeric and character data efficiently. These methods are categorized into numeric conversion methods and character operation methods.

1. Numeric Conversion Methods

These methods convert string representations of numbers into their respective primitive types.

- **int parseInt(String s)** → Converts a string into an integer.
- **long parseLong(String s)** → Converts a string into a long integer.
- **float parseFloat(String s)** → Converts a string into a floating-point number.
- **double parseDouble(String s)** → Converts a string into a double-precision number.

Example
```
String num = "100";
  int value = Integer.parseInt(num);  // Converts "100" to an integer 100
```

2. Character Operation Methods

These methods help in analyzing and modifying character data.

- **boolean isDigit(char ch)** → Checks if the character is a digit (0-9).
- **boolean isLetter(char ch)** → Checks if the character is a letter (A-Z, a-z).
- **boolean isLetterOrDigit(char ch)** → Checks if the character is either a letter or a digit.
- **boolean isLowerCase(char ch)** → Checks if the character is in lowercase.
- **boolean isUpperCase(char ch)** → Checks if the character is in uppercase.
- **boolean isWhitespace(char ch)** → Checks if the character is a whitespace.

Example
```
char ch = 'A';
  System.out.println(Character.isLetter(ch));  // true
  System.out.println(Character.isDigit(ch));   // false
```

3. Character Case Conversion Methods

These methods are used to convert the case of characters.

- **char toLowerCase(char ch)** → Converts uppercase letters to lowercase.
- **char toUpperCase(char ch)** → Converts lowercase letters to uppercase.

Example
```
char ch = 'a';
      System.out.println(Character.toUpperCase(ch));    // Output: 'A'
```

Class as a Composite Type

A class is a composite data type that combines variables and methods into a single unit. Unlike primitive types (like int, char), which store only a single value, a class can store multiple values and define behaviors.

Difference Between Primitive and Composite Types

Aspect	Primitive Data Type	Composite Data Type (Class)
Nature	Stores a single value (e.g., int, char).	Groups multiple variables and methods.
Functionality	No built-in methods or operations.	Allows user-defined methods for behavior.

Example : Primitive Type
```
int age = 20;
char grade = 'A';
```

Class as a User-Defined Data Type

A class allows programmers to create custom data types with specific attributes and behaviors. Objects of a class act as instances of this new type.

Example

```
class Student
{
   String name;
   int age;
   void display()
   {
      System.out.println("Name: " + name + ", Age: " + age);
   }
}
```

Autoboxing and Unboxing in Wrapper Classes

Autoboxing

Automatic conversion of primitive data types to the object of their corresponding wrapper classes is known as autoboxing.

e.g., Conversion of int to Integer, long to Long, double to Double etc.

Unboxing

It is just the reverse process of autoboxing. Automatically converting an object of a wrapper class to its corresponding primitive type is known as unboxing.

e.g., Conversion of Integer to Int, Long to long, Double to double etc.

EXAM ORIENTED QUESTIONS

TYPE - 1   01 Mark

Multiple Choice Questions

Q.1 Character class methods are found in the packages called: **ICSE 2025**
(a) java.util (b) java.lang
(c) java.awt (d) java.io

Q.2 Name the package that contains wrapper classes: **ICSE SQP 2024, ICSE SQP 2022 (Sem II)**
(a) java.lang (b) java.util
(c) java.io (d) java.awt

Q.3 _______ class is used to convert a primitive data type to its corresponding object. **ICSE 2022 (Sem II)**
(a) String (b) Wrapper
(c) System (d) Math

Q.4 The keyword used to call package in the program: **ICSE 2023**
(a) extends (b) export
(c) import (d) package

Q.5 Corresponding wrapper class of float data type is _______. **ICSE 2022 (Sem II)**
(a) FLOAT (b) float
(c) Float (d) Floating

Q.6 Corresponding wrapper class of int data type is .... **ICSE SQP 2022 (Sem II)**
(a) integer (b) INTEGER
(c) Int (d) Integer

Q.7 Which of the following is the wrapper class for the data type char? **ICSE SQP 2024**
(a) String (b) Char
(c) Character (d) Float

Q.8 The method to check if a character is an alphabet or not is **ICSE SQP 2023**
(a) isLetter(char) (b) isAlpha(char)
(c) isUppercase(char) (d) isLowercase(char)

Q.9 The output of Double.parseDouble("71.25") + 0.75 is:
(a) 72 (b) 72.0 (c) 71.0 (d) 71.75

Q.10 Which of the following converts "25" to 25.0? **ICSE 2025**
(a) Double Parsedouble("25")
(b) Double.parse("25")
(c) Double.parseDouble("25")
(d) Double.parseDouble(25)

Q.11 State the value of y after the following is executed

```
char x = '7';
y = Character.isLetter(x);
```

ICSE SQP 2022 (Sem II)
(a) false (b) 7
(c) true (d) '7'

Q.12 Return data type of isLetter(char) is __________ . **ICSE 2022 (Sem II)**
(a) Boolean (b) boolean
(c) bool (d) char

Q.13 What is the method to check whether a character is a letter or digit? **ICSE 2024**
(a) `isDigit(char)` (b) `isLetterOrDigit()`
(c) `isLetterOrDigit(char)` (d) `isLETTERorDIGIT(char)`

Q.14 What will be the output for:

```
System.out.print(Character.toLowerCase('1'));
```

ICSE SQP 2024
(a) 0 (b) 1
(c) A (d) true

Q.15 Method that converts a character to uppercase is __________ . **ICSE 2022 (Sem II)**
(a) toUpper( ) (b) ToUpperCase( )
(c) toUppercase( ) (d) toUpperCase(char)

Q.16 The method to convert a lowercase character to uppercase is: **ICSE SQP 2025**
(a) String.toUpperCase()
(b) Character.isUppercase (char)
(c) Character.toUpperCase(char)
(d) toUpperCase ()

Q.17 The image compares the use of primitive and composite data types. The Character class is used to perform operations on primitive char, while Book represents a real-world entity as a class. What is the key learning from this image?

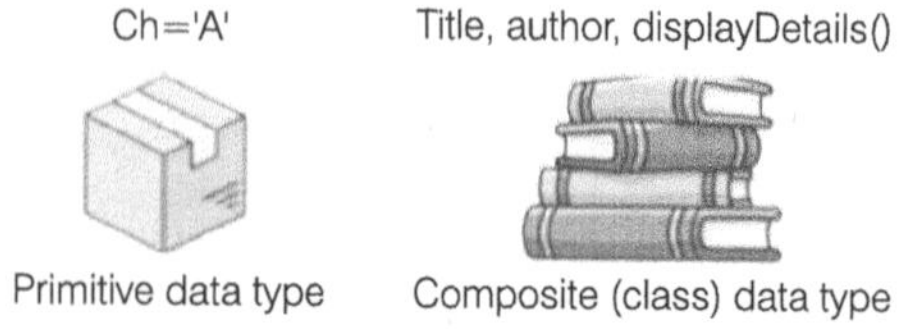

(a) Primitive data types can only be used with loops
(b) Wrapper classes like Character allow methods on primitives; classes like Book represent user-defined composite types
(c) All data types in Java are primitive by default
(d) Classes can only be used for storing numeric data

Q.18 When an object of a Wrapper class is converted to its corresponding primitive data type, it is called as

ICSE 2023

(a) boxing (b) explicit type conversion
(c) unboxing (d) implicit type conversion

Q.19 When primitive data type is converted to its corresponding object of its class, it is called as ....

ICSE SQP 2022 (Sem II), ICSE SQP 2024

(a) boxing (b) explicit type conversion
(c) unboxing (d) implicit type conversion

Q.20 What concepts are being demonstrated in the image?

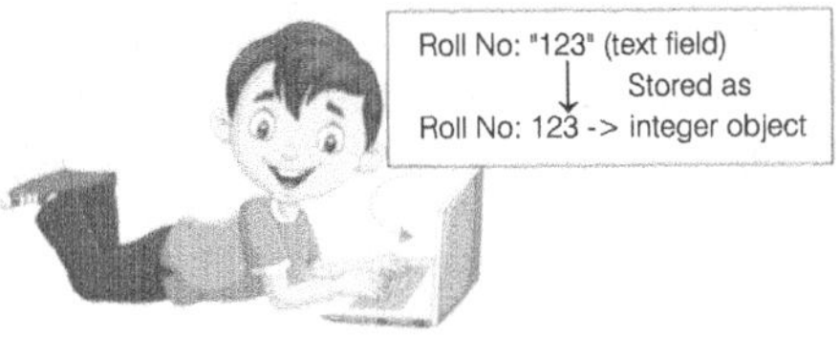

(a) Method overloading and data encapsulation
(b) parseInt method, Autoboxing and Unboxing
(c) String manipulation and object serialization
(d) Recursion and dynamic method dispatch

Answers

1. (b)	**2.** (a)	**3.** (b)	**4.** (c)	**5.** (c)
6. (d)	**7.** (c)	**8.** (a)	**9.** (b)	**10.** (c)
11. (a)	**12.** (b)	**13.** (c)	**14.** (b)	**15.** (d)
16. (c)	**17.** (b)	**18.** (c)	**19.** (a)	**20.** (b)

TYPE - 2 1 Mark

Assertion-Reason Type Questions

Directions (Q. Nos. 1-5) The following questions are Assertion-Reason based questions. Choose the answer based on the code given below

(a) Both Assertion (A) and Reason (R) are true and Reason (R) is a correct explanation of Assertion (A).
(b) Both Assertion (A) and Reason (R) are true and Reason (R) is not a correct explanation of Assertion (A).
(c) Assertion (A) is true and Reason (R) is false.
(d) Assertion (A) is false and Reason (R) is true.

Q.1 Assertion (A) Wrapper classes are essential for using primitive data types in collections like ArrayList.

Reason (R) ArrayLists can only store objects, and wrapper classes provide object representations of primitive types.

Q.2 Assertion (A) Integer class can be used in the program without calling a package. **ICSE SQP 2025**

Reason (R) It belongs to the default package java.lang.

Q.3 Assertion (A) Integer.parseInt("123") converts the string "123" into an Integer object.

Reason (R) parseInt() is a method of the Integer wrapper class.

Q.4 Assertion (A) Primitive data types have built-in methods for various operations.

Reason (R) Primitive types are objects, and objects have methods.

Q.5 Assertion (A) Classes in Java are classified as composite data types.

Reason (R) Classes encapsulate data (attributes, represented by variables) and behavior (methods) within a single, cohesive unit, thus composing a more complex data structure than primitive types.

Answers

1. (a) **2.** (a) **3.** (d) **4.** (c) **5.** (a)

TYPE - 3 1 Mark

Odd One Out

Q.1 Which of the following is NOT a Java package?
(a) java.lang (b) java.util
(c) java.io (d) ArrayList

Q.2 Which of the following is NOT a method of a wrapper class used for numeric conversion?
(a) parseInt() (b) isDigit()
(c) parseFloat() (d) parseDouble()

Q.3 Which of the following is NOT a character operation method?
(a) isLetter() (b) toLowerCase()
(c) isWhitespace() (d) isUpperCase()

Q.4 Which of the following is NOT a method that converts a string to a primitive type?
(a) parseInt() (b) parseLong()
(c) toUpperCase() (d) parseFloat()

Q.5 Which of the following is NOT a primitive data type?
(a) int (b) char (c) String (d) double

Q.6 Which of the following is NOT a characteristic of a composite data type (class)?
(a) Groups multiple variables and methods.
(b) Allows user-defined methods for behavior.
(c) Stores a single value.
(d) Allows programmers to create custom data types.

Answers

1. (d) **2.** (b) **3.** (b) **4.** (c) **5.** (c)
6. (c)

TYPE - 4 2 Marks

Short Answer Type Questions

Q.1 What is meant by a package? Name any two Java application programming interface packages. **ICSE 2014**

Or What is package? Give an example. **ICSE 2019, 06**

Ans. A package is a namespace that organises a set of related types (classes, interfaces, enumerations and annotations) providing access protection. It allows classes in the same package to access each other's package access members.

Two Java application programming interface packages are:

(i) java.lang (ii) java.io

Q.2 What are library classes? Give an example. **ICSE 2011**

Ans Predefined classes of Java, which get included in an application program themself are called library classes. They are also known as standard Java classes or built-in Java classes. These classes also have built-in member variables, constructors and methods like ordinary classes developed by programmer. These library classes are contained in packages.

e.g. java.io, java.lang, etc.

Q.3 Name any two library packages. **ICSE 2016**

Ans Two library packages are

(i) java.lang (ii) java.util

Q.4 What is a wrapper class? Give an example. **ICSE 2006**

Ans. Wrapper class is used to convert any primitive data type into object. A wrapper class also contains a number of methods, which may be used in the processing of the corresponding data type. e.g. the wrapper class for int data type is Integer.

Q.5 Name the wrapper classes of char type and boolean type. **ICSE 2015**

Ans.

Primitive Type	Wrapper Classes
char	Character
boolean	Boolean

Q.6 Name any two wrapper classes. **ICSE 2013**

Ans Wrapper classes are

(i) Integer (ii) Boolean

Q.7 What is the use of import statement in Java? **ICSE 2020**

Ans. The import statement in Java provides a mechanism to make classes and interfaces from other packages accessible within the current compilation unit, thereby simplifying their usage and preventing naming collisions.

Q.8 Predict the output of the following code snippet: **ICSE SQP 2024**

```
String a = "20";
String b = "23";
int p = Integer.parseInt(a);
int q = Integer.parseInt(b);
System.out.print(a + "*" + b);
```

Ans. Output

20*23

Q.9 A student is trying to convert the string present in x to a numerical value, so that he can find the square root of the converted value. However the code has an error. Name the error (syntax / logical / runtime). Correct the code so that it compiles and runs correctly. **ICSE SQP 2025**

```
String x= "25";
int y=Double.parseDouble(x);
double r=Math.sqrt(y);
System.out.println(r);
```

Ans. Syntax error in the line

```
int y=Double.parseDouble(x);
```

Corrected code

```
String x= "25";
double y=Double.parseDouble(x); //int
changed to double
double r=Math.sqrt(y);
System.out.println(r);
```

Q.10

```
String s1= "45.50";
String s2 = "54.50";
double d1 = Double.parseDouble(s1);
double d2 = Double.parseDouble(s2);
int x =(int)(d1+d2);
```

What is value of x ? **ICSE 2024**

Ans. Result in the output is 100.

Q.11 State the data type and value of res after the following is executed **ICSE 2019**

```
char ch = '9';
res = Character.isDigit(ch);
```

Ans. The data type of res is boolean and value of res after executing the code will be true.

Q.12 State the data type and value of y after the following code is executed **ICSE 2015**

```
char x = '7';
y = Character.isLetter(x);
```

Ans data type of y = boolean

value of y = false

Q.13 Predict the output of the following code snippet: **ICSE SQP 2025**

```
char ch='B',
char chr=Character.toLowerCase(ch);
int n=(int)chr-10;
System.out.println((char)n+"\t"+chr);
```

Ans. Output X b

Q.14 (i) int res = 'A'; **ICSE 2018**

What is the value of res?

(ii) Name the package that contains wrapper classes.

Ans. (i) Value of res is 65 which is the ASCII code of A. As res is an int variable and we are trying to assign it the character A so through implicit type conversion the ASCII code of A is assigned to res.

(ii) java.lang

Q.15 Primitive data types are built in data types which are a part of the wrapper classes. These wrapper classes are encapsulated in the java.lang package. Non-primitive datatypes like Scanner class are a part of the utility package for which and object needs to be created. **ICSE 2024**

(a) To which package the Character and Boolean classes belong?

(b) Write the statement to access the Scanner class in the program.

Ans. (a) java.lang

(b) import java.util.Scanner

Q.16 What is autoboxing in Java? Give an example. **ICSE 2020**

Ans. Autoboxing in Java is the automatic conversion between primitive data types (like int, double) and their corresponding wrapper classes (like Integer, Double). For example, assigning an int to an Integer variable involves autoboxing.

Example Integer obj = 10; // Autoboxing: int 10 is converted to Integer.

Q.17 Define boxing with an example. **ICSE SQP 2023**

Ans It is used to convert the primitive data type into corresponding objects.

e.g. Conversion of int to Integer.

```
Integer obj = new Integer ("2526");
```

TYPE - 5   2 Marks

Output Based Questions

Q.1 Predict the output of the following code snippet **ICSE 2023**

```
String P="20", Q="22";
int a = Integer.parseInt(P);
int b = Integer.valueOf(Q);
System.out.println(a+""+b);
```

(a) 20 (b) 20 22

(c) 2220 (d) 22

Ans. (b) 20 22

Q.2 Give the output of the following code: **ICSE 2022 (Sem II)**

```
String A ="56.0",B="94.0";
double C=Double.parseDouble(A);
double D= Double.parseDouble(B);
System.out.println((C+D));
```

(a) 100 (b) 150.0 (c) 100.0 (d) 150

Ans (b) 150.0

Q.3 Give the output of the following code. **ICSE SQP 2022 (Sem II)**

```
String A = "26.0", B = "74.0";
double C = Double.parseDouble(A);
double D = Double.parseDouble(B);
System.out.println((C+D));
```

(a) 26 (b) 74 (c) 100.0 (d) 2674

Ans (c) 100.0

Q.4 Give the output of the following code **ICSE 2019**

```
String P = "20", Q = "19";
int a = Integer.parseInt(P);
int b = Integer.valueOf(Q);
System.out.println(a + " " + b);
```

Ans **Output** 2019

Q.5 Give the output of the following Character class methods **ICSE 2023**

(a) Character.toUpperCase('a')

(b) Character.isLetterOrDigit ('#')

Ans (a) A (b) false

TYPE - 6   2 Marks

Differentiate

Q.1 Write a difference between the functions isUpperCase() and toUpperCase(). **ICSE 2018**

Or Differentiate between isUpperCase(char) and toUpperCase(char). **ICSE 2018, ICSE SQP 2017**

Ans.

isUpperCase()	toUpperCase()
Checks whether a given character is an uppercase letter or not.	Converts the character to its upper case form and all the digits and special characters will remain as it is.
It returns a Boolean data type.	Returns char or String type.

Q.2 Differentiate between Boxing and Unboxing. **SQP 2020, ICSE 2024**

Ans.

Boxing	Unboxing
Boxing is used to store value types in the Garbage-collected Heap.	Unboxing an Interface type of a value type that implements the interface.
Convert the value type to reference type.	Convert to reference type to value type.
Implicit Conversion	Explicit Conversion

ENCAPSULATION

Encapsulation binds **data (variables)** and **methods** within a class, while restricting direct access, and allowing controlled changes.

Importance

1. **Data Hiding** It prevents unauthorized access, which ensures data security.
2. **Security** It restricts direct modification, which allows controlled updates.
3. **Maintainability** Internal changes of code don't affect external code.
4. **Modularity & Reusability** Encapsulated classes can be reused without exposing internal details.

Encapsulation is achieved using **access specifiers** (private, protected, public), ensuring structured and secure programming.

Access Specifiers and Their Scope in Java

Access specifiers in Java define the visibility and accessibility of classes, methods, and variables. They help in controlling how different parts of a program interact, which ensures data security and preventing unauthorized access. By restricting access, they enhance code reliability and maintainability.

Interfaces in java

In Java, an interface is like a contract that defines methods without providing implementations. It can include method signatures, constants, default methods, static methods, and nested types. Interfaces allow different, unrelated classes to implement common functionality by following the contract.

Key Features

- **Abstract Methods** All methods are abstract and must be implemented by the class.
- **No Constructor** Interfaces cannot have constructors.
- **Multiple Inheritance** A class can implement multiple interfaces.

Types of Access Specifiers in Java

Java access specifiers (or modifiers) are keywords placed before class member declarations to control accessibility and enable encapsulation. They define who can use methods and variables.

Java provides four types of access specifier:

1. Public

The public access specifier is the most open access level. Classes, methods, and fields declared as public can be accessed from any class in a Java program, regardless of whether these classes are in the same package or a different package.

e.g.
```
public class Book  //public class
{
   public int x,y;
              //public instance variables
}
```

2. Protected

The protected access specifier cannot be applied to classes or interfaces. Methods and fields can be declared protected, however, methods and fields within an interface cannot be declared protected. A protected member can be accessed by subclasses in other packages or by any class within the same package.

e.g.
```
class Book
{
   protected boolean colour()
      //protected method
   {
      //implementation details
   }
}
```

3. Private

The private access specifier provides the lowest level of accessibility. Private methods and fields can only be accessed within the same class. They are not visible to or inherited by subclasses. This allows for encapsulation, hiding data from external access.

e.g.
```
class Book
{
   private double x, y;
         //private instance variables
}
```

4. Default (friendly)

The default access specifier occurs when no explicit access modifier is declared for a class, field, or method. In Java, this is also known as package-private.

e.g.
```
class Book
{
   int i; //default instance variable
}
```

Visibility Rules of Access Specifiers in Java

In Java, access specifiers are essential for encapsulation and data hiding. They control the visibility and accessibility of class members—variables, methods, and classes—ensuring data integrity and restricting unauthorized access.

Application to Variables, Methods, and Classes

The application of access specifiers extends to variables (fields), methods, and classes, each with its own implications.

- **Variables (Fields)** Access specifiers applied to fields determine the extent to which their values can be read or modified by other classes.
- **Methods** Access specifiers applied to methods define the scope within which they can be invoked.
- **Classes (Top-Level)** Only public and default (package-private) access specifiers are applicable to top-level classes.

The table below gives a simple comparison of the visibility levels provided by the private, protected, and public access specifiers:

Access Specifier	Within Same Class	Within Same Package	Within Subclass (Different Package)	Anywhere
private	Yes	No	No	No
protected	Yes	Yes	Yes	No
public	Yes	Yes	Yes	Yes
Default	Yes	Yes	No	No

Scope of Variables in Java

Variable scope determines a variable's lifetime and accessibility. It controls where a variable can be used within a program.

Thus, a Java variable can have one of the three scope:

1. Class Variables (Static Variables)

Class variables, also known as **static variables**, are declared using the static keyword. These variables belong to the class itself, rather than to individual instances (objects) of the class. As a result, they are shared among all objects of that class. Any modification to a class variable by one object is reflected in all other objects of the same class.

e.g.
```
class MyAddress
{
   static int count=0;
               //class variable
   public void increment()
   {
      count++;
   }
   public static void main(String args[])
   {
      MyAddress ma=new MyAddress();
      MyAddress ma1=new MyAddress();
      ma.increment();
      ma1.increment();
      System.out.println("ma : count is="+ma.count);
      System.out.println("ma1: count is="+ma1.count);
   }
}
```

Output

ma : count is = 2
ma1: count is = 2

Note *Static variables (or class variables) are common to all the instance (or object) of the same class.*

2. Instance Variables

Instance variables, also known as **non-static variables**, are declared without the **static** keyword. Each object of a class has its own copy of instance variables. Consequently, modifications made to an instance variable in one object do not affect the corresponding variable in other objects.

e.g.
```
class Address
{
   private String phone;   // Instance variable
   public void setphone(String phone)
   {
      this.phone = phone;
   }
}
class Main_class
{
   public static void main(String[] args)
   { // access the Address class
      Address a=new Address();
      a.setphone("001");
   }
}
```

3. Local Variables

Local variables are declared within a **method**, **constructor**, or **block of code**. Their scope is limited to the method, constructor, or block in which they are declared. They cease to exist when the method, constructor, or block completes execution.

e.g.

```
public class Calc
{
   public void Age()
   {
      int age = 0;        //local variable
      age = age + 7;
      System.out.println("Age is:"+age);
   }
   public static void main(String args[])
   {
      Calc m = new Calc();
      m.Age();
   }
}
```

Output Age is: 7

4. Argument Variables

These are the variables that are defined in the **header of a constructor** or **a method**. The scope of these variables is the method or constructor in which they are defined. Once the method finishes execution, these variables are destroyed.

e.g.

```
public class myprogram
{
   public static void main(string[] args)
   {
      double r;
      r = ToolBox.min (1.0, 4.0);
               //argument variable
   }
}
public class ToolBox
{
   public static double min(double a, double b)
   {
      double m= 0;
      if (a<b)
      {
         m = a ;
      }
      else
      {
            m = b;
      }
         return (m);
      }
   }
```

EXAM ORIENTED QUESTIONS

TYPE - 1 01 Mark

Multiple Choice Questions

Q.1 The process of binding the data and method together as one unit is called as: **ICSE SQP 2023**
(a) Encapsulation (b) Inheritance
(c) Polymorphism (d) Dynamic binding

Q.2 Which feature of encapsulation ensures that internal code changes do not affect external code?
(a) Data Hiding (b) Security
(c) Maintainability (d) Modularity

Q.3 Access specifiers are used for
(a) removing objects
(b) deallocating objects
(c) renaming objects
(d) restricting accessibility of class members

Q.4 The access modifier that gives most accessibility is **ICSE SQP 2022 (Sem II)**
(a) private (b) public
(c) protected (d) package

Q.5 Post office is an example for .... **ICSE 2025**
(a) public (b) local
(c) protected (d) private

Q.6 The access modifier that gives least accessibility is **ICSE 2022 (Sem II), ICSE 2024**
(a) private (b) public
(c) protected (d) package

Q.7 Which keyword is used to define a static variable in Java?
(a) final (b) static
(c) private (d) protected

Q.8 Which of the following variables is shared among all instances of a class?
(a) Local variable (b) Instance variable
(c) Static variable (d) Argument variable

Q.9 The variable that is accessible to all parts of the program is called
(a) local variable (b) global variable
(c) static variable (d) final variable

Q.10 Which type of variable is destroyed when the method or block finishes execution?
(a) Static variable (b) Instance variable
(c) Local variable (d) Class variable

Q.11 A data member of a class that carries a single shared value for all the objects of the class is called
(a) Class variable (b) Instance variable
(c) Static variable (d) Both (a) and (c)

Q.12 The variables declared in the function signature are named as
(a) Parameter variables (b) Argument variables
(c) Global variables (d) Return variables

Answers

1. (a)	**2.** (c)	**3.** (d)	**4.** (b)	**5.** (a)
6. (a)	**7.** (b)	**8.** (c)	**9.** (b)	**10.** (c)
11. (d)	**12.** (b)			

TYPE - 2 01 Mark

Assertion-Reason Type Questions

Directions (Q. Nos. 1-7) The following questions are Assertion-Reason based questions. Choose the answer based on the code given below
(a) Both Assertion (A) and Reason (R) are true and Reason (R) is a correct explanation of Assertion (A).
(b) Both Assertion (A) and Reason (R) are true and Reason (R) is not a correct explanation of Assertion (A).
(c) Assertion (A) is true and Reason (R) is false.
(d) Assertion (A) is false and Reason (R) is true.

Q.1 **Assertion (A)** Encapsulation ensures data security by preventing unauthorized access.
Reason (R) Encapsulation allows direct modification of variables from outside the class.

Q.2 **Assertion (A)** Interfaces in Java allow multiple inheritance.
Reason (R) A class can implement multiple interfaces, inheriting behaviors from all.

Q.3 **Assertion (A)** Private access specifier allows access to class members from any subclass.
Reason (R) Private members are only accessible within the same class.

Q.4 **Assertion (A)** The protected access specifier allows access within the same package and in subclasses of different packages.
Reason (R) Methods and fields declared protected can be inherited by subclasses, even if they are in different packages.

Q.5 Assertion (A) Static variables are unique to each object of a class.

Reason (R) Static variables belong to the class itself and are shared among all instances.

Q.6 Assertion (A) Local variables exist throughout the lifetime of the class.

Reason (R) Local variables are created when a method or block starts execution and are destroyed once it finishes.

Q.7 Assertion (A) In Java, the default access specifier is also known as package-private.

Reason (R) If no access modifier is specified, the class, method, or field is accessible only within the same package.

Answers

1. (c) **2.** (a) **3.** (d) **4.** (a) **5.** (d)
6. (d) **7.** (a)

TYPE - 3 — 01 Mark

Odd One Out

Q.1 Which of the following is NOT a benefit of encapsulation?
(a) Data Hiding (b) Modularity
(c) Global Variable Access (d) Maintainability

Q.2 Which of the following is NOT an access specifier in Java?
(a) public (b) static
(c) private (d) protected

Q.3 Which of the following is NOT a characteristic of interfaces?
(a) Constructors (b) Abstract Methods
(c) Multiple Inheritance (d) Constants

Q.4 Which of the following access specifiers allows access from anywhere?
(a) private (b) protected
(c) default (d) public

Q.5 Which of the following is NOT a place where local variables can be declared?
(a) Class Body (b) Methods
(c) Constructors (d) Blocks

Q.6 Which of the following is NOT a characteristic of static variables?
(a) Shared among instances
(b) Declared with static
(c) Unique to each object
(d) Belong to the class

Q.7 Which of the following is NOT a type of variable scope?
(a) Instance Variables (b) Class Variables
(c) Global Variables (d) Local Variables

Answers

1. (c) **2.** (b) **3.** (a) **4.** (d) **5.** (a)
6. (c) **7.** (c)

TYPE - 4 — 02 Marks

Short Answer Type Questions

Q.1 Define encapsulation. **ICSE SQP 2020, 16**

Ans. Encapsulation is a fundamental object-oriented programming concept where data (variables) and the methods that operates on that data are bundled together within a single unit, a class.

Q.2 Mention the types of access specifiers. **ICSE SQP 2020**

Or Name any two types of access specifier. **ICSE 2017, 16, 08**

Ans. Java provides four types of access specifier
(i) default (ii) public (iii) private (iv) protected

Q.3 Can a private member of a public class can be accessed by
(i) same class?
(ii) other class in the same package?

Ans (i) Yes, private member of a public class can be accessed by same class.
(ii) No, other classes are unable to access private member of a public class.

Q.4 Give reasons
(i) In what circumstances is a class derived publicly?
(ii) In what circumstances is a class derived privately?

Ans (i) In Java, a base class can be derived by a sub class by using only public mode of inheritance. When a class is derived publicly, the public and protected members of the base class are accessible to the derived class. Private members of the base class are not inherited by derived class.
(ii) Java does not support private and protected modes of inheritance. Classes are always derived publicly in Java.

Q.5 Consider the following class

```
public class MyClass
{
   public static int x = 3, y = 4;
   public int a = 2, b = 3;
}
```

(i) Name the variables for which each object of the class will have its own distinct copy.

(ii) Name the variables that are common to all object of the class. **ICSE 2014**

Ans. (i) 'a' and 'b'

(ii) 'x' and 'y'

Q.6 What is meant by private visibility of a method? **ICSE 2006**

Ans. Private visibility of a method means that methods is accessible only in same class and cannot be accessed by subclass or in other class.

TYPE - 5 — 02 Marks

Differentiate

Q.1 How are private members of a class different from public members? **ICSE 2018, 12**

Or

Differentiate between public and private modifiers for members of a class.

Ans. Difference between Public and Private Access Modifier

Public	Private
A public access specifier is the most open access level.	A private access specifier is the lowest level of accessibility.
It allows variables and methods visible to all classes.	Private methods and variables are not visible within the subclasses.
Public access specifier uses public keyword.	Private access specifier uses private keyword.

Q.2 Differentiate between private and protected visibility modifiers. **ICSE 2010**

Ans Differences between private and protected visibility modifiers

Private Visibility Modifier	Protected Visibility Modifier
It can be accessed by the same class to which the methods and fields belong.	It can be accessed by the subclass.
Private method and fields are not visible within the subclass.	Protected methods and fields are visible within subclass.

07

ARRAYS

An array is a data structure that holds a fixed number of elements of the same type. These elements are stored in a continuous block of memory, which makes accessing them fast.

For example, an integer array holds only integers, and a character array holds only characters.

Consider an integer array named abc with 5 elements:

abc

int	int	int	int	int
0	1	2	3	4

Accessing Array Elements: Subscripts

Individual elements in an array are accessed using their index, or subscript, within square brackets. For example, abc[n] refers to the element at index n. The subscript indicates both the element and its position in the array's sequence.

Types of Arrays

1. **Single-Dimensional Arrays (1D)** A 1D array is a linear collection of elements stored in a single row or column. Each element is accessed using a **single index**.
2. **Two-Dimensional Arrays (2D)** A 2D array is a collection of elements arranged in rows and columns, resembling a matrix. Each element is accessed using **two indices**.

Declaration, Initialization, and Input Handling

1D Array

- **Declaration** An array is declared by specifying the data type followed by the array name and its size. The size indicates the number of elements the array can hold.

  Syntax `Type array_name[];`
  or `Type[] array_name;`
  or `Type []array_name;`
  e.g. `int roll_No[];`
  or `int[] roll_No;`
  or `int []roll_No;`

- **Initialization** Initialization of an array involves assigning values to its elements. It can be done at the time of declaration or later through assignment statements.

  Syntax `arrayName[index] = value;`

  Example `int arr[ ] = {10, 20, 30, 40, 50};  // Direct initialization`

- **Accepting Data** The values of a 1D array can be input by using a loop and taking data from the user.

  Example
```
Scanner sc = new Scanner(System.in);
for(int i = 0; i < arr.length; i++)
{
    arr[i] = sc.nextInt();
}
```

2D Array

- **Declaration** A two-dimensional (2D) array is essentially an array of arrays. It is declared by specifying two dimensions: the number of rows and columns.

  Syntax `Type array_name[][];`
  or `Type[][] array_name;`
  or `Type [][]array_name;`
  or `Type[] array_name[];`
  e.g. `int a[][];` or `int[][] a;`
  or `int [][]a;` or `int[] a[];`

- **Initialization** A 2D array can be initialized at the time of declaration or later by explicitly assigning values to each element.

  Syntax `arrayName[row][column] = value;`

  Example `int matrix[ ][ ] = { {1, 2}, {3, 4}, {5, 6} };  // Direct initialization`

- **Accepting Data** Like 1D arrays, 2D arrays can also accept input through nested loops, where the outer loop iterates over rows and the inner loop iterates over columns.

  Example

```
Scanner sc = new Scanner(System.in);
for(int i = 0; i < 3; i++)
{
    for(int j = 0; j < 3; j++)
    {
        matrix[i][j] = sc.nextInt();
    }
}
```

Accepting Data in Array from User

In an array, the Scanner class is used to obtain input for primitive types like int, double, etc. and the data output is performed by System.out.println() function.

There are two ways to input the elements in the array

(i) Without using loop

(ii) Using loop

Operations on Arrays

1. Finding the Length of an Array

Java's length property returns the element count of an array, useful for traversal and operations.

For 1D arrays, it provides the total number of elements.

```
int[] numbers = {10, 20, 30, 40};
int length = numbers.length; // length will be 4
```

For a 2D array, the length property can be used for both rows and columns:

```
int rows = matrix.length; // number of rows, i.e., 3
int columns = matrix[0].length; // number of columns in the first row, i.e., 3
```

2. Performing Sum of Elements in Rows, Columns, and Diagonals (Right & Left) in a 2D Array

```
int[][] matrix =
{
    {1, 2, 3},
    {4, 5, 6},
    {7, 8, 9}
};
// Sum of elements in a row (e.g., first row)
int rowSum = 0;
for (int i = 0; i < matrix[0].length; i++)
```

```
{
    rowSum += matrix[0][i]; // Adding elements of the first row
}
// Sum of elements in a column (e.g., first column)
int colSum = 0;
for (int i = 0; i < matrix.length; i++)
{
    colSum += matrix[i][0]; // Adding elements of the first column
}
// Sum of right diagonal
int rightDiagonalSum = 0;
for (int i = 0; i < matrix.length; i++)
{
    rightDiagonalSum += matrix[i][i];
}
// Sum of left diagonal
int leftDiagonalSum = 0;
for (int i = 0; i < matrix.length; i++)
{
    leftDiagonalSum += matrix[i][matrix.length - i - 1];
}
```

3. Displaying a 2D Array in Matrix Format

```
int[][] matrix =
{
    {1, 2, 3},
    {4, 5, 6},
    {7, 8, 9}
};
for (int i = 0; i < matrix.length; i++)
{
    for (int j = 0; j < matrix[i].length; j++)
    {
        System.out.print(matrix[i][j] + " "); // Printing elements in each row
    }
    System.out.println(); // Moving to the next line after each row
}
```

Searching Techniques

It is the process to determine whether the given **item is present in the array** or **not**. There are two ways to search an item:

1. Linear Search

Linear Search is the simplest searching technique where each element of the array is checked sequentially until the target element is found or all elements are checked.

Code Segment for Linear Search

Loop variable

Size of array

Element to be search

```
for(c = 0; c < n; c++)
{
    if(array[c] == search)
    {
        System.out.println(search+ "is present at location"+ (c + 1) +".");
        break;
    }
}
```

```
    if(c==n)
        System.out.println(search+" is not present in array");
```

2. Binary Search

Binary search is an efficient algorithm for sorted arrays. It compares the target with the middle element and narrows the search to the left or right half, repeating until the element is found. Following the Divide and Conquer principle, it is faster than linear search for large datasets.

Following conditions to be followed in binary search:

(a) Array should be in sorted order

(b) If array[mid] = data; pos = mid

(c) If array[mid] < data; lb = mid+1

(d) If array[mid] > data; ub = mid - 1

(e) If lb > ub element not in array

where, lb = lower bound, ub = upper bound mid = mid value of an array, data = element to be search and pos = storing index.

Code Segment of Binary Search

```
pos=-1;
while(lb <= ub)
{
    mid = (lb+ub)/2;
    if(array[mid] == data)
    {
        pos = mid;
        break;
    }
    else if(data > array[mid])
        lb = mid + 1;
    else if(data < array[mid])
        ub = mid - 1;
}
if(pos == -1)
    System.out.println("\n number does not exist");
else
    System.out.println("\n index is" +pos);
```

Sorting Techniques

Sorting is the process of **arranging data in ascending** or **descending order**. There are two ways to sort the data

1. Selection Sort

Selection Sort is a comparison-based algorithm that repeatedly selects the smallest (or largest) element from the unsorted part of the array and swaps it with the first (or last) element of the unsorted section. This process continues until the array is fully sorted.

Code segment for selection sort

```
for (int i=0; i<arr.length - 1; i++)
{
    int index = i;
    for (int j=i+1; j<arr.length; j++)
    {
        if (arr[j] < arr[index])
        {
            index = j;    //searching for lowest index
        }
    }
```

```
        int smallerNumber = arr[index];
        arr[index] = arr[i];
        arr[i] = smallerNumber;
    }
```

2. Bubble Sort

Bubble Sort is another simple sorting algorithm. It repeatedly steps through the array, compares adjacent elements, and swaps them if they are in the wrong order. The process is repeated until no swaps are needed, indicating the array is sorted.

Code Segment for Bubble Sort

```
for(int k = 0 ; k < n; k++)
{
    for(int KK = 0; KK < n - k; KK++)
    {
        if(M[KK] > M[KK+1]
            // for descending order
        {
            temp = M[KK];
            M[kk] = M[KK+1];
            M[KK + 1] = temp;
        }
    }
}
```

Memory Required to Store the Elements

In one dimensional array, number of bytes required to store the element in the memory = size of the type of data * size of the array.

e.g. char A[4] will require $2 \times 4 = 8$ bytes of storing place because char data type requires 2 bytes and A[4] contains 4 elements.

REVISION NOTES

EXAM ORIENTED QUESTIONS

TYPE - 1 01 Mark

Multiple Choice Questions

Q.1 The element in x[4] of the array {3, 5, 7, 12, 16, 18, 20, 35, 42, 89} is **ICSE SQP 2023**
(a) 16 (b) 12 (c) 7 (d) 18

Q.2 Java statement to access the 5th element of an array is **ICSE SQP 2024**
(a) X[4] (b) X[5] (c) X[3] (d) X[0]

Q.3 Consider the array given below: **ICSE SQP 2025**

```
char ch[]={ 'A','E','I','O', 'U'};
```

Write the output of the following statements.

```
System.out.println(ch[0]*2);
```

(a) 65 (b) 130 (c) 'A' (d) 0

Q.4 A single dimensional array contains N elements. What will be the last subscript? **ICSE 2022 (Sem II)**
(a) N (b) N – 1
(c) N – 2 (d) N+1

Q.5

Name the above structure: **ICSE SQP 2025**
(a) One dimensional array
(b) Two dimensional array with 4 rows and 5 columns
(c) Three dimensional array
(d) Two dimensional array with 5 rows and 4 columns

Q.6 Identify the correct array declaration statement. **ICSE SQP 2022 (Sem II)**
(a) int a [10];
(b) int a [ ]= new int [10];
(c) int arr [i] = 10;
(d) int a [10] = new int [ ];

Q.7 A single dimensional array has 50 elements, which of the following is the correct statement to initialize the last element to 100. **ICSE SQP 2025**
(a) x[51]=100 (b) x[48]=100
(c) x[49]=100 (d) x[50]=100

Q.8

Consider the two dimensional array P[2][3], of peripherals (input/output devices) given above, state the index of the device Barcode Scanner. **ICSE 2025**
(a) P[1][1] (b) P[0][1]
(c) P[1][2] (d) P[0][0]

Q.9 What is the output of the Java code given below?

```
String color [ ] = {"Blue", "Red", "Violet"};
System.out.println(color[2].length());
```

ICSE 2024
(a) 6 (b) 5
(c) 3 (d) 2

Q.10 The index (subscript) of the last element of an array ar[ ] is: **ICSE 2025**
(a) ar.length( ) (b) ar[ ].length
(c) ar.length( ) – 1 (d) ar.length – 1

Q.11 The array int x[10] occupies **ICSE SQP 2023**
(a) 10 bytes (b) 40 bytes
(c) 20 bytes (d) 80 bytes

Q.12 The number of bytes occupied by a character array of four rows and three columns are **ICSE 2024**
(a) 12 (b) 24
(c) 96 (d) 48

Q.13 The number of bytes occupied by a character array of 10 elements. **ICSE SQP 2024**
(a) 20 bytes
(b) 60 bytes
(c) 40 bytes
(d) 120 bytes

Q.14 double *x* [] = {2.5, 4.5, 5.5, 6.4}; occupies .... bytes. **ICSE 2025**
(a) 16 (b) 4
(c) 8 (d) 32

Answers

1. (a)	**2.** (a)	**3.** (b)	**4.** (b)	**5.** (b)
6. (b)	**7.** (c)	**8.** (a)	**9.** (a)	**10.** (d)
11. (b)	**12.** (b)	**13.** (a)	**14.** (d)	

TYPE - 2 01 Mark

Assertion-Reason Type Questions

Directions (Q. Nos. 1-4) The following questions are Assertion-Reason based questions. Choose the answer based on the code given below

(a) Both Assertion and Reason are true and Reason is the correct explanation for Assertion.
(b) Both Assertion and Reason are true but Reason is not the correct explanation for Assertion.
(c) Assertion is true but Reason is false.
(d) Assertion is false but Reason is true.

Q.1 Assertion In Java, arrays are considered objects.
Reason Arrays in Java are derived from the Object class.

Q.2 Assertion A two-dimensional array in Java is essentially an array of arrays.
Reason Each element of a two-dimensional array can hold a reference to a one-dimensional array.

Q.3 Assertion Binary search can be efficiently performed on an unsorted array.
Reason Binary search requires the array to be sorted to effectively narrow down the search space.

Q.4 Assertion Selection sort generally performs fewer swaps than bubble sort.
Reason Bubble sort repeatedly compares and swaps adjacent elements, while selection sort finds the minimum element in each iteration and swaps it with the element at the beginning of the unsorted portion.

Answers

1. (a) **2.** (a) **3.** (d) **4.** (a)

TYPE - 3 01 Mark

Odd One Out

Q.1 Find the odd one out:
(a) int[] marks = new int[5];
(b) float data[] = new float[10];
(c) String[] names = {"A", "B", "C"};
(d) int sum = 0;

Q.2 Find the odd one out:
(a) Declaration (b) Initialization
(c) Sorting (d) Accessing elements

Q.3 Find the odd one out:
(a) marks[0] (b) marks[marks.length]
(c) marks[2] (d) marks[1]

Q.4 Find the odd one out:
(a) One-dimensional array (b) Multi-dimensional array
(c) Jagged array (d) Stack

Q.5 Find the odd one out:
(a) Traverse using for loop (b) Use length to find size
(c) Use .add() to insert (d) Initialize using {1, 2, 3}

Answers

1. (d) **2.** (c) **3.** (b) **4.** (d) **5.** (c)

TYPE - 4 02 Marks

Short Answer Type Questions

Q.1 What is an array? Write a statement to declare an integer array of 10 elements. **ICSE 2012**

Ans. Array is a collection of the same data type variables, which are referenced by a common name. An array is an object.

Declaration of integer array

```
int[] arr = new int[10];
```

Q.2 Consider the following array and answer the questions given below: **ICSE 2025**

```
int a[ ] = {12, 10, 8, 4, 6, 2, 3, 5, 7}
```

(a) What is the output of System.out.print(a[0]+a[5]);?
(b) What is the index (subscript) of the largest element of the array a[ ]?

Ans. (a) 12 + 7 = 19
(b) 0

Q.3 (a) Write the Java statement to initialise the first 6 odd numbers in a 3×2 array. **ICSE 2025**
(b) What is the result of x[0][1] + x[2][1] of the above array?

Ans. (a) int[][] oddNumbers = {{1, 3}, {5, 7}, {9, 11}};
(b) 1 + 3 + 5 = 9

Q.4 Consider the following two-dimensional array and answer the questions given below **ICSE 2024**

```
int x[][] = {{4, 3, 2}, {7, 8, 2}, {8, 3, 10}, {1, 2, 9}};
```

(a) What is the order of the array?
(b) What is the value of x[0][0]+ x[2][2]?

Ans. (i) The order of the array, it's a 2D array with 4 rows and 3 columns. Each row represents a separate array with 3 elements.
(ii) The program then prints the sum of two elements: x[0][0] and x[2][2].
x[0][0] refers to the element in the first row and first column, which is 4.
x[2][2] refers to the element in the third row and third column, which is 10.
So, the sum x[0][0] + x[2][2] is equal to 4 + 10 = 14.

Q.5 Consider the following program segment and answer the questions given below: **ICSE SQP 2025**

```
int x[ ][ ]={{2,4,5,6}, {5,7,8,1}, {34, 1,10, 9}};
```

(a) What is the position of 34?

(b) What is the result of x[2][3] + x[1][2]?

Ans. (a) x[2][0] (b) 17

Q.6 If array[]={1,9,8,5,2}; **ICSE 2008**

(i) What is array.length?

(ii) What is array[2]?

Ans. (i) array.length determines the length of array, so array.length = 5

(ii) array[2] = 8

Q.7 If int x [] = {4, 3, 7, 8, 9, 10}; what are the values of p and q? **ICSE 2016**

(i) p = x.length (ii) q =x[2] +x[5]*x[1]

Ans. (i) x.length determines the length of array x so p = 6

(ii) x [2] = 7, x[5] = 10, x [1] = 3

$q = x[2] + x[5] * x[1]$

$= 7 + 10 * 3 = 7 + 30$

$q = 37$

Q.8
```
int P [ ]={ 12,14,16,18};
int Q[ ]={ 20,22,24};
```

Place all elements of P array and Q array in the array R one after the other. **ICSE SQP 2024**

(a) What will be the size of array R [ ] ?

(b) Write index position of first and last element?

Ans. (a) To get the size of array R[], we add the sizes of P[] and Q[]

R[] size = P[] size + Q[] size = 4 + 3 = 7.

Therefore, the size of array R[] will be 7.

(b) The index position of the first element is 0, and the index position of the last element is 6.

Q.9 Consider the following array and answer the questions given below **ICSE SQP 2023**

```
int x[ ] = {23,45,67,12,45,89,24,12,9,7};
```

(i) What is the size of the array ?

(ii) What is the position of 89 ?

Ans. (i) Length-wise, the size is 10.

Memory-wise, the size is 40 bytes.

(ii) x[5]

Q.10 Consider the given array and answer the questions given below **ICSE 2023**

```
int x[ ] = {4,7,9,66,72,0,16};
```

(i) What is the length of the array?

(ii) What is the value in x[4] ?

Ans. (i) Length-wise, the size is 7.

Memory-wise, the size is 28 bytes.

(ii) 72

Q.11 State the number of bytes and bits occupied by a character array of 10 elements. **ICSE SQP 2020**

Ans. As size of char is 2 bytes, a character array of 10 elements occupies 2 × 10 = 20 bytes.

1 byte = 8 bits so 20 bytes convert to 8 × 20 = 160 bits.

Q.12 State the total size in bytes, of the arrays a[4] of char data type and p[4] of float data type. **ICSE 2011**

Ans. One char value takes 2 bytes so

size of char a[4] is 4 × 2 = 8 bytes

One float value takes 4 bytes so

size of float p[4] is 4 × 4 = 16 bytes

TYPE - 5

02 Marks

Differentiate

Q.1 State the difference between length and length() in Java. **ICSE 2020**

Ans.

	length	length()
Type	Property/Variable	Method
Used With	Arrays (e.g., int[], String[])	Strings (e.g., String)
Syntax	arrayName.length	stringName.length()
Purpose	Returns the number of elements in the array.	Returns the number of characters in the String.
Return Type	int	int
Example	int[] arr = {1, 2, 3}; int size = arr.length;	String str = "Java"; int len = str.length();

Q.2 Differentiate between Binary Search and Linear Search techniques. **ICSE SQP 2020, ICSE SQP 2017, ICSE 2019**

Ans.

Linear Search	Binary Search
This process can be carried on unsorted array.	This is applied only on sorted arrays.
Linear search, searches an element in a sequential manner.	In binary search, an array is divided into two halves and then the element is searched.

Q.3 Differentiate between searching and sorting. **ICSE 2019**

Ans.

Searching	Sorting
It is the process to determine whether the given item is present in the array or not.	It is a process of arranging data in ascending or descending order.
It includes linear search and binary search.	It includes bubble sort, quick sort, insertion sort etc.

TYPE - 6 15 Marks

Long Answer Type Questions

Q.1 Define a class to declare an array of size twenty of double data type, accept the elements into the array and perform the following:

- Calculate and print the product of all the elements.
- Print the square of each element of the array.

ICSE 2022 (Sem II)

Ans.

```
import java.util.*;
public class SquareProduct
{
  public static void main(String [] args)
  {
    double numbers[]=new double[20];
    Scanner sc=new Scanner(System.in);
    double prod=1.0,sq=0.0;
    int i;
    System.out.println("Enter 20
                               numbers :");
    for(i=0;i<20;i++)
    numbers[i]=sc.nextDouble();
    for(i=0;i<20;i++)
    {
      prod*=numbers[i];
      System.out.println("Product of
          all the elements =" + prod);
    }
    System.out.println("Square of :"+
                          numbers[i] + "="
                  + numbers[i]*numbers[i]);
  }
}
```

Q.2 Define a class to declare an array of size 20 of double datatype, accept the elements into the array and perform the following:

- Calculate and print the sum of all the elements.
- Calculate and print the highest value of the array.

ICSE SQP 2022 (Sem II)

Ans.

```
import java.util.Scanner;
public class DoubleArray
{
  public static void main(String[] args)
  {
     Scanner scanner = new Scanner(System.in);
     double[] arr = new double[20];
      // Accepting elements into the array
     System.out.println("Enter 20 double
                                    values:");
     for (int i = 0; i < arr.length; i++)
     {
       arr[i] = scanner.nextDouble();
     }
    // Calculating the sum of all elements
     double sum = 0;
     for (int i = 0; i < arr.length; i++)
     {
       sum += arr[i];
     }
     System.out.println("Sum of all
                       elements: " + sum);
       // Calculating the highest value
                               of the array
     double max = arr[0];
     for (int i = 1; i < arr.length; i++)
     {
       if (arr[i] > max)
       {
         max = arr[i];
       }
     }
     System.out.println("Highest value
                   in the array: " + max);
  }
}
```

Output

Enter 20 double values:
2.3
1.2
3.5
7.8
5.6
9.0
0.5
2.2
4.1
1.0
3.2
2.1
8.7
6.5
4.3
7.6
0.9
5.4
1.8
3.6
Sum of all elements: 72.5
Highest value in the array: 9.0

Q.3 Define a class to accept values in integer array of size 10. Find sum of one digit number and sum of two digit numbers entered. Display them separately. **ICSE 2023**

Example: Input:

a [] = {2, 12, 4, 9, 18, 25, 3, 32, 20, 1}

Output:

Sum of one digit numbers

2 + 4 + 9 + 3 + 1= 19

Sum of two digit numbers

12 + 18 + 25 + 32 + 20 = 107

Ans.
```
import java.util.Scanner;
public class Example
{
 public static void main (String[] args)
 {
     Scanner sc = new Scanner (System.in);
     int [] arr = new int[10];
             // Taking input array from user
     System.out.println("Enter 10 integer
                                    values:");
     for (int i = 0; i < 10; i++)
     {
       arr[i] = sc.nextInt();
     }
     // Calculating sum of one-digit and
            two-digit numbers in the array
     int oneDigitSum = 0;
     int twoDigitSum = 0;
     for (int i = 0; i < 10; i++)
     {
       if (arr[i] >= 0 && arr[i] <= 9)
       {
         oneDigitSum += arr[i];
       } else if (arr[i] >= 10 && arr[i]
                                    <= 99)
       {
         twoDigitSum += arr[i];
       }
     }
     // Printing sum of one-digit and
            two-digit numbers in the array
     System.out.println("Sum of one-digit
   numbers in the array: " + oneDigitSum);
     System.out.println("Sum of two-digit
   numbers in the array: " + twoDigitSum);
   }
 }
```

Output

Enter 10 integer values:

23

4

6

5

33

76

5

89

66

54

Sum of one-digit numbers in the array: 20

Sum of two-digit numbers in the array: 341

Q.4 Define a class to accept values into a double array of size 20 and print the range of the array, range is the difference between the largest and the smallest elements of the array. **ICSE SQP 2023**

Ans.
```
import java.util.Scanner;
class Range
{
 public static void main (String[] args)
 {
     Scanner in = new Scanner(System.in);
     double a [] = new double [20];
     double large = 0.0;
     double small = 0.0;
     System.out.println("Enter 20
                                 numbers:");
     for (int i = 0; i < a.length; i++)
     {
       a[i] = Double.parseDouble
                            (in.nextLine());
       if (i == 0)
       {
         large = a[i];
         small = a[i];
       }
       else
       {
         if (large < a[i])
           large = a[i];
         if (small > a[i])
           small = a[i];
       }
     }
     double range = large - small;
     System.out.println("Range = " + range);
   }
}
```

Output

Enter 20 numbers:1

2

3

4

5

6

7
8
9
10
11
12
13
14
15
16
17
18
19
20
Range = 19.0

Q.5 Write a program to input and store integer elements in a double dimensional array of size 4 × 4 and find the sum of all the elements. **ICSE SQP 2020**

7 3 4 5
5 4 6 1
6 9 4 2
3 2 7 5

Sum of all the elements: 73

Ans.

```
import java.util.Scanner;
public class arraySum
{
  public static void main(String args[])
  {
      Scanner in = new Scanner(System.in);
      int arr[][] = new int[4][4];
      long sum = 0;
      System.out.println("Enter the
                elements of 4x4 array:");
      for (int i = 0; i < 4; i++)
      {
         for (int j = 0; j < 4; j++)
         {
            arr[i][j] = in.nextInt();
         }
      }
      for (int i = 0; i < 4; i++)
      {
         for (int j = 0; j < 4; j++)
         {
            sum += arr[i][j];
         }
      }
      System.out.println("Sum of all the
                        elements: " + sum);
  }
}
```

Output

Enter the elements of 4 × 4 array:
7 3 4 5
5 4 6 1
6 9 4 2
3 2 7 5
Sum of all the elements: 73

Q.6 Define a class to accept values into a 3×3 array and check, if it is a special array. An array is a special array if the sum of the even elements = sum of the odd elements. **ICSE SQP 2024**

Example

A[][]={{ 4 ,5, 6}, { 5 ,3, 2}, { 4, 2, 5}};

Sum of even elements = 4+6+2+4+2 =18

Sum of odd elements = 5+5+3+5=18

Ans.

```
import java.util.Scanner;
class SpecialArrayChecker
{
   public static boolean isSpecialArray(int[][] arr)
   {
     int sumEven = 0;
     int sumOdd = 0;
     for (int i = 0; i < arr.length; i++)
     {
       for (int j = 0; j < arr[i].length; j++)
       {
         if (arr[i][j] % 2 == 0)
         {
           sumEven += arr[i][j];
         }
         else
         {
           sumOdd += arr[i][j];
         }
       }
     }
     return sumEven == sumOdd;
   }
   public static void main(String[] args)
   {
     int[][] arr = new int[3][3];
     Scanner scanner = new Scanner(System.in);
       // Accept values into the array
     System.out.println("Enter 3x3 array elements:");
     for (int i = 0; i < arr.length; i++)
     {
       for (int j = 0; j < arr[i].length; j++)
       {
         arr[i][j] = scanner.nextInt();
       }
     }
       // Check if it is a special array
```

```
        boolean isSpecial = isSpecialArray(arr);
        // Display the result
        if (isSpecial)
        {
          System.out.println("The array is a
                                   special array.");
        }
        else
        {
          System.out.println("The array is not
                                   a special array.");
        }
    }
}
```

Q.7 Write a program to input and store integer elements in a double dimensional array of size 3 × 3 and find the sum of elements in the left diagonal. **ICSE 2020**

Example

1	3	5
4	6	8
9	2	4

Output : Sum of the left diagonal elements = (1 + 6 + 4) = 11

Ans.

```
import java.util.Scanner;
public class LeftDiagonalSum
{
  public static void main(String[] args)
  {
    int[][] array = new int[3][3];
    Scanner scanner = new Scanner
                         (System.in);
    System.out.println("Enter the elements
                    of the 3x3 array:");
    for (int i = 0; i < 3; i++)
    {
      for (int j = 0; j < 3; j++)
      {
        array[i][j] = scanner.nextInt();
      }
    }
    int diagonalSum = 0;
    for (int i = 0; i < 3; i++)
    {
      diagonalSum += array[i][i];
    }
    System.out.println("Sum of the left
      diagonal elements = " + diagonalSum);
  }
}
```

Q.8 Define a class to accept values into an integer array of order 4×4 and check whether it is a DIAGONAL array or not. An array is DIAGONAL if the sum of the left diagonal elements equals the sum of the right diagonal elements. Print the appropriate message. **ICSE 2024**

Example

3 4 2 5	Sum of the left diagonal elements =
2 5 2 3	$3+5+2+1=11$
5 3 2 7	Sum of the right diagonal elements =
1 3 7 1	$5+2+3+1=11$

Ans.

```
import java.util.Scanner;
public class DiagonalArrayCheck
{
  public static void main(String[] args)
  {
    Scanner scanner = new
                        Scanner(System.in);
    int[][] array = new int[4][4];
    System.out.println("Enter values
                        for a 4x4 array:");
    // Accepting values into the array
    for (int i = 0; i < 4; i++)
    {
      for (int j = 0; j < 4; j++)
      {
        array[i][j] = scanner.nextInt();
      }
    }
    // Checking if it's a diagonal array
    boolean isDiagonal = true;
    int leftDiagonalSum = 0;
    int rightDiagonalSum = 0;
    for (int i = 0; i < 4; i++)
    {
      leftDiagonalSum += array[i][i];
      rightDiagonalSum += array[i][3 - i];
    }
    if (leftDiagonalSum !
                        = rightDiagonalSum)
    {
      isDiagonal = false;
    }
    // Printing the appropriate message
    if (isDiagonal)
    {
      System.out.println("The array is
                        a DIAGONAL array.");
    }
    else
    {
```

```
            System.out.println("The array
                      is NOT a DIAGONAL array.");
        }
    }
}
```

Q.9 Define a class to accept values into a 4×4 integer array. Calculate and print the NORM of the array. **ICSE 2025**

NORM is the square root of sum of squares of all elements.

1	2	1	3
5	2	1	6
3	6	1	2
3	4	6	3

Sum of squares of elements $= 1 + 4 + 1 + 9 + 25$

$+ 4 + 1 + 36 + 9 + 36 + 1 + 4 + 9 + 16 + 36 + 9 = 201$

NORM = Squareroot of 201

$= 14.177446878757825$

Ans.

```
import java.util.Scanner;
class NormCalculator
{
  int[][] arr = new int[4][4];
  // Method to accept values using Scanner
  public void acceptValues()
  {
    Scanner sc = new Scanner(System.in);
    System.out.println("Enter 16 integers for
                                the 4x4 array:");
    for (int i = 0; i < 4; i++)
    {
      for (int j = 0; j < 4; j++)
      {
        arr[i][j] = sc.nextInt();
      }
    }
  }
  // Method to calculate and print NORM
  public void calculateNorm()
  {
    int sum = 0;
    for (int i = 0; i < 4; i++)
    {
      for (int j = 0; j < 4; j++)
      {
        sum += arr[i][j] * arr[i][j];
          // square of each element
      }
    }
    double norm = Math.sqrt(sum);
    System.out.println("NORM = " + norm);
  }
  // Main method
  public static void main(String[] args)
  {
    NormCalculator obj = new NormCalculator();
    obj.acceptValues();
    obj.calculateNorm();
  }
}
```

Output

Enter 16 integers for the 4x4 array:

2 3 4 5

6 7 8 9

2 3 4 5

6 2 1 5

NORM = 20.09975124224178

Q.10 Write a program to accept name and total marks of N number of students in two single subscript array name[] and totalmarks[]. **[ICSE 2018]**

Calculate and print:

1. The average of the total marks obtained by N number of students.

   [average = (sum of total marks of all the students)/N]
2. Deviation of each student's total marks with the average.

   [deviation = total marks of a student – average]

Ans.

```
import java.util.Scanner;
public class SDAMarks
{
  public static void main(String args[])
  {
    Scanner in = new Scanner(System.in);
    System.out.print("Enter number of students: ");
    int n = in.nextInt();
    String name[] = new String[n];
    int totalmarks[] = new int[n];
    int grandTotal = 0;
    for (int i = 0; i < n; i++)
    {
      in.nextLine();
      System.out.print("Enter name of student "
                                 + (i+1) + ": ");
      name[i] = in.nextLine();
      System.out.print("Enter total marks
                      of student " + (i+1) + ": ");
      totalmarks[i] = in.nextInt();
      grandTotal += totalmarks[i];
    }
    double avg = grandTotal / (double)n;
    System.out.println("Average = " + avg);
```

```java
        for (int i = 0; i < n; i++)
        {
            System.out.println("Deviation for "
             + name[i] + " = " + (totalmarks[i] - avg));
        }
    }
}
```

Q.11 Write a program to input and store roll numbers, names and marks in 3 subjects of n number of students in five single dimensional arrays and display the remark based on average marks as given below **ICSE 2015**

Average Marks	Remark
85 — 100	Excellent
75 — 84	Distinction
60 — 74	First Class
40 — 59	Pass
Less than 40	Poor

Ans.

```java
import java.util.Scanner;
public class AvgMarks
{
    public static void main(String args[])
    {
        Scanner in = new Scanner(System.in);
        System.out.print("Enter number of students: ");
        int n = in.nextInt();
        int rollNo[] = new int[n];
        String name[] = new String[n];
        int s1[] = new int[n];
        int s2[] = new int[n];
        int s3[] = new int[n];
        double avg[] = new double[n];
        for (int i = 0; i < n; i++)
        {
            System.out.println("Enter student"
                              + (i+1) + " details:");
            System.out.print("Roll No: ");
                rollNo[i] = in.nextInt();
                in.nextLine();
            System.out.print("Name: ");
                name[i] = in.nextLine();
            System.out.print("Subject 1 Marks: ");
                s1[i] = in.nextInt();
            System.out.print("Subject 2 Marks: ");
                s2[i] = in.nextInt();
            System.out.print("Subject 3 Marks: ");
                s3[i] = in.nextInt();
            avg[i] = (s1[i] + s2[i] + s3[i]) / 3.0;
        }
        System.out.println("Roll No\tName\tRemark");
        for (int i = 0; i < n; i++)
        {
            String remark;
            if (avg[i] < 40)
                remark = "Poor";
            else if (avg[i] < 60)
                remark = "Pass";
            else if (avg[i] < 75)
                remark = "First Class";
            else if (avg[i] < 85)
                remark = "Distinction";
            else
                remark = "Excellent";
            System.out.println(rollNo[i] + "\t"
                + name[i] + "\t" + remark);
        }
    }
}
```

Q.12 Write a program to create an array to store 10 integers and print the largest integer and the smallest integer in that array. **ICSE SQP 2017**

Ans.

```java
import java.util.Scanner;
public class MinMaxIntegerArray
{
    public static void main(String[] args)
    {
        Scanner scanner = new Scanner(System.in);
        int[] numbers = new int[10];
          // Declare an array to hold 10 integers
          // Input: Populate the array with
                                 10 integers from the user
        System.out.println("Enter 10 integers:");
        for (int i = 0; i < 10; i++)
        {
            System.out.print("Enter number " + (i + 1)
                                                    + ": ");
            numbers[i] = scanner.nextInt();
        }
        scanner.close();
        // Initialize min and max with the first
                                   element of the array.
        int min = numbers[0];
        int max = numbers[0];
        // Find the minimum and maximum values
        for (int i = 1; i < 10; i++)
        {
            if (numbers[i] < min)
            {
                min = numbers[i];
            }
            if (numbers[i] > max)
            {
                max = numbers[i];
            }
        }
```

```
    // Output: Print the results
    System.out.println("Smallest Integer: "+ min);
    System.out.println("Largest Integer: " + max);
  }
}
```

Q.13 Define a class to accept values into 4x4 array and find and display the sum of each row. **ICSE SQP 2025**

Example

A[][]={{1,2,3,4},{5,6,7,8},{1,3,5,7},{2,5,3,1}}

Output

sum of row 1 = 10 (1+2+3+4)

sum of row 2 = 26 (5+6+7+8)

sum of row 3 = 16 (1+3+5+7)

sum of row 4 = 11 (2+5+3+1)

Ans.

```
import java.util.Scanner;
public class DDARowSum
{
  public static void main(String args[])
  {
    Scanner in = new Scanner(System.in);
    int arr[][] = new int[4][4];
    System.out.println("Enter 4x4 DDA elements:");
    for (int i = 0; i < 4; i++)
    {
      for (int j = 0; j < 4; j++)
      {
        arr[i][j] = in.nextInt();
      }
    }
    for (int i = 0; i < 4; i++)
    {
      int rowSum = 0;
      for (int j = 0; j < 4; j++)
      {
        rowSum += arr[i][j];
      }
      System.out.println("Sum of Row" + (i+1)
                         + " = " + rowSum);
    }
  }
}
```

Q.14 Define a class to declare an integer array of size n and accept the elements into the array. Search for an element input by the user using linear search technique, display the element if it is found, otherwise display the message "NO SUCH ELEMENT". **ICSE SQP 2022 (Sem II)**

Ans.

```
import java.util.Scanner;
public class LinearSearch
{
  private int[] arr;
  private int n;
  public LinearSearch(int size)
  {
    n = size;
    arr = new int[n];
  }
  public void accept()
  {
    Scanner input = new Scanner
                    (System.in);
    System.out.println("Enter " + n + "
                    elements:");
    for (int i = 0; i < n; i++)
    {
      arr[i] = input.nextInt();
    }
  }
  public void search(int x)
  {
    boolean found = false;
    for (int i = 0; i < n; i++)
    {
      if (arr[i] == x)
      {
        System.out.println(x + " found
                    at index " + i);
        found = true;
        break;
      }
    }
    if (!found)
    {
      System.out.println("NO SUCH
                    ELEMENT");
    }
  }
  public static void main(String[] args)
  {
    Scanner input = new Scanner
                    (System.in);
    System.out.print("Enter the size of
                    the array: ");
    int size = input.nextInt();
    LinearSearch obj = new
                    LinearSearch(size);
    obj.accept();
    System.out.print("Enter the element
                    to search: ");
    int element = input.nextInt();
    obj.search(element);
  }
}
```

Output

Enter the size of the array: 5

Enter 5 elements:

45

67
43
89
78
Enter the element to search: 67
67 found at index 1

Q.15 Define a class to perform binary search on a list of integers given below, to search for an element input by the user, if it is found display the element along with its position, otherwise display the message "Search element not found".

2, 5, 7, 10, 15, 20, 29, 30, 46, 50 **ICSE 2022 (Sem II)**

Ans.
```
import java.util.*;
public class Search
{
   public static void main(String[] args)
   {
      int intarray[]=new int[10];
      Scanner sc=new Scanner(System.in);
      int beg=0,mid=-1,end=9,se=0,i,
                                found=-1;
      System.out.println("Enter 10
           integers in ascending order ");
      for (i=0;i<=9;i++)
      intarray[i]=sc.nextInt();
      System.out.println("Enter search
                              element ");
      se=sc.nextInt();
      while (beg<=end)
      {
         mid=(beg+end)/2;
         if (intarray[mid]==se)
         {
            found=1;
            break;
         }
         else if(se>intarray[mid])
            beg=mid+1;
         else
            end=mid-1;
      }
      if (found==1)
      System.out.println("Found at :"+
                                (mid+1));
      else
         System.out.println("Search
                element not found!!!");
   }
}
```

Q.16 Define a class to accept values into an array of double data type of size 20. Accept a double value from user and search in the array using linear search method. If value is found display message "Found" with its position where it is present in the array. Otherwise display message "not found". **ICSE 2023**

Ans.
```
import java.util.Scanner;
public class LinearSearch
{
  public static void main(String args[])
  {
    Scanner in = new Scanner(System.in);
    double arr[] = new double[20];
    int l = arr.length;
    int i = 0;
    System.out.println("Enter array elements: ");
    for (i = 0; i < l; i++)
    {
      arr[i] = in.nextDouble();
    }
    System.out.print("Enter the number to search: ");
    double n = in.nextDouble();
    for (i = 0; i < l; i++)
    {
      if (arr[i] == n)
      {
        break;
      }
    }
    if (i == l)
    {
      System.out.println("Not found");
    }
    else
    {
      System.out.println(n + " found at index " + i);
    }
  }
}
```

Q.17 Define a class to search for a value input by the user from the list of values given below. If it is found display the message "Search successful", otherwise display the message "Search element not found" using Binary search technique.

5.6, 11.5, 20.8, 35.4, 43.1, 52.4, 66.6, 78.9, 80.0, 95.5. **ICSE SQP 2025**

Ans.
```
import java.util.Scanner;
public class BinarySearch
{
  void search(double[] arr, double key)
  {
    int low = 0;
    int high = arr.length - 1;
    boolean found = false;
    while (low <= high)
    {
      int mid = (low + high) / 2;
```

```
        if (arr[mid] == key)
        {
          found = true;
            break;
        }
        else if (arr[mid] < key)
        {
          low = mid + 1;
        }
        else
        {
          high = mid - 1;
        }
      }
      if (found)
      {
        System.out.println("Search successful");
      }
      else
      {
        System.out.println("Search element not found");
      }
    }
    public static void main(String[] args)
    {
      Scanner in = new Scanner(System.in);
      double[] values = {5.6, 11.5, 20.8, 35.4,
                43.1, 52.4, 66.6, 78.9, 80.0, 95.5};
      System.out.print("Enter the value to search: ");
      double key = in.nextDouble();
      BinarySearch obj = new BinarySearch();
      obj.search(values, key);
    }
}
```

Q.18 Define a class to initialise the following data in an array.
Search for a given character input by the user, using the Binary Search technique. **ICSE 2025**

Print "Search Successful" if the character is found otherwise print "Search is not Successful"

'A', 'H', 'N', 'P', 'S', 'U', 'W','Y', 'Z', 'b', 'd'

Ans.

```
import java.util.Arrays;
import java.util.Scanner;
class BinarySearchChar
{
    char[] arr = {'A', 'H', 'N', 'P', 'S', 'U',
                  'W', 'Y', 'Z', 'b', 'd'};
    // Method to perform binary search
    public void searchChar()
    {
      Scanner sc = new Scanner(System.in);
      System.out.print("Enter a character to
                                    search: ");
      char key = sc.next().charAt(0);
      // Sort the array before binary search
      Arrays.sort(arr);
      int left = 0, right = arr.length - 1;
      boolean found = false;
      while (left <= right)
      {
        int mid = (left + right) / 2;
        if (arr[mid] == key)
        {
          found = true;
            break;
        }
        else if (arr[mid] < key)
        {
          left = mid + 1;
        }
        else
        {
          right = mid - 1;
        }
      }
      // Output result
      if (found)
      {
        System.out.println("Search Successful");
      }
      else
      {
        System.out.println("Search is not
                                  Successful");
      }
    }
    // Main method
    public static void main(String[] args)
    {
      BinarySearchChar obj = new BinarySearchChar();
      obj.searchChar();
    }
}
```

Output

Enter a character to search: B

Search is not Successful

Q.19 Define a class to accept 10 integers and arrange them in descending order using bubble sort. Print the original array and the sorted array. **ICSE 2023**

Ans.

```
import java.util.*;
public class Integers
{
    public static void main(String[] args)
    {
        Scanner sc = new Scanner(System.in);
        int[] a = new int[10];
```

```
            int i, j, temp;
            System.out.println("Enter ten integers:");

            for (i = 0; i < 10; i++)
            {
                System.out.print("Enter integer "
                                    + (i + 1) + ": ");
                a[i] = sc.nextInt();
            }
            System.out.println("\nOriginal Array:");
            for (i = 0; i < 10; i++)
            {
                System.out.print(a[i] + "\t");
            }
            System.out.println();
            // Add a newline for better formatting
            for (i = 0; i < 9; i++)
            { // Optimized loop condition
                for (j = 0; j < 9 - i; j++)
                 { // Optimized loop condition
                    if (a[j] < a[j + 1])
                    {
                        temp = a[j];
                        a[j] = a[j + 1];
                        a[j + 1] = temp;
                    }
                }
            }
            System.out.println("\nSorted Array
                                (Descending Order):");
            for (i = 0; i < 10; i++)
            {
                System.out.print(a[i] + "\t");
            }
            System.out.println(); // Add a newline
                                  for better formatting
            sc.close(); // It's good practice to
            close the Scanner when you're done with it
        }
    }
```

Q.20 Write a program to input name and percentage of 35 students of class X in two separate one dimensional arrays. Arrange students details according to their percentage in the descending order using selection sort method. Display name and percentage of first ten toppers of the class. **ICSE SQP 2020**

Ans.

```
import java.util.Scanner;
public class StudentPercentage
{
  public static void main(String args[])
  {
    Scanner in = new Scanner(System.in);
    //Initialize the 2 SDA
    String names[] = new String[35];
    double percentage[] = new double[35];
    /*
    * Accept student details from user and store
    * in corresponding SDA
    */
    for (int i = 0; i < names.length; i++)
    {
      System.out.print("Enter name of student "
                                    + (i + 1) + ": ");
      names[i] = in.nextLine();
      System.out.print("Enter percentage of
                          student " + (i + 1) + ": ");
      percentage[i] = in.nextDouble();
      in.nextLine();
    }
    //Selection Sort in Descending Order
    for (int i = 0; i < percentage.length - 1; i++)
    {
      int maxIdx = i;
      for (int j = i + 1; j < percentage.length; j++)
      {
        if (percentage[j] > percentage[maxIdx])
        maxIdx = j;
      }
      double t = percentage[i];
      percentage[i] = percentage[maxIdx];
      percentage[maxIdx] = t;
      String name = names[i];
      names[i] = names[maxIdx];
      names[maxIdx] = name;
    }
    //Display first ten toppers
    System.out.println("Name\tPercentage");
    for (int  i = 0; i < 10; i++)
    {
      System.out.println(names[i] + '\t'
                                    + percentage[i]);
    }
  }
}
```

Q.21 Define a class to accept values in integer array of size 10. Sort them in an ascending order using selection sort technique. Display the sorted array. **ICSE SQP 2024**

Ans.

```
import java.util.Scanner;
public class tSelectionSort
{
    public static void main(String args[])
    {
        Scanner in = new Scanner(System.in);
        int arr[] = new int[10];
        System.out.println("Enter 10 integers: ");
```

```java
        for (int i = 0; i < 10; i++)
        {
            arr[i] = in.nextInt();
        }
        for (int i = 0; i < 9; i++)
        {
            int idx = i;
            for (int j = i + 1; j < 10; j++)
            {
                if (arr[j] < arr[idx])
                    idx = j;
            }
            int t = arr[i];
            arr[i] = arr[idx];
            arr[idx] = t;
        }
        System.out.println("Sorted Array:");
        for (int i = 0; i < 10; i++)
        {
            System.out.print(arr[i] + " ");
        }
    }
}
```

Q.22 Define a class pin code and store the given pin codes in a single dimensional array. Sort these pin codes in ascending order using the Selection Sort technique only. Display the sorted array. **ICSE 2024**

110061, 110001, 110029, 110023, 110055, 110006, 110019, 110033

Ans.

```java
public class Pincode
{
    public static void main(String args[])
    {
        int[] arr = {110061, 110001,
                     110029, 110023,
                     110055, 110006,
                     110019, 110033};
        for (int i = 0; i < 7; i++)
        {
            int idx = i;
            for (int j = i + 1; j < 8; j++)
            {
                if (arr[j] < arr[idx])
                    idx = j;
            }
            int t = arr[i];
            arr[i] = arr[idx];
            arr[idx] = t;
        }
        System.out.println("Sorted Array:");
        for (int i = 0; i < 8; i++)
        {
            System.out.print(arr[i] + " ");
        }
    }
}
```

08

STRING HANDLING

A String in Java is a sequence of characters enclosed in **double quotes** ("") and treated as a **single data type.** It is an object of the String class, which provides various built-in methods for efficient text manipulation.

e.g. `String name = "Hello World";`

String Class in Java

In Java, String is a **pre-defined class,** and it is part of the java.lang package. It is used to store and manipulate sequences of characters. As String is an object, it provides various built-in methods for efficient handling.

e.g. Java offers three classes to work with character data:

1. **Character Class** can hold single character data.
2. **String Class** can hold unchanging string, i.e. once initialised, its contents cannot be modified.
3. **StringBuffer Class** can hold mutable strings, i.e. can be changed or modified.

String Declaration and Initialization in Java

Java offers two primary methods for declaring and initializing strings:

1. String Literals

Strings created using literals are stored in the String Pool, a special area within the heap memory.

Example
```
String str1 = "Java";
String str2 = "Java";     // str2 references the same object as str1
```

2. Using the new Keyword

Using the new keyword explicitly creates a new String object in heap memory, even if an identical string already exists.

Example
```
String str3 = new String("Java");     // Creates a distinct new object
```

Methods of String Class

Function	Format	Description	Example
charAt( )	a.charAt(n);	Returns the character at the specified index (n[th] position as it starts counting from 0th position).	a = "computer"; a.charAt(5); **Output** t
compareTo( )	a1.compareTo(a2);	Compare two strings lexicographically. It returns negative if a1 < a2 positive if a1 > a2 zero if a1 = a2	a1 = "Computer Application"; a2 = "Computer Application"; a1. compareTo (a2); **Output** 0
concat( )	a1.concat(a2);	Concatenates the specified string to the end of the current string object.	a1 = "good"; a2 = "bye"; a1.concat(a2); **Output** goodbye

Function	Format	Description	Example
endsWith( )	p.endsWith (b);	Returns True if the string p contains a suffix specified by string b.	p = "COMPUTER"; b = "FUN"; boolean x = p.endsWith(b); **Output** False
equals( )	a1.equals(a2);	Check whether contents of two strings are equal or not.	a1 = "Rajendra"; a2 = "Rajendra"; a1. equals(a2); **Output** True
equals IgnoreCase( )	a1.equalsIgnore Case(a2);	Returns True, if a1 and a2 are equal after ignoring cases of the strings and otherwise False, if they are unequal.	a1 = "Computer"; a2 = "COMPUTER"; a1. equalsIgnoreCase(a2); **Output** True

indexOf( )	a.indexOf('m');
	Or
	a.indexOf('m', n);
		Returns the position of the first occurrence of 'm' in the string a.
		Or
		Returns the position of 'm' in the string from n^{th} position.
			a = "Computer";
			a.indexOf('m');
			Output 2
			Or
			a = "prime number";
			a.indexOf('m', 5);
			Output 8
			(The next occurrence of 'm' in the string from 5th position is at 8th location).

lastIndexOf( )	int n = s.lastIndexOf('A');	Returns position of last occurrence of letter.	String s = "MALAYALAM"; int n = s.lastIndexOf('A'); **Output** 7
length( )	s.length( );	Returns the length of character present in the string.	String s = "MALAYALAM"; s.length( ); **Output** 9
replace( )	a.replace('m', 'n');	Replaces all the occurrences of one character or string with other character or string.	a = "Computer"; a.replace ('m', 'n'); **Output** Conputer
startsWith( )	p.startsWith(b);	Returns True if the string p starts with specified string b.	p = "Arihant Publication"; b = "Arihant"; boolean x = p.startsWith(b); **Output** True
int compare ToIgnoreCase (String str)	s1.compareToIgnore Case (s2);	Compares two strings lexicographically, ignoring case differences	s1="HELLO"; s2="hello"; s1.compareToIgnoreCase(s2); **Output** zero
substring( )	a.substring(m, n);	Returns a substring, out of n –1 characters leaving first m character of the string.	a = "Vidyalaya"; a.substring (3, 8); **Output** yalay
toLowerCase( )	a.toLowerCase( );	Converts all the characters of the string in lowercase.	a = "ARIHANT"; a.toLowerCase ( ); **Output** arihant
toUpperCase( )	a.toUpperCase( );	Converts all the characters of the string in uppercase.	a = "arihant"; a.toUpperCase( ); **Output** ARIHANT

Function	Format	Description	Example
valueOf( )	String.valueOf(b);	Returns string represented by the value of the passed argument.	b = true; String.valueOf(b); **Output** true

trim( )	a.trim( );	Removes the whitespaces from the beginning and ending of the current or this string.	a = "# arihant #" //here, # denotes whitespace
			a.trim( );
			Output arihant

Java String Arrays

A string array in Java is an object that stores a fixed-size collection of string elements, which is crucial for various programming tasks.

String Array Declaration

Square brackets is used to declare a string array. There are two ways of using it.

e.g.
```
string[]  stringArray;
```
Or
```
string   stringArray[];
```

String Array Initialization

There are multiple ways to initialize a string array. Initialization can also be done at the same time as the declaration.

e.g.
```
string[] stringArray ={"AA", "BB", "CC", "DD"};
```

Another syntax to declare and initialize a string array together is by using the new operator.

e.g.
```
string []  stringArray=new string [] {"AA", "BB", "CC", "DD"};
```

Java program that demonstrates extracting and modifying characters in a string

```
public class StringManipulation
{
    public static void main(String[] args)
    {
        String str = "Hello, Java!";
        // Extracting characters
        char extractedChar = str.charAt(7);
        System.out.println("Character at index 7: " + extractedChar);
        String substring = str.substring(7, 11);
        System.out.println("Extracted substring: " + substring);
        // Modifying characters
        String replacedStr = str.replace('a', 'o');
        System.out.println("After replacement: " + replacedStr);
        String upperCaseStr = str.toUpperCase();
        System.out.println("Uppercase: " + upperCaseStr);
        String lowerCaseStr = str.toLowerCase();
        System.out.println("Lowercase: " + lowerCaseStr);
    }
}
```

String Sorting Techniques

1. Bubble Sort (Sorting Strings in Alphabetical Order)

A comparison-based sorting algorithm that repeatedly swaps adjacent elements if they are in the wrong order.

```
import java.util.Arrays;
public class BubbleSortStrings
```

```
{
    public static void main(String[] args)
    {
        String[] arr = { "Banana", "Apple", "Mango", "Cherry" };
        int n = arr.length;
        for (int i = 0; i < n - 1; i++)
        {
            for (int j = 0; j < n - i - 1; j++)
            {
                if (arr[j].compareTo(arr[j + 1]) > 0)
                {
                    String temp = arr[j];
                    arr[j] = arr[j + 1];
                    arr[j + 1] = temp;
                }
            }
        }
        System.out.println("Sorted Array: " + Arrays.toString(arr));
    }
}
```

2. Selection Sort

A sorting algorithm that selects the smallest element from the unsorted part and swaps it with the first unsorted element.

```
import java.util.Arrays;
public class SelectionSortStrings
{
    public static void main(String[] args)
    {
        String[] arr = { "Banana", "Apple", "Mango", "Cherry" };
        int n = arr.length;
        for (int i = 0; i < n - 1; i++)
        {
            int minIndex = i;
            for (int j = i + 1; j < n; j++)
            {
                if (arr[j].compareTo(arr[minIndex]) < 0)
                {
                    minIndex = j;
                }
            }
            String temp = arr[minIndex];
            arr[minIndex] = arr[i];
            arr[i] = temp;
        }
        System.out.println("Sorted Array: " + Arrays.toString(arr));
    }
}
```

Searching in Strings Using Linear Search

A search algorithm that sequentially checks each string in an array until the target string is found or the array ends.

```
import java.util.Scanner;
public class LinearSearchString
{
    public static void main(String[] args)
    {
        String[] arr = { "Apple", "Banana", "Cherry", "Mango", "Orange" };
        Scanner sc = new Scanner(System.in);
        System.out.print("Enter the string to search: ");
        String key = sc.nextLine();
        sc.close();
        int index = -1;
        for (int i = 0; i < arr.length; i++)
        {
            if (arr[i].equalsIgnoreCase(key))
            {
                index = i;
                break;
            }
        }
        if (index != -1)
        {
            System.out.println("String found at index: " + index);
        }
        else
        {
            System.out.println("String not found in the array.");
        }
    }
}
```

EXAM ORIENTED QUESTIONS

TYPE - 1 01 Mark

Multiple Choice Questions

Q.1 The output of the statement "talent". compare To("genius") is
(a) 11 (b) –11 (c) 0 (d) 13

Q.2 The method compareTo() returns __________ when two strings are equal and in lowercase. **ICSE SQP 2024**
(a) true (b) 0 (c) 1 (d) false

Q.3 What is the output of the statement given below? "ANGER". compareTo("ANGEL") **ICSE 2025**
(a) 3 (b) – 6 (c) 6 (d) 0

Q.4 The String class method to join two strings is **ICSE 2023**
(a) concat(String) (b) <string>.joint(string)
(c) concat(char) (d) Concat()

Q.5 "ICSE" + toLowerCase("Exam")
Which of the following is the correct output, considering Java's concat() behavior and case sensitivity?
(a) ICSE exam (b) Icseexam
(c) ICSE exam (d) ICSEexam

Q.6 Give the output of the following code.
```
System.out.println("Good".concat("Day"));
```
ICSE 2022 (Sem II)
(a) GoodDay (b) Good Day
(c) Goodday (d) goodDay

Q.7 Give the output of the following String methods.
```
"SUCESS" indexOf('S')+
"SUCESS".lastIndexOf('S')
```
ICSE 2022 (Sem II)
(a) 0 (b) 5 (c) 6 (d) – 5

Q.8 Which of the following returns a String? **ICSE SQP 2025**
(a) length() (b) charAt(int)
(c) replace(char, char) (d) indexOf(String)

Q.9 The output of the statement "CONCENTRATION". indexOf ('T') is
(a) 9 (b) 7 (c) 6 (d) (–1)

Q.10 Give the output of the following string methods
```
"MISSISSIPPI.indexOf('S')+"MISSISSIPPI".lastIndex
Of('I')
```
ICSE SQP 2022 (Sem II)
(a) 10 (b) 12 (c) 20 (d) 11

Q.11 The statement used to find the total number of Strings present in the string array String s[] is: **ICSE SQP 2025**
(a) s.length (b) s.length()
(c) length(s) (d) len(s)

Q.12 The output of the function "COMPOSITION". substring (3, 6) **ICSE 2023**
(a) POSI (b) POS
(c) MPO (d) MPOS

Q.13 The output of the method "DETERMINATION". substring(2, 6) is **ICSE SQP 2023**
(a) "TERM" (b) term
(c) "Term" (d) "TERMI"

Q.14 What will be the output of the following code?
```
System.out.println("Lucknow".substring(0,
4));
```
ICSE 2022 (Sem II)
(a) Lucknow (b) Luckn (c) Luck (d) luck

Q.15 The output of "Remarkable". substring(6) is **ICSE SQP 2024**
(a) mark (b) emark (c) marka (d) able

Q.16 The method to convert a string to upper case is **ICSE SQP 2023**
(a) toUpperCase(char) (b) toUPPERCASE(String)
(c) toUpperCase(String) (d) touppercase(String)

Answers

1. (d)	2. (b)	3. (c)	4. (a)	5. (d)
6. (a)	7. (c)	8. (c)	9. (b)	10. (b)
11. (a)	12. (b)	13. (a)	14. (c)	15. (d)
16. (c)				

TYPE - 2 01 Mark

Assertion-Reason Type Questions

Directions (Q. Nos. 1-10) The following questions are Assertion-Reason based questions. Choose the answer based on the code given below
(a) Both Assertion (A) and Reason (R) are true and Reason (R) is a correct explanation of Assertion (A).
(b) Both Assertion (A) and Reason (R) are true and Reason (R) is not a correct explanation of Assertion (A).
(c) Assertion (A) is true and Reason (R) is false.
(d) Assertion (A) is false and Reason (R) is true.

Q.1 Assertion (A) Strings created using the new keyword are always stored in the String Pool.

Reason (R) The new keyword explicitly creates a new String object in the heap memory, bypassing the String Pool.

Q.2 Assertion (A) String arrays in Java can dynamically resize to accommodate more elements.

Reason (R) String arrays in Java have a fixed size determined at the time of creation.

Q.3 Assertion (A) String literals are stored in the heap memory.

Reason (R) String literals are stored in the String Pool, a special area within the heap memory.

Q.4 Assertion (A) The charAt() method returns the entire substring starting from the given index.

Reason (R) The charAt() method returns the character at the specified index, not a substring.

Q.5 Assertion (A) The compareTo() method is used to check if two strings have the same content.

Reason (R) The compareTo() method returns an integer representing the lexicographical comparison between two strings.

Q.6 Assertion (A) The replace() method modifies the original String object.

Reason (R) Strings in Java are immutable, and the replace() method returns a new String object with the replacements.

Q.7 Assertion (A) The equalsIgnoreCase() method is used in Linear Search to perform a case-sensitive search.

Reason (R) The equalsIgnoreCase() method performs a case-insensitive comparison, ignoring the case of characters.

Q.8 Assertion (A) In Bubble Sort for Strings, strings are compared using the == operator.

Reason (R) In Bubble Sort for Strings, strings are compared using the compareTo() method for lexicographical ordering.

Q.9 Assertion (A) Selection Sort for Strings swaps the smallest element with the first unsorted element in each iteration.

Reason (R) Selection Sort finds the minimum element in the unsorted part and places it at the beginning of the unsorted part.

Q.10 Assertion (A) Linear Search in a String array checks all elements until the target is found or the array ends.

Reason (R) Linear Search sequentially checks each element in the array, making it suitable for unsorted arrays.

Answers

1. (d)	**2.** (d)	**3.** (d)	**4.** (d)	**5.** (c)
6. (d)	**7.** (d)	**8.** (d)	**9.** (c)	**10.** (c)

TYPE - 3 — 01 Mark

Odd One Out

Q.1 Find odd one out:

(a) String str1 = "Java";
(b) String str2 = "Java";
(c) String str3 = new String("Java");
(d) String str4 = "Java".toString();

Q.2 Find odd one out:

(a) Strings are immutable and cannot be changed once created.
(b) Strings in Java are primitive data types.
(c) String objects can be created using either literals or the new keyword.
(d) The String class belongs to the java.lang package and has built-in methods.

Q.3 Find odd one out:

(a) charAt() (b) compareTo()
(c) equals() (d) concat()

Q.4 Find odd one out:

(a) equalsIgnoreCase() (b) compareTo()
(c) endsWith() (d) equals()

Q.5 Find odd one out:

(a) toLowerCase() (b) toUpperCase()
(c) trim() (d) valueOf()

Q.6 Find odd one out:

(a) startsWith()
(b) compareToIgnoreCase()
(c) substring()
(d) trim()

Answers

1. (c)	**2.** (b)	**3.** (a)	**4.** (c)	**5.** (d)
6. (c)				

TYPE - 4 — 02 Marks

Short Answer Type Questions

Q.1 What will be the output for the following program segment? **ICSE 2006**

```
String s = new String("abc");
System.out.println(s.toUpperCase());
```

Ans. Output

ABC

Q.2 How can you declare string array in Java? **ICSE 2005**

Ans. Square brackets is used to declare a string array. There are two ways of using it:

e.g. `String[ ] stringArray;`

Or

```
String stringArray[ ];
```

Q.3 When there is no explicit initialisation, what are the default values set for variables in the following cases? **ICSE SQP 2024**

(a) Integer variable (b) String variable

Ans. (a) **Integer variable** The default value is 0 (zero).

(b) **String variable** The default value is null.

Q.4 Write the output of the following String methods:

`String x = "Galaxy ", y = "Games ";` **ICSE SQP 2025**

(a) `System.out.println (x.charAt(0)==y.charAt(0));`

(b) `System.out.println (x.compareTo(y));`

Ans. (a) true (b) – 1

Q.5 The following code to compare two strings is compiled, the following syntax error was displayed - incompatible types – int cannot be converted to boolean. Identify the statement which has the error and write the correct statement. Give the output of the program segment. **ICSE 2024**

```
void calculate()
{
  String a = "KING", b = "KINGDOM";
  boolean  x = a.compareTo(b);
  System.out.println(x);
}
```

Ans. The statement boolean x = a.compareTo(b); has the error. compareTo() returns an int, not a boolean.

Correct Statement: int x = a.compareTo(b);

Q.6 Give the output of the following String class methods. **ICSE 2023**

(i) "COMMENCEMENT".lastIndexOf('M')

(ii) "devote".compareTo("DEVOTE")

Ans. (i) 8

(ii) 32

Q.7 Write a Java statement for each to perform the following task. **ICSE SQP 2020**

(i) Find and display the position of the last space in a string str.

(ii) Extract the second character of the string str.

Ans. (i) `System.out.println(str.lastIndexOf(" "));`

(ii) `System.out.println(str.charAt(1));`

Q.8 What will be the output of the following program segments? **ICSE SQP 2017**

(i)
```
String s = "application";
int p = s.indexOf('a');
System.out.println(p);
System.out.println(p+s);
```

(ii)
```
String st = "PROGRAM";
System.out.println(st.indexOf
                    (st.charAt(4)));
```

Ans. (i) 0

0application

(ii) 4

Q.9 Give the output of the following string functions. **ICSE 2016**

(i) "MISSISSIPPI".indexOf('S')+"MISSISSIPPI".lastIndexOf('I')

(ii) "CABLE".compareTo("CADET")

Ans. (i) 12 (ii) – 2

Q.10 State the values stored in the variable str1 and str2. **ICSE 2013**

```
String s1 = "good";
String s2 = "world/matters";
String str1 = s2.substring(5).replace
                            ('t','n');
String str2 = s1.concat(str1);
```

Ans. str1 = /manners

str2 = good/manners

Q.11 What will be following code output? **ICSE 2012**

```
String s = "malayalam";
System.out.println(s.indexOf('m'));
System.out.println(s.lastIndexOf('m'));
```

Ans. The output will be

0

8

Q.12 Write a statement each to perform the following task on a string **ICSE 2011**

(i) Find and display the position of the last space in a string.

(ii) Convert a number stored in a string variable x to double data type.

Ans. (i) `i = s.lastIndexOf(' ');`

(ii) `Double.parseDouble(s);`

Q.13 State the purpose and return data type of the following string functions. **ICSE 2010**

(i) `indexOf()` (ii) `compareTo()`

Ans. (i) **indexOf( )** This function returns the index of the character presented in a string.

Syntax `int variable = String.indexOf(character);`

This function returns an integer value.

(ii) **compareTo( )** It is also a type of function which compares two strings. It is not only checks the equality of the strings but also checks whether a string is bigger or smaller than other or not.

Syntax `int variable = String1.compareTo(String2);`

This function can return an integer value depending upon the condition you want to check.

Q.14 Write a statement each to perform the following task on a string **ICSE 2010**

(i) Extract the second last character of a word stored in the variable wd.

(ii) Check if the second character of a string str is in uppercase.

Ans. (i) `char c = wd.charAt(wd.length() - 2)`

(ii)
```
if(character.isUpperCase (s.charAt(1)))
{
   ......
}
```

Q.15 What do the following functions return for
```
String x = "hello";
String y = "world";
```
(i) `System.out.println(x+y);`

(ii) `System.out.println(x.length());`

(iii) `System.out.println(x.charAt(3));`

(iv) `System.out.println(x.equals(y));`

Ans. (i) helloworld (ii) 5

(iii) l (iv) false

Q.16
```
String x[ ] = {"Artificial intelligence", "IOT", "Machine learning", "Big data"};
```
Give the output of the following statements. **ICSE 2019**

(i) `System.out.println(x[3]);`

(ii) `System.out.println(x.length);`

Ans. (i) Big Data

(ii) 4

Q.17 Write the output for the following:
```
String s1 = "Life is Beautiful";
System.out.println(s1.endsWith("L"));
```
Ans. False

Q.18
```
String x[] = {"SAMSUNG", "NOKIA", "SONY", "MICROMAX", "BLACKBERRY"};
```
ICSE 2017

Give the output of the following statements.

(i) `System.out.println(x[1]);`

(ii) `System.out.println(x[3].length());`

Ans. (i) **Output** NOKIA (ii) **Output** 8

Q.19 Write the output of the following String method: **ICSE 2025**
```
String x="talent";
String y = "matrix";
System.out.print(x.substring(3).concat
                              (y.substring(3));
```
Ans. Output endrix

Q.20 (i) Name one string method which results in positive integer only. **ICSE 2025**

(ii) Name one string method which results in a character.

Ans. (i) length()

(ii) charAt(int index)

Q.21 Give the output of the following String class method.
```
"REDUCE".compareTo("REVOLT") + "ANTARTICA"
.lastIndexOf('A')
```
ICSE SQP 2023

Ans. – 10

Q.22 Give the output of the following Java statements. **ICSE SQP 2020**

(i) "TRANSPARENT".toLowerCase()

(ii) "TRANSPARENT" .compareTo("TRANSITION")

Ans. (i) transparent

(ii) 7

Q.23 Write the return data type of the following functions. **ICSE 2019**

(i) startsWith( ) (ii) random( )

Ans. (i) boolean (ii) double

Q.24 Give the output of the following string functions. **ICSE 2018**

(i) "ACHIEVEMENT".replace('E', 'A')

(ii) "DEDICATE".compareTo("DEVOTE")

Ans. (i) ACHIAVAMANT (ii) –18

Q.25 Give the output of the following String class method. **ICSE SQP 2023**
```
"MISSISSIPPI".replace('S', 't').toLowerCase()
```
Ans. mittittippi

Q.26 Write the output for the following:
```
String s1 = "phoenix";
String s2 = "island";
System.out.println(s1.substring (0).
                 concat (s2.substring(2)));
System.out.println(s2.toUpperCase( ));
```
ICSE 2019

Ans. phoenixland

ISLAND

Q.27 Write the output for the following **ICSE 2017**
```
String s="Today is Test";
System.out.println(s.indexOf('T'));
System.out.println(s.substring(0,7)
                        +" "+"Holiday");
```
Ans. Output

0

Today i Holiday

Q.28 State the output when the following program segment is executed. **ICSE 2015**
```
String a = "Smartphone", b = "Graphic Art";
String h = a. substring(2,5);
String k = b. substring(8).toUpperCase();
```

```
System.out.println(h);
System.out.println(k.equalsIgnoreCase(h));
```

Ans. art
True

Q.29 What is the data type returned by the library functions? **ICSE 2014**

(i) compareTo( ) (ii) equals( )

Ans. (i) **compareTo( )** returns an int data type.
(ii) **equals( )** returns boolean data type.

Q.30 State the value of characteristic and mantissa when the following code is executed. **ICSE 2014**

```
String s = "4.3756";
int n = s.indexOf('.');
int characteristic = Integer.parseInt
                     (s.substring (0, n));
int mantissa = Integer.valueOf
                     (s.substring (n + 1));
```

Ans. characteristic = 4
mantissa = 3756

Q.31 State the output of the following program segment. **ICSE 2012**

```
String s = "Examination";
int n = s.length();
System.out.println(s.startsWith
                   (s.substring(5, n)));
System.out.println(s.charAt(2)
                   == s.charAt(6));
```

Ans. False
True

Q.32 State the method that **ICSE 2012**

(i) converts a string to a primitive float data type.
(ii) determines if the specified character is an uppercase character.

Ans. (i) `Float.parseFloat( );`
(ii) `Character.isUpperCase(char);`

Q.33 State the data type and values of a and b after the following segment is executed. **ICSE 2012**

```
String s1="Computer", s2="Applications";
a=(s1.compareTo(s2));
b=(s1.equals(s2));
```

Ans. a = (s1.compareTo(s2));
compareTo method returns int value
a = 2 [because C = 3, A = 1. So, difference = 3 – 1 = 2]
b = (s1.equals(s2));
equals method returns boolean value
Both strings are not equal.
So, b = false

Q.34 Give the output of the following **ICSE 2011**

```
String n = "Computer Knowledge";
String m = "Computer Applications";
System.out.println(n.substring(0,8)
                   .concat(m.substring(9)));
System.out.println(n.endsWith("e"));
```

Ans. Computer Applications
true

Q.35 Write the return data type of the following functions. **ICSE 2018**

(i) endsWith() (ii) log()

Ans (i) Return data type of function endsWith() is boolean.
(ii) Return data type of function log() is double.

Q.36 If, `String x = "Computer";` **ICSE 2008**
`String y = "Applications";`

What do the following return for

(i) `System.out.print(x.substring(1, 5));`
(ii) `System.out.print(x.indexOf(x.charAt(4)));`
(iii) `System.out.print(y+x.substring(5));`
(iv) `System.out.print(x.equals(y));`

Ans. (i) omput (ii) 4
(iii) Applicationster (iv) False

Q.37 What is the output of the following **ICSE 2007**

```
String S1 = "Hi";
String S2 = "Hi";
String S3 = "three";
String S4 = "HI";
System.out.println(S1 + "equals" + S2 + "
→" + S1.equals(S2));
System.out.println(S1 + "equals" + S3 + "
→" + S1.equals(S3));
System.out.println(S1 + "equals" + S4 + "
→" + S1.equals(S4));
System.out.println(S1 +
        "equalsIgnoreCase" + S4 + "→" +
              S1.equalsIgnoreCase(S4));
```

Ans. HiequalsHi → True
Hiequalsthree → False
HiequalsHI → False
HiequalsIgnoreCaseHI → true

Q.38 State the data type and value of y after the following code is executed:

```
char x = '7';
y = Character.isLetter(x);
```

Ans. Data type of y = boolean
Value of y = false.

Q.39 Write the output of the following statements. **ICSE 2011**

(i) `System.out.println(Character.isUpperCase('R'));`
(ii) `System.out.println(Character.toUpperCase('j'));`

Ans. The output will be
(i) true (ii) J

Q.40 Write the return type of the following library functions: **ICSE 2016**

(i) is LetterorDigit(char)

(ii) replace (char, char)

Ans. (i) boolean

(ii) String

Q.41 Write the output of the following string methods:

(a) "ARTIFICIAL".indexOf('I')

(b) "DOG and PUPPY".trim().length **ICSE SQP 2024**

Ans. (a) 3 (b) 13

Q.42 Consider the following String array and give the output. **ICSE 2018**

```
String arr[ ]= {"DELHI", "CHENNAI",
          "MUMBAI", "LUCKNOW", "JAIPUR"};
System.out.println(arr[0].length()>
                   arr[3].length());
System.out.print(arr[4].substring(0,3));
```

Ans. Output

False

JAI

Q.43 Give the output of the following program segment and specify how many times the loop is executed. **ICSE 2025**

```
String s = "JAVA";
for(i=0;i<s.length();i+ =2)
System.out.println(s.substring(i));
```

Ans. Output

J

JA

JAV

JAVA

Number of times the loop is executed: 4

Q.44 Name a string function which removes the blank spaces provided in the prefix and suffix of a string.

Ans. trim()

Q.45 State the output of the following program segment. **ICSE 2014**

```
String str1= "great";
String str2 = "minds";
System.out.println(str1.substring(0,2)
        .concat(str2.substring(1)));
System.out.println("WH" +
     (str1.substring(2).toUpperCase()));
```

Ans. grinds

WHEAT

Q.46 Write the prototype of a function search which takes two arguments a string and a character and returns an integer value. **ICSE SQP 2020**

Ans. int search (string str, char ch)

TYPE - 5 02 Marks

Differentiate

Q.1 Differentiate between compareTo() and equals() methods.

Ans. Differences between compareTo() and equals() method.

compareTo()	equals()
It compares two strings lexicographically.	It checks if contents of two strings are same or not.
The result is a negative, positive or zero integer value depending on whether the String object precedes, follows or is equal to the String argument	The result is true if the contents are same otherwise it is false.

Q.2 State the differences between == operator and equals() method.

Ans. Differences between = = operator and equals ( ) method are as follows:

Feature	== Operator	equals() Method
Purpose	Compares object references (memory addresses).	Compares the actual content of objects.
Default Behavior	Checks if two variables point to the same object in memory.	Checks if the objects have the same content (often overridden in classes).
String Comparison	Checks if two string variables refer to the same string object in the string pool.	Checks if two strings have the same sequence of characters.
Example (Java)	String str1 = "hello"; String str2 = str1; str1 == str2; // true	String str1 = new String("hello"); String str2 = new String("hello"); str1.equals(str2); // true

TYPE - 6 15 Marks

Long Answer Type Questions

Q.1 Define a class to accept a string and print the characters with the uppercase and lowercase reversed, but all the other characters should remain the same as before.

Example : Input : WelCoMe_2022

Output : wELcOmE_2022 **ICSE 2022 (Sem II)**

Ans.
```
import java.util.*;
public class UpperLowert
{
  public static void main(String[] args)
  {
    String str="", newstr="";
    Scanner sc=new Scanner(System.in);
    char c;
    int i;
    System.out.println("Enter a string:");
    str=sc.nextLine();
    for(i=0;i<str.length();i++)
    {
      c=str.charAt(i);
      if(Character.isLetter(c) &&
            Character.isUpperCase(c))
       newstr+=Character.toLowerCase(c);
      else if (Character.isLetter(c)
           && Character.isLowerCase(c))
       newstr+=Character.toUpperCase(c);
      else
       newstr+=c;
    }
      Systerm.out.println("Converted
                    String :"+newstr);
  }
}
```

Q.2 Define a class to accept two strings of same length and form a new word in such a way that, the first character of the first word is followed by the first character of the second word and so on.

Example : Input : String 1-BALL

String 2-WORD

Output : BWAOLRLD **ICSE 2022 (Sem II)**

Ans.
```
import java.util.*;
public class Alternate
{
  public static void main(String[] args)
  {
    String s1="",s2="",newstr="";
    s1=sc.nextLine()+"";
    if(s1.length()!=s2.length())
    {
      System.out.println("Strings
        should be of same length!!!");
      return;
    }
    else
    {
      for(int i=0;i<s1.length();i++)
      {
        c1=s1.char At(i);
        c2=s2.char At(i);
        newstr+=c1;
        newstr+=c2;
      }
      System.out.println("New string:
                           "+newstr);
    }
  }
}
```

Q.3 Define a class to accept two strings, convert them into uppercase, check and display whether two strings are equal or not, if the two strings are not equal, print the string with the highest length or print the message both the strings are of equal length.

ICSE SQP 2022 (Sem II)

Ans.
```
import java.util.*;
public class StringComparer
{
  public static void compareStrings
            (String str1, String str2)
  {
    String upperStr1 = str1.toUpperCase();
    String upperStr2 = str2.toUpperCase();
    if (upperStr1.equals(upperStr2))
    {
      System.out.println("The two
                strings are equal.");
    }
    else
    {
      int length1 = upperStr1.length();
      int length2 = upperStr2.length();
      String longerString = (length1 >
      length2) ? upperStr1 : upperStr2;
      System.out.println("The two
            strings are not equal.");
      System.out.println("The longer
         string is: " + longerString);
    }
  }
  public static void main(String[] args)
  {
    String str1 = "Hello";
    String str2 = "World";
    compareStrings(str1, str2);
  }
}
```

Output

The two strings are not equal.

The longer string is: WORLD

Q.4 Define a class to accept a string, convert it into lowercase and check whether the string is a palindrome or not.

A palindrome is a word which reads the same backward as forward.

Example: madam, racecar etc. **ICSE SQP 2022 (Sem II)**

Ans.
```
import java.util.Scanner;
public class PalindromeChecker
{
   public static void main(String[] args)
   {
      Scanner scanner = new Scanner
                             (System.in);
      System.out.print("Enter a string: ");
      String input = scanner.nextLine()
                           .toLowerCase();
      if (isPalindrome(input))
      {
         System.out.println("The string
                          is a palindrome.");
      }
      else
      {
         System.out.println("The string
                       is not a palindrome.");
      }
   }
   private static boolean isPalindrome
                              (String str)
   {
      int length = str.length();
      for (int i = 0; i < length / 2; i++)
      {
         if (str.charAt(i) != str.charAt
                           (length - 1 - i))
         {
            return false;
         }
      }
      return true;
   }
}
```

Output 1

Enter a string: madam

The string is a palindrome.

Output 2

Enter a string: world

The string is not a palindrome.

Q.5 Define a class to declare an array to accept and store ten words. Display only those words which begin with the letter 'A' or 'a' and also end with the letter 'A' or 'a'. **ICSE 2022 (Sem II)**

Example:

Input : Hari, Anita, Akash, Amrita, Alina, Devi, Rishab, John, Farha, AMITHA

Output : Anita
Amrita
Alina
AMITHA

Ans.
```
import java.util.*;
public class Words
{
   public static void main(String[] args)
   {
      String s="",str="";
      Scanner sc=new Scanner(System.in);
      System.out.println("Enter the
                                    string");
      s=sc.nextLine()+"";
      char cb,ce;
      int l=s.length();
      for(int i=0; i<s.length();i++)
      {
         char c=s.charAt(i);
         if(c!='')
         {
            str+=s.charAt(i);
         }
         else
         {
            cb=str.charAt(0);
            ce=str.charAt(str.length()-1);
            if ((cb=='a' || cb =='A')&&
                       (ce=='a' || ce=='A'))
            System.out.println(str);
            str="";
         }
      }
   }
}
```

Q.6 Define a class to accept and store 10 strings into the array and print the strings with even number of characters. **ICSE SQP 2022 (Sem II)**

Ans.
```
import java.util.Scanner;
public class StringArray
{
   public static void main(String[] args)
   {
      String[] strings = new String[10];
      Scanner scanner = new Scanner
                               (System.in);
      System.out.println("Enter 10
                                 strings:");
      for (int i = 0; i < strings.length;
                                       i++)
      {
         strings[i] = scanner.nextLine();
      }
```

```
        System.out.println("Strings with
              even number of characters:");
        for (String s : strings)
        {
            if (s.length() % 2 == 0)
            {
                System.out.println(s);
            }
        }
    }
}
```

Output

Enter 10 strings:
suman
bhavana
sapna
adishree
farah
gautam
harsha
rakesh
shivani
supriya
Strings with even number of characters:
adishree

Q.7 Special words are those words which start and end with the same letter. **ICSE 2016**

Examples:
EXISTENCE
COMIC
WINDOW

Palindrome words are those words which read the same from left to right and *vice-versa.*

Examples:
MALAYALAM
MADAM
LEVEL
ROTATOR
CIVIC

All palindromes are special words, but all special words are not palindromes.

Write a program to accept a word check and print whether the word is a palindrome or only special word or none of them.

Ans.

```
import java.util.Scanner;
public class SpecialPalindrome
{
    public static void main(String args[])
    {
        Scanner in = new Scanner(System.in);
        System.out.print("Enter a word: ");
        String str = in.next();
        str = str.toUpperCase();
        int len = str.length();
        if (str.charAt(0) == str.charAt
                                (len - 1))
        {
            boolean isPalin = true;
            for (int i = 1; i < len / 2; i++)
            {
                if (str.charAt(i)
                    != str.charAt(len - 1 - i))
                {
                    isPalin = false;
                    break;
                }
            }
            if (isPalin)
            {
                System.out.println
                            ("Palindrome");
            }
            else
            {
                System.out.println("Special");
            }
        }
        else
        {
            System.out.println("Neither
                  Special nor Palindrome");
        }
    }
}
```

Q.8 Write a program that encodes a word into Piglatin. To translate word into a Piglatin word, convert the word into uppercase and then place the first vowel of the original word as the start of the new word along with the remaining alphabets. The alphabets present before the vowel being shifted towards the end followed by "AY".

Sample input (1) : London, Sample output (1) : ONDONLAY

Sample input (2) : Olympics, Sample output (2) : OLYMPICSAY **ICSE 2013**

Ans.

```
public class PigLatinEncoder
{
    public static String
            encodePigLatin(String word)
    {
        // Convert the word to uppercase
                for easier vowel checking
        String wordUpper = word
                        .toUpperCase();
        final String VOWELS = "AEIOU";
        int firstVowelIndex = -1;
        // Find the index of the first vowel
        for (int i = 0; i < wordUpper
                        .length(); i++)
```

```
        {
           if (VOWELS.indexOf
                  (wordUpper.charAt(i)) != -1)
           {
              firstVowelIndex = i;
                break;
           }
        }
        if (firstVowelIndex == -1)
        {
           return wordUpper + "AY";
              // No vowels, just add "AY"
        }
        // Rearrange the word according
                          to Pig Latin rules
        String firstPart = wordUpper
              .substring(firstVowelIndex);
        String secondPart = wordUpper
            .substring(0, firstVowelIndex);
        String pigLatinWord = firstPart
                        + secondPart + "AY";
        return pigLatinWord;
    }
    public static void main(String[] args)
    {
        String[] testWords = {"London",
              "Olympics", "apple", "rhythm",
                             "STRAWBERRY"};
        for (String word : testWords)
        {
           String pigLatinWord =
                      encodePigLatin(word);
           System.out.println("Original
          word: " + word + ", Pig Latin: " +
                              pigLatinWord);
        }
        // Get user input (optional)
        System.out.print("Enter a word to
                encode into Pig Latin: ");
        java.util.Scanner scanner = new
              java.util.Scanner(System.in);
        String userWord = scanner
                                .nextLine();
        scanner.close(); // Close the
           scanner to prevent resource leaks
        String pigLatinWord = encodePigLatin
                                (userWord);
        System.out.println("Original word:
            " + userWord + ", Pig Latin: " +
                              pigLatinWord);
    }
}
```

Q.9 Write a program to accept a string. Convert the string to uppercase count and output the number of double letter sequences that exist in the string.

Sample Input : "SHE WAS FEEDING THE LITTLE RABBIT WITH AN APPLE

Sample Output : 4 **ICSE 2012**

Ans.

```
import java.util.Scanner;
public class DoubleLetterCounter
{
   public static int
            countDoubleLetters(String str)
   {
      if (str == null || str.length() < 2)
      {
         return 0; // Empty or
               single-character string has
                         no double letters.
      }
      String upperStr =
         str.toUpperCase(); // Convert to
                                uppercase
      int count = 0;
      for (int i = 0; i <
            upperStr.length() - 1; i++)
      {
         if (upperStr.charAt(i) ==
                upperStr.charAt(i + 1))
         {
            count++;
         }
      }
      return count;
   }
   public static void main(String[] args)
   {
      Scanner scanner = new
                      Scanner(System.in);
      System.out.println("Enter a string: ");
      String inputString = scanner.nextLine();
      scanner.close();
      int doubleLetterCount =
         countDoubleLetters(inputString);
      System.out.println("Number of
            double letter sequences: " +
                       doubleLetterCount);
   }
}
```

Q.10 Write a program to accept a word and convert it into lowercase, if it is in uppercase and display the new word by replacing only the vowels with the character following it.

Example:

Sample Input : Computer

Sample Output : Cmmpttrr **ICSE 2011**

Ans.

```
import java.util.Scanner;
public class VowelReplacement
{
   public static void main(String[] args)
   {
      Scanner scanner = new
                      Scanner(System.in);
      System.out.print("Enter a word: ");
      String word = scanner.nextLine();
```

```
        scanner.close();
        // Convert the word to lowercase
        word = word.toLowerCase();
        // Convert the word to a character
              array for easier manipulation
        char[] charArray = word.toCharArray();
        // Iterate through the character
                   array and replace vowels
        for (int i = 0; i <
                     charArray.length; i++)
        {
          char currentChar = charArray[i];
          if (isVowel(currentChar))
          {
            if (i < charArray.length - 1)
            {
              charArray[i] = charArray[i + 1];
                   // Replace vowel with
                           next character
            }
            //If the vowel is the last
              letter, we don't replace it.
          }
        }
        // Convert the modified character
                     array back to a string
        String result = new
                        String(charArray);
        System.out.println("Modified word:
                              " + result);
      }
      // Helper method to check if a
                       character is a vowel
      private static boolean isVowel(char c)
      {
        return c == 'a' || c == 'e' ||
          c == 'i' || c == 'o' || c == 'u';
      }
    }
```

Q.11 Write a program to input a sentence and print the number of characters found in the longest word of the given sentence.
Example: if s = "India is my country" then the output should be 7. **ICSE 2009**

Ans.

```
import java.util.Scanner;
public class LongestWordLength
{
    public static void main(String[] args)
    {
        Scanner scanner = new
                       Scanner(System.in);
        System.out.print("Enter a
                            sentence: ");
        String sentence =
                      scanner.nextLine();
        scanner.close();
        String[] words =
         sentence.split("\\s+"); // Split
                the sentence into words
        int maxLength = 0;
        for (String word : words)
        {
            int wordLength =
                          word.length();
            if (wordLength > maxLength)
            {
                maxLength = wordLength;
            }
        }
        System.out.println("Length of
        the longest word: " + maxLength);
    }
}
```

Q.12 Write a program to enter a sentence from the keyboard and count the number of times a particular word occurs in it. Display the frequency of the search word.

Example

Input: Enter a sentence : the quick brown fox jumps over the lazy dog

Enter a word to be searched : the

Output: Searched word occurs : 2 times. **ICSE 2007**

Ans.

```
import java.util.Scanner;
public class WordFrequencyCounter
{
    public static void main(String[] args)
    {
        Scanner scanner = new
                      Scanner(System.in);
        System.out.print("Enter a
                           sentence: ");
        String sentence =
                      scanner.nextLine();
        System.out.print("Enter a word
                      to be searched: ");
        String searchWord =
                          scanner.next();
        scanner.close();
        int count = 0;
        String[] words =
         sentence.split("\\s+"); // Split
                the sentence into words
        for (String word : words)
        {
          if (word.equalsIgnoreCase
                          (searchWord))
          { // Use equalsIgnoreCase for
            case-insensitive comparison
              count++;
          }
        }
```

```
        System.out.println("Searched
        word occurs : " + count + " times");
    }
}
```

Q.13 Write a program using a method Palin(), to check whether a string is a Palindrome or not. A Palindrome is a string that reads the same from left to right and *vice-versa*. e.g. MADAM, ARORA, ABBA, etc. **ICSE 2007**

Ans.

```
import java.util.Scanner;
public class PalindromeChecker
{
    public static void main(String[] args)
    {
        Scanner scanner = new
                    Scanner(System.in);
        System.out.print("Enter a string: ");
        String inputString =
                    scanner.nextLine();
        scanner.close();
        if (Palin(inputString))
        {
         System.out.println(inputString
              + " is a palindrome.");
        } else {
        System.out.println(inputString
            + " is not a palindrome.");
        }
    }
    // Method to check if a string is
                        a palindrome
    public static boolean Palin(String str)
    {
        // Remove spaces and convert
     to lowercase for accurate comparison
        str = str.replaceAll("\\s+",
                    "").toLowerCase();
        int left = 0;
        int right = str.length() - 1;
        while (left < right)
        {
            if (str.charAt(left) !=
                    str.charAt(right))
            {
             return false; // Not a
                        palindrome
            }
            left++;
            right--;
        }
        return true; // It is a palindrome
    }
}
```

Q.14 Write a program to input any given string to calculate the total number of characters and vowels present in the string and also reverse the string

Example

Input: Enter string : SNOWY

Output: Total number of characters : 05

Number of vowels : 01

Reverse string : YWONS **ICSE 2005**

Ans.

```
import java.util.Scanner;
public class StringOperations
{
    public static void main(String[] args)
    {
        Scanner scanner = new Scanner(System.in);
        System.out.print("Enter a string: ");
        String inputString = scanner.nextLine();
        scanner.close();
        int charCount = inputString.length();
        int vowelCount = countVowels(inputString);
        String reversedString =
                    reverseString(inputString);
        System.out.println("Total number of
                    characters : " + charCount);
        System.out.println("Number of vowels : "
                            + vowelCount);
        System.out.println("Reverse string : "
                        + reversedString);
    }
    // Method to count the number of vowels in
                                a string
    public static int countVowels(String str)
    {
        int count = 0;
        for (int i = 0; i < str.length(); i++)
        {
            char c = str.charAt(i);
            if (isVowel(c))
            {
                count++;
            }
        }
        return count;
    }
    // Helper method to check if a character is
                                a vowel
    private static boolean isVowel(char c)
    {
        c = Character.toLowerCase(c);
                // Consider both uppercase and
                            lowercase vowels
        return c == 'a' || c == 'e' || c == 'i'
                    || c == 'o' || c == 'u';
    }
    // Method to reverse a string
    public static String reverseString(String str)
```

```java
    {
        StringBuilder reversed = new
                             StringBuilder();
        for (int i = str.length() - 1; i >= 0; i--)
        {
            reversed.append(str.charAt(i));
        }
        return reversed.toString();
    }
}
```

Q.15 Define a class to accept a String and print the number of digits, alphabets and special characters in the string. **ICSE 2023**

Example : S = "KAPILDEV@83"

Output : Number of digits–2

Number of alphabets–8

Number of special characters–1

Ans.

```java
import java.util.Scanner;
public class Example
{
    public static void main(String[] args)
    {
        Scanner sc = new Scanner(System.in);
        System.out.println("Enter a
                             string:");
        String str = sc.nextLine();
        int specialCharCount = 0;
        int digitCount = 0;
        int alphabetCount = 0;
        for (int i = 0; i < str.length(); i++)
        {
            char c = str.charAt(i);
            if (Character.isDigit(c))
            {
                digitCount++;
            }
            else if (Character.isLetter(c))
            {
                alphabetCount++;
            }
            else
            {
                specialCharCount++;
            }
        }
        System.out.println("Number of
                  digits: " + digitCount);
        System.out.println("Number of
              alphabets: " + alphabetCount);
        System.out.println("Number of
                   special characters: " +
                        specialCharCount);
    }
}
```

Q.16 Write a program to accept a sentence and print only the first letter of each word of the sentence in capital letters separated by a full stop. **ICSE SQP 2017**

Example:

INPUT SENTENCE : "This is a cat"

OUTPUT : T.I.A.C.

Ans.

```java
import java.util.Scanner;
public class CapitalizeFirstLetter
{
    public static void main(String[] args)
    {
        Scanner scanner = new Scanner
                                (System.in);
        System.out.print("Enter a
                              sentence: ");
        String sentence = scanner.nextLine();
          // Split the sentence into words
        String[] words = sentence.split(" ");
          // Create a StringBuilder to
             store the capitalized letters
         StringBuilder capitalizedLetters
                  = new StringBuilder();
          // Loop through each word in the
                                 sentence
         for (String word : words)
         {
           // Get the first letter of the
                    word and capitalize it
             char firstLetter = Character
               .toUpperCase(word.charAt(0));
           // Append the capitalized letter
                      to the StringBuilder
             capitalizedLetters.append
                 (firstLetter).append(".");
         }
        // Print the capitalized letters,
               removing the last full stop
        System.out.println
           (capitalizedLetters.deleteCharAt
                 (capitalizedLetters.
              length() - 1).toString());
    }
}
```

Q.17 Define a class to accept a string and print the same in reverse, also print the number of vowels in the string.

Example : S = "BEAUTIFUL"

Output – "LUFITUAEB"

No. of vowels = 5 **ICSE SQP 2023**

Ans.

```java
import java.util.Scanner;
class reverse
{
    public static void main (String[] args)
    {
```

```
        Scanner in = new Scanner (System.in);
        System.out.print("Enter the string
                                        = ");
        String s = in.nextLine();
        int j = 0;
        String r = "";
        for (int i = s.length() - 1; i
                                  >= 0; i--)
        {
            char ch = s.charAt(i);
            r += ch;
            if ("AEIOUaeiou".indexOf(ch)>= 0)
                j++;
        }
        System.out.println(("Reverse of
                            the string = "+ r);
        System.out.println("No. of vowels
                                   = " + j);
    }
}
```

Q.18 Write a program to input a string and convert it into uppercase and print the pair of vowels and number of pair of vowels occurring in the string. **ICSE SQP 2020**

Example:

Input:

"BEAUTIFUL BEAUTIES"

Output:

Pair of vowels: EA, AU, EA, AU, IE

No. of pair of vowels: 5

Ans.

```
import java.util.Scanner;
public class VowelPair
{
    static boolean isVowel(char ch)
    {
        ch = Character.toUpperCase(ch);
        if (ch == 'A' ||ch == 'E'
        ||ch == 'I' || ch == 'O' ||ch == 'U')
            return true;
        return false;
    }
    public static void main(String args[])
    {
        Scanner in = new Scanner(System.in);
        System.out.println("Enter the
                                sentence : ");
        String str = in.nextLine();
        str = str.toUpperCase();
        int count = 0;
        System.out.print("Pair of vowels: ");
        for (int i = 0; i < str.length()
                                   - 1; i++)
        {
            if (isVowel(str.charAt(i)) &&
                isVowel(str.charAt(i + 1)))
            {
                count++;
                System.out.print(str.charAt(i));
                System.out.print(str.charAt
                              (i+1) + " ");
            }
        }
        System.out.print("\nNo. of pair
                        of vowels: " + count);
    }
}
```

Q.19 Define a class to accept a string and convert it into uppercase. Count and display the number of vowels in it. **ICSE SQP 2024**

Input : robotics

Output : ROBOTICS

Number of vowels : 3

Ans.

```
import java.util.Scanner;
class StringManipulator
{
    public static void main(String[] args)
    {
        Scanner scanner = new Scanner(System.in);
          // Accept a string from the user
        System.out.print("Enter a string: ");
        String input = scanner.nextLine();
          // Convert the string to uppercase
        String uppercaseString = input.toUpperCase();
          // Count the number of vowels
        int vowelCount = 0;
        for (int i = 0; i < uppercaseString.length();
                                              i++)
        {
          char c = uppercaseString.charAt(i);
          if (c == 'A' || c == 'E' || c == 'I' || c
                              == 'O' || c == 'U')
          {
            vowelCount++;
          }
        }
        // Display the uppercase string and
                          the number of vowels
        System.out.println("Uppercase string: "
                          + uppercaseString);
        System.out.println("Number of vowels: "
                               + vowelCount);
    }
}
```

Q.20 Write a program to input a sentence and convert it into uppercase and display each word in a separate line.

Example : Input : India is may country

Output : INDIA

IS

MY

COUNTRY

Ans.

```
import java.util.Scanner;
public class UppercaseWords
{
  public static void main(String[] args)
  {
    Scanner scanner = new Scanner(System.in);
    System.out.print("Input: ");
    String sentence = scanner.nextLine();
    String uppercaseSentence =
                    sentence.toUpperCase();
    String[] words =
              uppercaseSentence.split(" ");
    System.out.println("Output: ");
    for (String word : words)
    {
      System.out.println(word);
    }
    scanner.close();
  }
}
```

Q.21 Define a class to accept a string and convert the same to uppercase, create and display the new string by replacing each vowel by immediate next character and every consonant by the previous character. The other characters remain the same. **ICSE SQP 2025**

Example : Input : #IMAGINATION@2024

Output : #JLBFJMBSJPM@2024

Ans.

```
class Convert
{
  String s;
    // Constructor to initialize the string
  Convert(String z)
  {
    s = z;
  }
  // Method to perform the conversion
  void convert()
  {
    int i, l = s.length();
    char ch;
    String ns = "";
    for (i = 0; i < l; i++)
    {
      ch = s.charAt(i);
      if (Character.isLetter(ch))
      {
        if ("AEIOUaeiou".indexOf(ch) >= 0)
          ns = ns + (char) (ch + 1);
        else
          ns = ns + (char) (ch - 1);
      }
      else
      {
        ns = ns + ch;
      }
    }
    System.out.print(ns);
  }
  public static void main(String[] args)
  {
    Convert obj = new Convert("Example");
    obj.convert();  // Call the convert method
  }
}
```

Q.22 Write a program to input a sentence and convert it into uppercase and count and display the total number of words starting with a letter 'A'.

Example:

Sample Input : ADVANCEMENT AND APPLICATION OF INFORMATION TECHNOLOGY ARE EVER CHANGING.

Sample Output : Total number of words starting with letter 'A' = 4. **ICSE 2019**

Ans.

```
import java.util.*;
class Print_Vowel
{
   public static void main(String args[])
   {
      Scanner sc=new Scanner(System.in);

      System.out.print("Enter any
                              sentence: ");
      String s=sc.nextLine();
      s = s+" ";
      int l=s.length();
      s=s.toUpperCase();
      int pos=0,count=0;
      char ch1, ch2;
      String w;
      for(int i=0; i<l; i++)
      {
         ch1 = s.charAt(i);
         if(ch1 == ' ')
         {
            w = s.substring(pos,i);
            // extracting words one by one
            ch2 = w.charAt(0);
            if(ch2=='A' )
```

```
                {
                    count++;
                }
                pos = i+1;
            }
        }
        System.out.print("No. of words
                starting with A :"+count);
    }
}
```

Q.23 Write a program in Java to accept a string in lower case and change the first letter of every word to upper case. Display the new string. **ICSE 2018**

Sample input: we are in cyber world

Sample output: We Are In Cyber World

Ans.

```
import java.util.*;
class Convert
{
    public static void main(String args[])
    {
        Scanner sc=new Scanner(System.in);
        System.out.println("Enter any
                                    String ");
        String str=sc.nextLine();
        String s1="";
        s1=s1+(Character.toUpperCase
                        (str.charAt(0)));
        for(int i=1;i<str.length();i++)
        {
            if(str.charAt(i)==' ')
            {
                s1=s1+str.charAt(i)+
                        (Character.toUpperCase
                            (str.charAt(i+1)));
                i++;
            }
            else
            s1=s1+(Character.toLowerCase
                            (str.charAt(i)));
        }
        System.out.println(s1);
    }
}
```

Q.24 Design a class to overload a function check() as follows **ICSE 2017**

(i) **void check (String str, char ch)** to find and print the frequency of a character in a string.

Example:

Input:	Output:
str = "success"	number of s present is = 3
ch = 's'	

(ii) **void check(String s1)** to display only vowels from string s1, after converting it to lower case.

Example:

Input:

s1 = "computer"

Output : o u e

Ans.

```
class Overload
{
    void check(String str, char ch)
    {
        int l=str.length();
        int count=0;
        for(int i=0;i<l;i++)
        {
            char c=str.charAt(i);
            if(c==ch)
            {
                count++;
            }
        }
        System.out.println("Number of
                "+ch+" present is = "+count);
    }
    void check(String s1)
    {
        int l=s1.length();
        for(int i=0;i<l;i++)
        {
            char c=Character.toLowerCase
                                (SL.charAt(i));
            if(c=='a'||c=='e'||c=='i'
                            ||c=='o'||c=='u')
            {
                System.out.print(c+" ");
            }
        }
    }
}
```

Q.25 Consider the following statement.
"January 26 is celebrated as the Republic Day of India".
Write a program to change 26 to 15, January to August, Republic to Independence and finally print "August 15 is celebrated as the Independence Day of India". **ICSE 2006**

Ans.

```
import java.io.*;
class Rep
{
    public static void main(String args[])
    {
        String s = "January 26 is
                celebrated as the Republic
                                Day of India";
        String h = "August 15";
        String str = "Independence";
```

```
        System.out.println("Original string");
        System.out.println(s);
        s = h + s.substring(10,32) + str
                    + s.substring(40);
        System.out.println("After
                    replacements string is");
        System.out.println(s);
    }
}
```

Q.26 Write a program to initialise the seven Wonders of the World alongwith their locations in two different arrays. Search for a name of the country input by the user. If found, display the name of the country alongwith its Wonder, otherwise display "Sorry Not Found! **ICSE 2016**

Seven wonders - CHICHEN ITZA, CHRIST THE REDEEMER, TAJMAHAL, GREAT WALL OF CHINA, MACHU PICCHU, PETRA, COLOSSEUM

Locations - MEXICO, BRAZIL, INDIA, CHINA, PERU, JORDAN, ITALY

Example - Country Name : INDIA Output : INDIA - TAJMAHAL

Country Name : USA Output : Sorry Not Found!

Ans.

```
import java.util.Scanner;
public class 7Wonders
{
    public static void main(String args[])
    {
        String wonders[] = {"CHICHEN ITZA",
              "CHRIST THE REDEEMER", "TAJMAHAL",
            "GREAT WALL OF CHINA", "MACHU
                  PICCHU", "PETRA", "COLOSSEUM"};
        String locations[] = {"MEXICO", "BRAZIL",
      "INDIA", "CHINA", "PERU", "JORDAN","ITALY"};
        Scanner in = new Scanner(System.in);
        System.out.print("Enter country: ");
        String c = in.nextLine();
        int i;
        for (i = 0; i < locations.length; i++)
        {
            if (locations[i].equals(c))
            {
                System.out.println(locations[i]
                         + " - " + wonders[i]);
                break;
            }
        }
        if (i == locations.length)
           System.out.println("Sorry Not Found!");
    }
}
```

Q.27 Write a program to input twenty names in an array. Arrange these names in descending order of alphabets, using the bubble sort technique.

Ans.

```
import java.util.Scanner;
public class NameSorter
{
    public static void main(String[] args)
    {
        Scanner scanner = new Scanner(System.in);
        String[] names = new String[20];
        // Input: Accept 20 names from the user
        System.out.println("Enter 20 names:");
        for (int i = 0; i < 20; i++)
       {
            System.out.print("Enter name "
                              + (i + 1) + ": ");
            names[i] = scanner.nextLine();
        }
        scanner.close();
        // Sort the names in descending order
                              using bubble sort
        bubbleSortDescending(names);
        // Output: Print the sorted names
        System.out.println("\nSorted names in
                           descending order:");
        for (String name : names)
       {
            System.out.println(name);
        }
    }
    // Method to sort an array of strings in
             descending order using bubble sort
    public static void
             bubbleSortDescending(String[] arr)
    {
        int n = arr.length;
        for (int i = 0; i < n - 1; i++)
        {
            for (int j = 0; j < n - i - 1; j++)
            {
                // Use compareTo() for string
                comparison.  For descending order,
                // swap if the first string is
                          "less than" the second.
                if (arr[j].compareTo(arr[j + 1])
                                            < 0)
                {
                    // Swap arr[j] and arr[j+1]
                    String temp = arr[j];
                    arr[j] = arr[j + 1];
                    arr[j + 1] = temp;
                }
            }
        }
    }
}
```

Q.28 Define a class and store the given city names in a single dimensional array. Sort these names in alphabetical order using the Bubble Sort technique only.

INPUT : Delhi, Bangalore, Agra, Mumbai, Calcutta.

OUTPUT : Agra, Bangalore, Calcutta, Delhi, Mumbai. **ICSE 2008**

Ans.
```
import java.io.*;
class Name
{
  public static void main(String args[])
                              throws IOException
  {
    String city[] = {"Delhi", "Bangalore",
             "Agra", "Mumbai", "Kolkata"};
    String temp;
    int i, j, n = 5;
    for(i= 1; i< n-1; i++)
    {
      for(j= 0; j<=n-i-1; j++)
      {
        if((city[j].compareTo(city[j+1]))
                                       > 0)
        {
          temp = city[j];
          city[j] = city[j+1];
          city[j + 1] = temp;
        }
      }
    }
    for(int K = 0; K <  n; K++)
    {
      System.out.println(city[K]);
    }
  }
}
```

Q.29 Define a class to accept the names of 10 students in an array and check for the existence of the given name in the array using linear search, if found print the position of the name, if not found print the appropriate message. Also print the names which begins with the word "SRI". **ICSE SQP 2023**

Ans.
```
import java.util.Scanner;
class Search
{
  public static void main(String[] args)
  {
    Scanner in = new Scanner(System.in);
    String a[] = new String[10];
    int count = 0;
    int pos = 0;
    System.out.println("Enter 10 names:");
    for (int i = 0; i < a.length; i++)
    a[i] = in.nextLine();
    System.out.print("Enter name to
                         be searched: ");
    String key = in.nextLine();
    boolean found = false;
    for (int i=0; i < a.length; i++)
    {
      if (key.equalsIgnoreCase(a[i])
                             && !found)
      {
        found = true;
        pos = i;
      }
      if (a[i].startsWith("SRI"))
      count++;
    }
    if (found)
      System.out.println("Found
            at position: " + (pos + 1));
    else
      System.out.println("Not found!");
      System.out.println("No. of names
         beginning with SRI = " + count);
  }
}
```

Output

Enter 10 names:
suman
bhavana
sapna
adishree
farah
gautam
harsha
rakesh
shivani
supriya
Enter name to be searched: supriya
Found at position: 10
No. of names beginning with SRI = 0

Q.30 Write a program to store 10 names in an array. Arrange these in alphabetical order by sorting. Print the sorted list. Take single word names, all in capital letters, e.g. SAMSON, AJAY, LUCY, etc. **ICSE SQP 2017**

Ans.
```
import java.util.Scanner;
public class NameSorter
{
    public static void main(String[] args)
    {
        Scanner scanner = new Scanner(System.in);
        String[] names = new String[10];
        // Input: Accept 10 names from the user
                         (all in capital letters)
```

```java
        System.out.println("Enter 10 names
                    (all in capital letters):");
        for (int i = 0; i < 10; i++)
        {
            System.out.print("Enter name " +
                                (i + 1) + ": ");
            names[i] = scanner.nextLine();
        }
        scanner.close();
        // Sort the names in alphabetical order
                                using bubble sort
        bubbleSortAlphabetical(names);
        // Output: Print the sorted names
        System.out.println("\nSorted names in
                            alphabetical order:");
        for (String name : names)
        {
            System.out.println(name);
        }
    }
    // Method to sort an array of strings in
            alphabetical order using bubble sort
    public static void bubbleSortAlphabetical
                                    (String[] arr)
    {
        int n = arr.length;
        for (int i = 0; i < n - 1; i++)
        {
            for (int j = 0; j < n - i - 1; j++)
            {
                // Use compareTo() for string
                  comparison.  For ascending order
                                    (alphabetical).
                // swap if the first string is
                        "greater than" the second.
                if (arr[j].compareTo(arr[j + 1]) > 0)
                {
                    // Swap arr[j] and arr[j+1]
                    String temp = arr[j];
                    arr[j] = arr[j + 1];
                    arr[j + 1] = temp;
                }
            }
        }
    }
}
```

Q.31 Define a class to declare a character array of size ten, accept the character into the array and perform the following.

(i) Count the number of uppercase letters in the array and print.

(ii) Count the number of vowels in the array and print. **ICSE SQP 2022**

Ans.

```java
import java.util.Scanner;
public class CharacterArrayOperations
{
    public static void main(String[] args)
    {
        Scanner scanner = new Scanner(System.in);
        // Accept the string from the user
        System.out.println("Enter a string:");
        String inputString = scanner.nextLine();
        scanner.close();
        int uppercaseCount = 0;
        int vowelCount = 0;
        // Iterate through the string, character
                                    by character
        for (int i = 0; i < inputString.length();
                                            i++)
        {
            char c = inputString.charAt(i);
         // Get the character at the current index
            if (isUpperCase(c))
            {
                uppercaseCount++;
            }
            if (isVowel(c))
            {
                vowelCount++;
            }
        }
        // Print the results
        System.out.println("Number of uppercase
                letters: " + uppercaseCount);
        System.out.println("Number of vowels: "
                                + vowelCount);
    }
    // Helper method to check if a character is
                                        a vowel
    private static boolean isVowel(char c)
    {
        // Convert to lowercase without using
                                toLowerCase()
        if (c >= 'A' && c <= 'Z')
        {
            c = (char) (c + 32); // Add 32 to
                    get lowercase ASCII value
        }
        return c == 'a' || c == 'e' || c == 'i'
                    || c == 'o' || c == 'u';
    }
    //Helper method to check if a character is
                                    uppercase
    private static boolean isUpperCase(char c)
    {
        return c >= 'A' && c <= 'Z';
    }
}
```

Q.32 Define a class to declare a character array of size ten. Accept the characters into the array and display the characters with highest and lowest ASCII (American Standard Code for Information Interchange) value. **ICSE 2022**

EXAMPLE :

INPUT:

'R', 'z', 'q', 'A', 'N', 'p', 'm', 'U', 'Q', 'F'

OUTPUT :

Character with highest ASCII value = z

Character with lowest ASCII value = A

Ans.
```
import java.util.Scanner;
public class ASCIIVal
{
    public static void main(String[] args)
    {
        Scanner in = new Scanner(System.in);
        char ch[] = new char[10];
        int len = ch.length;
        System.out.println("Enter 10
                               characters:");
        for (int i = 0; i < len; i++)
        {
            ch[i] = in.nextLine().charAt(0);
        }
        char h = ch[0];
        char l = ch[0];
        for (int i = 1; i < len; i++)
        {
            if (ch[i] > h)
            {
                h = ch[i];
            }
            if (ch[i] < l)
            {
                l = ch[i];
            }
        }
        System.out.println("Character with
                     highest ASCII value: " + h);
        System.out.println("Character with lowest
                             ASCII value: " + l);
    }
}
```

Q.33 Define a class to accept 10 characters from a user. Using bubble sort technique arrange them in ascending order. Display the sorted array and original array. **[ICSE 2023] [ICSE 2019]**

Ans.
```
import java.util.Scanner;
public class CharBubbleSort
{
    public static void main(String args[])
    {
        Scanner in = new Scanner(System.in);
        char ch[] = new char[10];
        System.out.println("Enter 10 characters:");
        for (int i = 0;  i < ch.length; i++)
        {
            ch[i] = in.nextLine().charAt(0);
        }
        System.out.println("Original Array");
        for (int i = 0;  i < ch.length; i++)
        {
            System.out.print(ch[i] + " ");
        }
       //Bubble Sort
        for (int i = 0; i < ch.length - 1; i++)
        {
            for (int j = 0; j < ch.length - 1 -
                                        i; j++)
            {
                if (ch[j] > (ch[j + 1]))
                {
                    char t = ch[j];
                    ch[j] = ch[j + 1];
                    ch[j + 1] = t;
                }
            }
        }
        System.out.println("\nSorted Array");
        for (int i = 0;  i < ch.length; i++)
        {
            System.out.print(ch[i] + " ");
        }
    }
}
```

Q.34 Define a class to accept a String and Print if it is a Super string or not. A String is Super if the number of uppercase letters are equal to the number of lower case letters. **ICSE 2025**

[Use Character & String methods only]

Example: "COmmITmeNt"

Number of Uppercase letters -5

Number of Lowercase letters-5

String is a Super String

Ans.
```
import java.util.Scanner;
class SuperStringChecker
{
    // Method to accept a string and check if it
                             is a Super String
    public void checkSuperString()
    {
        Scanner sc = new Scanner(System.in);
        System.out.print("Enter a string: ");
        String input = sc.nextLine();
        int upperCount = 0;
        int lowerCount = 0;
```

```java
// Count uppercase and lowercase
                                characters
for (int i = 0; i < input.length(); i++)
{
    char ch = input.charAt(i);
    if (Character.isUpperCase(ch))
    {
        upperCount++;
    }
    else if (Character.isLowerCase(ch))
    {
        lowerCount++;
    }
}
// Display results
System.out.println("Number of Uppercase
                letters = " + upperCount);
System.out.println("Number of Lowercase
                letters = " + lowerCount);
if (upperCount == lowerCount)
{
    System.out.println("String is a
                            Super String");
}
else
{
    System.out.println("String is NOT
                        a Super String");
}
}
// Main method
public static void main(String[] args)
{
    SuperStringChecker obj = new
                    SuperStringChecker();
    obj.checkSuperString();
}
}
```

Output

Enter a string: COmmiTMENT

Number of Uppercase letters = 7

Number of Lowercase letters = 3

String is NOT a Super String

Question Paper 2025

Specimen Question Paper

QUESTION PAPER 2025
COMPUTER APPLICATIONS

General Instructions

Maximum Marks : 100

Time allowed : Two hours

Answer to this paper must be written on the paper provided separately.
You will not be allowed to write during the first 15 minutes. This time is to be spent in reading the question paper.
The time given at the head of this paper is the time allowed for writing the answers.
This paper is divided into two sections. Attempt all questions from Section A and any four questions from Section B.
The intended marks for questions or parts of questions are given in brackets [ ].

Section A

(Attempt **all** questions from this section) **(40 Marks)**

Question 1

Select the correct answers to the questions from the given options. **(20)**

(Do not copy the question, write the correct answer only)

(i) Character class methods are found in the package called
(a) java.util (b) java.lang (c) java.awt (d) java.io

(ii) `System.out.println('Z' + 32);` will display
(a) z (b) Z (c) 122 (d) 154

(iii) double *x* [] = {2.5, 4.5, 5.5, 6.4}; occupies .... bytes.
(a) 16 (b) 4 (c) 8 (d) 32

(iv) The output 42/6% 2 is:
(a) 1 (b) 10 (c) 2 (d) 0

(v)

Consider the two dimensional array P[2][3], of peripherals (input/output devices) given above, state the index of the device Barcode Scanner.
(a) P[1][1] (b) P[0][1] (c) P[1][2] (d) P[0][0]

(vi) Which of the following is user defined data type?

1. array	3. class
2. double	4. boolean

(a) only 1 (b) 1 and 3 (c) only 2 (d) only 4

(vii) Select the infinite loop:

(a) for(int i = 1; i< = 10; i + +)
(b) for(int i = 2; i! = 0; i – = 3)
(c) for(int i = 5; i< = 5; i + +)
(d) for(int i = 1; i > = 1; i – –)

(viii) The output of Math.max(– 7, Math.min(–5, – 4)) is

(a) – 5 (b) – 4 (c) – 7 (d) error

(ix) Which of the following is true for the given object creation statement?

```
Game cricket = new Game( );
```

(a) Game is an object of cricket class
(b) New keyword creates object Game
(c) Game is a class and cricket is an object
(d) Game and cricket are objects

(x) Post office is an example for .... access specifier.

(a) public (b) local (c) protected (d) private

(xi) **Assertion (A)** In switch case break statement avoids fall through.

Reason (R) break statement helps to execute only one case at a time.

(a) Both (A) and (R) are true and (R) is a correct explanation of (A).
(b) Both (A) and (R) are true and (R) is not a correct explanation of (A).
(c) (A) is true and (R) is false.
(d) (A) is false and (R) is true.

(xii) A physical education teacher asks the students to do the side stretch as shown below, 10 times. Which programming construct the teacher uses?

(a) if (b) switch (c) for (d) if else if

(xiii) The index (subscript) of the last element of an array ar[ ] is:

(a) ar.length( ) (b) ar[ ].length (c) ar.length( ) – 1 (d) ar.length – 1

(xiv) **Assertion (A)** A clock is a real-life example of nested loops.

Reason (R) The hour hand moves through 12 positions, while the minute hand moves through 60 positions within each hour.

(a) Both (A) and (R) are true and (R) is a correct explanation of (A).
(b) Both (A) and (R) are true and (R) is not a correct explanation of (A).
(c) (A) is true and (R) is false.
(d) (A) is false and (R) is true

(xv) Which of the following pairs of methods will cause a compile-time error due to incorrect method overloading?

(a) void test(int a, int b) and void test(double a, double b)
(b) void test(int a, double b) and void test(double a, int b)
(c) void test(int a, double b) and void test(int a)
(d) void test(int a) and int test(int a)

(xvi) Which of the following converts "25" to 25.0?

(a) Double.Parsedouble("25")
(b) Double.parse("25")
(c) Double.parseDouble("25")
(d) Double.parseDouble(25)

(xvii) Consider the program segment:

```
int p=0;
for(p=4;p>0;p- =2);
```

```
System.out.print(p);
System.out.println(p);
```

The above statements will display:

(a) 42 (b) 4200 (c) 0
0 (d) 00

(xviii) `System.out.println("I said,\ "It\'s wise to obey elders.\"");`

The output of the above statement is:

(a) I said,'It is wise to obey elders'. (b) I said, "It's wise to obey elders."
(c) I said, It's wise to elders. (d) "'It's wise to obey elders."'

(xix) What is the output of the statement given below?

```
"ANGER".compareTo("ANGEL")
```

(a) 3 (b) – 6 (c) 6 (d) 0

(xx) Consider the following program segment in which the statements are jumbled.

Choose the correct order of statements to calculate and return the factorial of 4.

```
for (k=1;k<=4;k+ +)  ———→  1
return fa;  ———→           2
long fa=1, k;  ———→        3
fa*=k;  ———→               4
```

(a) 1, 2, 3, 4 (b) 3, 1, 4, 2 (c) 3, 1, 2, 4 (d) 1, 3, 2, 4

Question 2

(i) Write the java expression to find the product of square root of *P* and the square root of *Q* using the methods of Math class. **[2]**

(ii) Write the output of the following String method:

```
String x=" talent"; String y="matrix";
System.out.print(x.substring(3).concat (y.substring(3));
```
[2]

(iii) Write the Java statement for creating an object named 'sifra' of the class 'Robot', which takes three double parameters. **[2]**

(iv) Convert the given loop into exit controlled loop. **[2]**

```
int a,b;
for (a=10,b=1; a>=1;a- =2)
{
  b+ =a;
  b+ +;
}
System.out.print(b);
```

(v) Consider and give the output of the following program: **[2]**

```
class report
{
  int a,b;
  report( )
  {
     a=10;
     b=15;
  }
  report(int x, int y)
  {
     a=x;
     b=y;
  }
  void print( )
  {
     System.out.println(a*b);
  }
  static void main( )
  {
     report r = new report( );
     r.print( );
     report p = new report(4, 5);
     p.print( );
  }
}
```

(vi) (a) Name one String method which results in positive integer only. **[2]**

(b) Name one String method which results in a character.

(vii) John was asked to write a Java code to calculate the surface area of a cone, the following code was written by him: **[2]**

Surface area of cone is $A = \pi r l$

$$l = \sqrt{r^2 + h^2}$$

```
class area
{
 double area (double r, double h)
 {
    double l, a;
    a=22.0/7*r*l;
    l=Math.sqrt(r*r+h*h);
    return a;
 }
}
```

Specify the type of the error in the above program, correct and write the program to be error free.

(viii) Consider the following array and answer the questions given below: **[2]**

```
int a[ ] = {12, 10, 8, 4, 6, 2, 3, 5, 7}
```

(a) What is the output of System.out.print(a[0]+a[5]);?

(b) What is the index (subscript) of the largest element of the array a[ ]?

(ix) (a) Write the Java statement to initialise the first 6 odd numbers in a 3×2 array. **[2]**

(b) What is the result of x[0][1] + x[2][1] of the above array?

(x) Give the output of the following program segment and specify how many times the loop is executed.

```
String s = "JAVA";
for(i=0;i<s.length();i+ =2)
System.out.println(s.substring(i));
```

[2]

Section B

(Attempt **any four** questions from this section) **(60 Marks)**

Question 3

Define a class named CloudStorage with the following specifications **[15]**

Member Variables	
int acno	stores the user's account number
int space	stores the amount of storage space in GB purchased by the user.
double bill	stores the total price to be paid by the user
Member Methods	
void accept()	prompts the user to input their account number and storage space using Scanner class methods only.
void calculate()	calculates the bill total price based on the storage space purchased using the pricing table provided:
void display()	displays the account number, storage space and bill to be paid

Pricing table (for void calculate()):

Storage range	Price per GB (Rs)
First 15 GB	15
Next 15 GB	13
Above 30 GB	11

Write a main method to create an object of the class and invoke the methods of the class with respect to the object.

Question 4

Define a class to accept values into a 4 × 4 integer array. Calculate and print the NORM of the array. **[15]**

NORM is the square root of sum of squares of all elements.

1	2	1	3
5	2	1	6
3	6	1	2
3	4	6	3

Sum of squares of elements = 1+ 4 + 1+ 9 + 25
+ 4 + 1+ 36 + 9 + 36 + 1+ 4 + 9 + 16 + 36 + 9= 201

NORM = Squareroot of 201
= 14.177446878757825

Question 5

Define a class to accept a String and Print if it is a Super string or not. A String is Super if the number of uppercase letters are equal to the number of lower case letters. **[15]**

[Use Character & String methods only]

Example: "COmmITmeNt"

Number of Uppercase letters -5

Number of Lowercase letters-5

String is a Super String

Question 6

Define a class to initialise the following data in an array.

Search for a given character input by the user, using the Binary Search technique. **[15]**

Print "Search Successful" if the character is found otherwise print "Search is not Successful"

'A', 'H', 'N', 'P', 'S', 'U', 'W','Y', 'Z', 'b', 'd'

Question 7

Define a class to overload the method print( ) as follows: **[15]**

void print( )	To print the given format using nested loops. @#@#@ @#@#@ @#@#@ @#@#@
double print(double a, double b)	To display the sum of numbers between a and b with difference of 0.5 eg. if a = 1.0, b = 4.0 output is: 1.0 + 1.5 + 2.0 + 2.5 + ... + 4.0
int print(char ch1, char ch2)	compare the two characters and return the ASCII code of the largest character.

Question 8

Define a class to accept a number. Check if the sum of the largest digit and the smallest digit is an even number or an odd number. Print appropriate messages. **[15]**

Sample Input:	6425	3748
Largest digit:	6	8
Smallest digit:	2	3
Sample Output:	Sum is even	Sum is odd

Answers

1. (i) (b) java.lang

(ii) (c) 122

(iii) (d) 32

(iv) (a) 1

(v) (a) P[1][1]

(vi) (b) 1 and 3

(vii) (b) for(int i = 2; i! = 0; i -- = 3)

(viii) (a) – 5

(ix) (c) Game is a class and cricket is an object

(x) (a) public

(xi) (a) Both (A) and (R) are true and (R) is a correct explanation of (A).

(xii) (c) for

(xiii) (d) ar.length – 1

(xiv) (a) Both (A) and (R) are true and (R) is a correct explanation of (A).

(xv) (d) void test(int a) and int test(int a)

(xvi) (c) Double.parseDouble("25")

(xvii) (d) 00

(xviii) (b) I said, "It's wise to obey elders."

(xix) (c) 6

(xx) (b) 3, 1, 4, 2

2. (i) `Math.sqrt(P)*Math.sqrt(Q)`

(ii) **Output** endrix

(iii) `Robot sifra = new Robot (1.0,2.0,3.0);`

(iv)
```
int a, b;
a = 10;
b = 1;
do{
    b = b + a;
    b++;
    a -= 2;
} while (a >= 1);
System.out.println(b);
```

(v) **Output**

150

20

(vi) (a) length()

(b) charAt(int index)

(vii)
```
class area
{
    double surfaceArea(double r, double h)
    {
        double l = Math.sqrt(r * r + h * h);
        // Correct slant height calculation
        return Math.PI * r * (r + l);
        // Correct total surface area formula
    }
}
```

(viii) (a) 12 + 7 = 19

(b) 0

(ix) (a) int[][] oddNumbers = {{1, 3}, {5, 7}, {9, 11}};

(b) 1 + 3 + 5 = 9

(x) **Output**

J

JA

JAV

JAVA

Number of times the loop is executed: 4

3.
```
import java.util.Scanner;
class CloudStorage
{
  // Member Variables
   int acno;
   int space; // in GB
   double bill;
   // Method to accept user input
   void accept()
    {
       Scanner sc = new Scanner(System.in);
       System.out.print("Enter account number: ");
       acno = sc.nextInt();
       System.out.print("Enter storage space purchased (in GB): ");
       space = sc.nextInt();
       sc.close();
   }
   // Method to calculate bill
   void calculate()
   {
       int remaining = space;
       bill = 0;
       if (remaining > 30)
       {
           bill += (remaining - 30) * 11;
           remaining = 30;
       }
       if (remaining > 15)
       {
           bill += (remaining - 15) * 13;
           remaining = 15;
       }
       if (remaining > 0)
```

```
            {
                bill += remaining * 15;
            }
        }
        // Method to display results
        void display()
        {
            System.out.println("\nAccount No: " + acno);
            System.out.println("Storage Space (GB): " + space);
            System.out.println("Total Bill (Rs): " + bill);
        }
        // Main method to test the class
        public static void main(String[] args)
        {
            CloudStorage cs = new CloudStorage();
            cs.accept();
            cs.calculate();
            cs.display();
        }
    }
```

4.

```
import java.util.Scanner;
class NormCalculator
{
   int[][] arr = new int[4][4];
   // Method to accept values using Scanner
   public void acceptValues()
   {
     Scanner sc = new Scanner(System.in);
     System.out.println("Enter 16 integers for the 4x4 array:");
     for (int i = 0; i < 4; i++)
     {
       for (int j = 0; j < 4; j++)
       {
         arr[i][j] = sc.nextInt();
       }
     }
   }
   // Method to calculate and print NORM
   public void calculateNorm()
   {
     int sum = 0;
     for (int i = 0; i < 4; i++)
     {
       for (int j = 0; j < 4; j++)
       {
         sum += arr[i][j] * arr[i][j];
           // square of each element
       }
     }
     double norm = Math.sqrt(sum);
     System.out.println("NORM = " + norm);
   }
   // Main method
   public static void main(String[] args)
   {
     NormCalculator obj = new NormCalculator();
```

```
        obj.acceptValues();
        obj.calculateNorm();
    }
}
```

Output

Enter 16 integers for the 4 × 4 array:
2 3 4 5
6 7 8 9
2 3 4 5
6 2 1 5
NORM = 20.09975124224178

5.

```
import java.util.Scanner;
class SuperStringChecker
{
    // Method to accept a string and check if it is a Super String
    public void checkSuperString()
    {
        Scanner sc = new Scanner(System.in);
        System.out.print("Enter a string: ");
        String input = sc.nextLine();
        int upperCount = 0;
        int lowerCount = 0;
        // Count uppercase and lowercase characters
        for (int i = 0; i < input.length(); i++)
        {
            char ch = input.charAt(i);
            if (Character.isUpperCase(ch))
            {
                upperCount++;
            }
            else if (Character.isLowerCase(ch))
            {
                lowerCount++;
            }
        }
        // Display results
        System.out.println("Number of Uppercase letters = " + upperCount);
            System.out.println("Number of Lowercase letters = " + lowerCount);
            if (upperCount == lowerCount)
            {
                System.out.println("String is a Super String");
            }
            else
            {
                System.out.println("String is NOT a Super String");
            }
        }
        // Main method
        public static void main(String[] args)
        {
            SuperStringChecker obj = new SuperStringChecker();
            obj.checkSuperString();
        }
    }
```

Output

Enter a string: COmmiTMENT

Number of Uppercase letters = 7

Number of Lowercase letters = 3

String is NOT a Super String

6.
```
import java.util.Arrays;
import java.util.Scanner;
class BinarySearchChar
{
   char[] arr = {'A', 'H', 'N', 'P', 'S', 'U', 'W', 'Y', 'Z', 'b', 'd'};
   // Method to perform binary search
   public void searchChar()
   {
     Scanner sc = new Scanner(System.in);
     System.out.print("Enter a character to search: ");
     char key = sc.next().charAt(0);
     // Sort the array before binary search
     Arrays.sort(arr);
     int left = 0, right = arr.length - 1;
     boolean found = false;
     while (left <= right)
     {
       int mid = (left + right) / 2;
       if (arr[mid] == key)
       {
          found = true;
            break;
       }
       else if (arr[mid] < key)
       {
          left = mid + 1;
       }
       else
       {
          right = mid - 1;
       }
     }
     // Output result
     if (found)
     {
       System.out.println("Search Successful");
     }
     else
     {
       System.out.println("Search is not Successful");
     }
   }
   // Main method
   public static void main(String[] args)
   {
     BinarySearchChar obj = new BinarySearchChar();
     obj.searchChar();
   }
}
```

Output

Enter a character to search: B

Search is not Successful

7.
```
import java.util.Scanner;
class Printer
{
  public void print()
  {
    for (int i = 0; i < 5; i++)
    {
      for (int j = 0; j < 5; j++)
      {
        System.out.print("@");
      }
      System.out.println();
    }
  }
  public void print(double a, double b)
  {
    if (a > b)
    {
      double temp = a;
        a = b;
        b = temp;
    }
    for (double i = a; i <= b; i += 0.5)
    {
      System.out.print(i);
      if (i + 0.5 <= b)
      {
        System.out.print(" + ");

      }
    }
    System.out.println();
  }
  public int print(char ch1, char ch2)
  {
    if (ch1 > ch2)
    {
      return (int) ch1;
    }
    else
    {
      return (int) ch2;
    }
  }
  public static void main(String[] args)
  {
    Scanner scanner = new Scanner(System.in);
    Printer printer = new Printer();
    System.out.println("Calling print() with no arguments:");
    printer.print();
    System.out.println();
    System.out.println("Calling print(double a, double b):");
    System.out.print("Enter the value of a: ");
```

```
        double a = scanner.nextDouble();
        System.out.print("Enter the value of b: ");
        double b = scanner.nextDouble();
        printer.print(a, b);
        System.out.println();
        System.out.println("Calling print(char ch1, char ch2):");
        System.out.print("Enter the first character: ");
        char char1 = scanner.next().charAt(0);
        System.out.print("Enter the second character: ");
        char char2 = scanner.next().charAt(0);
        int largestASCII = printer.print(char1, char2);
        System.out.println("ASCII code of the largest character: " + largestASCII);
        scanner.close();
    }
}
```

Output

Calling print() with no arguments:
@@@@@
@@@@@
@@@@@
@@@@@
@@@@@
Calling print(double a, double b):
Enter the value of a: 1.0
Enter the value of b: 4.0
1.0 + 1.5 + 2.0 + 2.5 + 3.0 + 3.5 + 4.0
Calling print(char ch1, char ch2):
Enter the first character: a
Enter the second character: c
ASCII code of the largest character: 99

8.

```
import java.util.Scanner;
class DigitSumCheck
{
    int num;
    // Method to accept input
    void accept()
    {
        Scanner sc = new Scanner(System.in);
        System.out.print("Enter a number: ");
        num = sc.nextInt();
        sc.close();
    }
    // Method to find largest and smallest digit and check the sum
    void checkSumEvenOdd()
    {
        int temp = num;
        int largest = 0;
        int smallest = 9;
        while (temp > 0)
        {
            int digit = temp % 10;
            if (digit > largest)
```

```
            {
               largest = digit;
            }
            if (digit < smallest)
            {
               smallest = digit;
            }
            temp /= 10;
         }
         int sum = largest + smallest;
         System.out.println("Largest digit: " + largest);
         System.out.println("Smallest digit: " + smallest);
         if (sum % 2 == 0)
         {
           System.out.println("Sum is even");
         }
         else
         {
           System.out.println("Sum is odd");
         }
      }
      // Main method
      public static void main(String[] args)
      {
        DigitSumCheck obj = new DigitSumCheck();
        obj.accept();
        obj.checkSumEvenOdd();
      }
   }
```

SPECIMEN QUESTION PAPER

FULLY SOLVED

(COMPUTER APPLICATIONS)

General Instructions

Maximum Marks : 100

Time allowed : Two hours

Answer to this paper must be written on the paper provided separately.
You will not be allowed to write during the first 15 minutes.
This time is to be spent in reading the question paper.
The time given at the head of this paper is the time allowed for writing the answers.
This paper is divided into two sections. Attempt all questions from Section A and any four questions from Section B.
The intended marks for questions or parts of questions are given in brackets [ ].

Section A

(Attempt **all** questions from this section) **(40 Marks)**

Question 1

Choose the correct answer to the questions from the given options.
(Do not copy the questions, write the correct answer only.) **(20)**

(i)

Name the above structure: *• Analysis*

(a) One dimensional array
(b) Two dimensional array with 4 rows and 5 columns
(c) Three dimensional array
(d) Two dimensional array with 5 rows and 4 columns

(ii) "Java compiled code (byte code) can run on all operating systems" – Name the feature. *• Understanding*

(a) Robust and Secure
(b) Object Oriented
(c) Platform Independent
(d) Multithreaded

(iii) The size of '\n' is: *• Recall*

(a) 2 bytes
(b) 4 bytes
(c) 8 bytes
(d) 16 bytes

(iv) Identify the operator that gets the highest precedence while evaluating the given expression: • *Analysis*

$a + b \% c * d - e$

(a) + (b) % (c) – (d) *

(v) Which of the following is a valid Java keyword? • *Understanding*

(a) If (b) BOOLEAN (c) static (d) Switch

(vi) The output of the following code is: • *Analysis*

```
System.out.println(Math.ceil(6.4)+Math.floor(-1 - 2));
```

(a) 3.0 (b) 4 (c) 3 (d) 4.0

(vii) Which of the following returns a String? • *Understanding*

(a) length() (b) charAt(int) (c) replace(char, char) (d) indexOf (String)

(viii) Which of the following is not true with regards to a switch statement? • *Understanding*

(a) checks for an equality between the input and the case labels
(b) supports floating point constants
(c) break is used to exit from the switch block
(d) case labels are unique

(ix) Consider the array given below:

```
char ch[]={ 'A','E','I','O', 'U'};
```

Write the output of the following statements. • *Analysis*

```
System.out.println(ch[0]*2);
```

(a) 65 (b) 130 (c) 'A' (d) 0

(x) To execute a loop 10 times, which of the following is correct? • *Analysis*

(a) for (int i=11;i<=30;i+=2) (b) for (int i=11;i<=30;i+=3)
(c) for (int i=11;i<20;i++) (d) for (int i=11;i<=21;i++)

(xi) A single dimensional array has 50 elements, which of the following is the correct statement to initialize the last element to 100. • *Analysis*

(a) x[51]=100 (b) x[48]=100 (c) x[49]=100 (d) x[50]=100

(xii) Method prototype for the method compute which accepts two integer arguments and returns true/false. • *Understanding*

(a) void compute (int a, int b) (b) boolean compute (int a, int b)
(c) Boolean compute (int a,b) (d) int compute (int a, int b)

(xiii) The statement that brings the control back to the calling method is: • *Recall*

(a) break (b) System.exit(0) (c) continue (d) return

(xiv) The default value of a boolean variable is: • *Recall*

(a) False (b) 0 (c) false (d) True

(xv) The method to convert a lowercase character to uppercase is: • *Recall*

(a) String.toUpperCase() (b) Character.isUppercase (char)
(c) Character.toUpperCase(char) (d) toUpperCase ()

(xvi) **Assertion (A)** Integer class can be used in the program without calling a package.
Reason (R) It belongs to the default package java.lang. • *Application*

(a) Both Assertion (A) and Reason (R) are true and Reason (R) is a correct explanation of Assertion (A)
(b) Both Assertion (A) and Reason (R) are true and Reason (R) is not a correct explanation of Assertion(A)
(c) Assertion (A) is true and Reason (R) is false
(d) Assertion (A) is false and Reason (R) is true

(xvii) A student executes the following code to increase the value of a variable '*x*' by 2.

He has written the following statement, which is incorrect. • *Analysis*

```
x = +2;
```

What will be the correct statement?

A. *x* + = 2;

B. *x* = 2;

C. *x* = *x* + 2;

(a) Only A (b) Only C (c) All the three (d) Both A and C

(xviii) The statement used to find the total number of Strings present in the string array String s[] is:

(a) s.length (b) s.length() (c) length(s) (d) len(s) • *Analysis*

(xix) Consider the following program segment in which the statements are jumbled, choose the correct order of statements to swap two variables using the third variable. • *Analysis*

```
void swap(int a, int b)
{
  a = b;  → (1)
  b = t;   → (2)
  int t = 0;  → (3)
  t = a;  → (4)
}
```

(a) (1) (2) (3) (4) (b) (3) (4) (1) (2) (c) (1) (3) (4) (2) (d) (2) (1) (4) (3)

(xx) **Assertion (A)** An argument is a value that is passed to a method when it is called. • *Application*

Reason (R) Variables which are declared in a method prototype to receive values are called actual parameters.

(a) Both Assertion (A) and Reason (R) are true and Reason (R) is a correct explanation of Assertion (A)
(b) Both Assertion (A) and Reason (R) are true and Reason (R) is not a correct explanation of Assertion(A)
(c) Assertion (A) is true and Reason (R) is false
(d) Assertion (A) is false and Reason (R) is true

Question 2.

(i) Rewrite the following code using single if statement. **[2]** • *Understanding*

```
if (code= = 'g')
  System.out.println ("GREEN");
else if (code=='G')
  System.out.println ("GREEN ");
```

(ii) Evaluate the given expression when the value of a=2 and b=3 **[2]** • *Analysis*

```
b* = a + + - + + b + + + a;
System.out.println ("a= "+a);
System.out.println ("b= "+b);
```

(iii) A student executes the following program segment and gets an error. Identify the statement which has an error, correct the same to get the output as WIN. **[2]** • *Analysis*

```
boolean x = true;
switch(x)
{
  case 1: System.out.println("WIN");
  break;
  case 2: System.out.println ("LOOSE");
}
```

(iv) Write the Java expression for $\sqrt[3]{x} + \sqrt{y}$ [2]

• *Understanding*

(v) How many times will the following loop execute? Write the output of the code: [2]

• *Analysis*

```
int x = 10;
while (true)
{
  System.out.println (x++*2);
  if (x%3==0)
  break;
}
```

(vi) Write the output of the following String methods: [2]

• *Analysis*

```
String x = "Galaxy ", y = "Games ";
```

(a) System.out.println (x.charAt(0)==y.charAt(0));

(b) System.out.println (x.compareTo(y));

(vii) Predict the output of the following code snippet: [2]

• *Analysis*

```
char ch='B';
char chr= Character.toLowerCase(ch);
int n=(int) chr-10;
System.out.println((char)n+" \t"+chr);
```

(viii) A student is trying to convert the string present in x to a numerical value, so that he can find the square root of the converted value. However the code has an error. Name the error (syntax/logical/ runtime). Correct the code so that it compiles and runs correctly. [2]

• *Analysis*

```
String x= "25";
int y=Double.parseDouble (x);
double r=Math.sqrt (y);
System.out.println (r);
```

(ix) Consider the following program segment and answer the questions below:

• *Analysis*

```
class calculate
{
  int a; double b;
  calculate()
  {
    a=0;
    b=0.0;
  }
    calculate(int x, double y)
    {
      a=x;
      b=y;
    }
    void sum()
    {
      System.out.println(a*b);
  }
}
```

Name the type of constructors used in the above program segment? [2]

(x) Consider the following program segment and answer the questions given below:

• *Analysis*

```
int x[ ][ ]={{2,4,5,6}, {5,7,8,1}, {34, 1,10, 9}};
```

(a) What is the position of 34?

(b) What is the result of x[2][3] + x[1][2]? [2]

Section B

(Attempt **any four** questions from this section) **(60 Marks)**

Question 3

Define a class with the following specifications: **[15]**

• *Understanding/Application*

Class name	Bank
Member variables	
double p	stores the principal amount
double n	stores the time period in years
double r	stores the rate of interest
double a	stores the amount
Member methods	
void accept ()	input values for p and n using Scanner class methods only.
void calculate ()	calculate the amount based on the following conditions:

Time in (Years)	**Rate %**
Upto ½	9
> ½ to 1 year	10
> 1 to 3 years	11
> 3 years	12

$$a = p\left(1 + \frac{r}{100}\right)^{n}$$

void display ()	display the details in the given format. Principal Time Rate Amount XXX XXX XXX XXX

Write the main method to create an object and call the above methods.

Question 4.

Define a class to search for a value input by the user from the list of values given below. If it is found display the message "Search successful", otherwise display the message "Search element not found" using Binary search technique. **[15]**

5.6, 11.5, 20.8, 35.4, 43.1, 52.4, 66.6, 78.9, 80.0, 95.5

• *Understanding/Application*

Question 5.

Define a class to accept a string and convert the same to uppercase, create and display the new string by replacing each vowel by immediate next character and every consonant by the previous character. The other characters remain the same.

Example : Input : #IMAGINATION@2024

Output : #JLBFJMBSJPM@2024

[15]

• *Understanding/Application*

Question 6.

Define a class to accept values into 4 × 4 array and find and display the sum of each row.

• Understanding/Application

Example

A[][]={1,2,3,4},{5,6,7,8},{1,3,5,7},{2,5,3,1}}

Output

sum of row 1 = 10 (1 + 2 + 3 + 4)

sum of row 2 = 26 (5 + 6 + 7 + 8)

sum of row 3 = 16 (1 + 3 + 5 + 7)

sum of row 4 = 11 (2 + 5 + 3 + 1) [15]

Question 7.

Define a class to accept a number and check whether it is a SUPERSPY number or not. A number is called SUPERSPY if the sum of the digits equals the number of the digits. [15]

Example1:

Input: 1021

Output: SUPERSPY number

[SUM OF THE DIGITS = 1 + 0 + 2 + 1 = 4,

NUMBER OF DIGITS = 4]

Example2:

Input: 125

Output: Not an SUPERSPY number [1+2+5 is not equal to 3]

• Understanding/Application

Question 8.

Define a class to overload the method display() as follows: [15]

void display()	To print the following format using nested loop. 1 2 1 2 1 1 2 1 2 1 1 2 1 2 1
void display (int n, int m)	To print the quotient of the division of m and n if m is greater than n otherwise print the sum of twice n and thrice m.
double display (double a, double b, double c)	To print the value of z where $z = p \times q,\ p = \dfrac{a+b}{c},\ q = a + b + c$

• Understanding/Application

SPECIMEN QUESTION PAPER

Answers

1. (i) (b) Name the given structure is two dimensional array with 4 rows and 5 columns.

   (ii) (c) Java's bytecode can run on any operating system that has a Java Virtual Machine (JVM) installed. This ensures that Java programs can be executed on different platforms without needing to be recompiled.

   (iii) (a) In many systems, especially in UTF-16 encoding, the newline character '\n' is represented using 2 bytes. However, it's typically 1 byte in ASCII and UTF-8 encoding, but among the provided options, 2 bytes is the closest.

   (iv) (b) Identify the operator that gets the highest precedence while evaluating the given expression: a + b % c * d – e is %.

   (v) (c) In Java, static is a reserved keyword used to define class-level methods and variables. If and Switch should be lowercase (if and switch), and BOOLEAN should be boolean.

   (vi) (d) Math.ceil(6.4) returns the smallest integer greater than or equal to 6.4, which is 7.0. Math.floor(-1 - 2) computes -1 - 2 which is -3, and Math.floor(-3) is -3.0.
   Adding these: 7.0 + (-3.0) = 4.0

   (vii) (c) replace(char, char) returns a String where all occurrences of the specified character are replaced with another character.

   (viii) (b) The switch statement in Java does not support floating-point constants (i.e., float or double). It supports byte, short, int, char, and enumerated types.

   (ix) (b) ch[0] refers to the character 'A'. In Java, characters are internally represented by their ASCII values. The ASCII value of 'A' is 65.Multiplying this value by 2 gives 65 * 2 = 130.So, the output of the statement is 130.

   (x) (a) for (int i=11;i<=30;i+=2) loop starts at 11 and increments by 2 each time. It will execute a total of 10 times (i.e., 11, 13, 15, 17, 19, 21, 23, 25, 27, 29).

   (xi) (c) For a single-dimensional array with 50 elements, the valid indices range from 0 to 49. To initialize the last element to 100, you should use the index 49.So, the correct statement is x[49] = 100.

   (xii) (b) The method prototype for the method compute, which accepts two integer arguments and returns a boolean value (true/false), is boolean compute(int a, int b).

   (xiii) (d) The statement that brings the control back to the calling method is return.

   (xiv) (c) The default value of a boolean variable in Java is false.

   (xv) (c) The Character.toUpperCase(char) method is used to convert a single lowercase character to its uppercase equivalent. The other options are either incorrect or not directly related to this specific conversion.

   (xvi) (a) The Integer class can be used in a Java program without explicitly importing it because it is part of the java.lang package, which is automatically imported by default. The Integer class belongs to the java.lang package, which is a default package that is automatically available to all Java programs. Hence, Both Assertion (A) and Reason (R) are true and Reason (R) is a correct explanation of Assertion (A).

   (xvii) (d) The incorrect statement x = +2; assigns the value 2 to x, rather than increasing its current value by 2. The correct statements to increase the value of x by 2 are: x += 2; (This is the shorthand for x = x + 2;) and x = x + 2; (This explicitly adds 2 to the current value of x.)

   (xviii) (a) The statement used to find the total number of elements in a string array String s[] is s.length.

(xix) (b) To swap two variables using a third variable, you need to follow these steps:

1. Assign the value of the first variable to the third variable.
2. Assign the value of the second variable to the first variable.
3. Assign the value of the third variable to the second variable.

Given the jumbled statements, the correct order to achieve this is: (3) (4) (1) (2)

(xx) (c) An argument is a value that is passed to a method when it is called. This is true. Variables declared in a method prototype to receive values are called parameters (or formal parameters), not actual parameters. The term "actual parameters" refers to the arguments passed to the method, not the variables in the method definition.Hence, Assertion (A) is true and Reason (R) is false.

2. (i)
```
if (code = = 'g'||code = = 'G')
System.out.println("GREEN");
```

(ii) 4, 6

(iii) Statement with error – boolean x = true; To get the required output – int x = 1;

(iv) Math.cbrt(x) + Math.sqrt(y)

(v) Loop is executed two times
20
22

(vi) (a) true
(b) –1

(vii) X b

(viii) Syntax error, double y = Double.parseDouble(x)

(ix) Default constructor, Parameterized Constructor

(x) (a) x[2][0]
(b) 17

3.
```
import java.util.*;
class Bank
{
  double p, n, r, a;
  Scanner ob = new Scanner(System.in);
  void accept()
  {
    System.out.println ("Enter principal");
    p = ob.nextDouble();
    System.out.println("Enter number of years");
    n = ob.nextDouble();
  }
  void calculate()
  {
    if (n <= 0.5)
      r = 9;
    else if (n > 0.5 && n < 1)
      r = 10;
    else if (n >= 1 && n <= 3)
      r = 11;
```

```java
        a = p * Math.pow(1 + r / 100, n);
    }
    void display()
    {
        System.out.println("Principal"+ "\t" + "Rate" + "\t" + "Time" + "\t" + "Amount");
        System.out.println(p + "\t" + r + "\t" + n + "\t" + a);
    }
    public static void main(String[] args)
    {
        Bank b = new Bank();
        b.accept();
        b.calculate();
        b.display();
    }
}
```

4.

```java
class Binary
{
    double x[] = {5.6, 11.5, 20.8, 35.4, 43.1, 52.4, 66.6, 78.9, 80.0, 95.5};
    double n;
    Binary(double z)
    {
        n = z;
    }
    void search()
    {
        int f = 0, l = x.length - 1, m;
        while (f <= l)
        {
            m = (f + l) / 2;
            if (x[m] == n)
            {
                System.out.println("Search Successful");
                System.exit(0);
            }
            if (x[m] < n)
                f = m + 1;
            else
                l = m - 1;
        }
        System.out.println("Search Unsuccessful");
    }
    public static void main(String[] args)
    {
        Binary binarySearch = new Binary(43.1); // Example search
        binarySearch.search();
    }
}
```

5.

```java
class Convert
{
    String s;
    // Constructor to initialize the string
    Convert(String z)
```

```
    {
        s = z;
    }
    // Method to perform the conversion
    void convert()
    {
        int i, l = s.length();
        char ch;

        String ns = "";
        for (i = 0; i < l; i++)
        {
            ch = s.charAt(i);
            if (Character.isLetter(ch))
            {
                if ("AEIOUaeiou".indexOf(ch) >= 0)
                    ns = ns + (char) (ch + 1);
                else
                    ns = ns + (char) (ch - 1);
            }
            else
            {
                ns = ns + ch;
            }
        }
        System.out.print(ns);
    }
    public static void main(String[] args)
    {
        Convert obj = new Convert("Example");
        obj.convert();  // Call the convert method
    }
}
```

6.

```
class SumRow
{
    int x[][];
        // Correct declaration of the 2D array
        // Constructor to initialize the array
    SumRow(int z[][])
    {
        x = z; // Correctly assigning the parameter to the class variable
    }
    // Method to calculate and print the sum of each row
    void calculate()
    {
        int r, c, s;
        for (r = 0; r < x.length; r++)
        { // Use x.length to handle different sizes of arrays
            s = 0;
                // Initialize sum for each row
            for (c = 0; c < x[r].length; c++)
            { // Use x[r].length to handle different column sizes
                s += x[r][c]; // Accumulate the sum for the current row
            }
            System.out.println("Sum of row " + r + " = " + s); // Print the sum of the current row
        }
    }
```

```
    public static void main(String[] args)
    {
      int[][] array =
      {
        {1, 2, 3, 4},
        {5, 6, 7, 8},
        {9, 10, 11, 12},
        {13, 14, 15, 16}
      };
      SumRow sr = new SumRow(array);
      sr.calculate(); // Call the method to calculate and print row sums
    }
}
```

7.

```
class Superspy
{
  int n;
  Superspy(int x)
  {
    n = x;
  }
  boolean isSuperspy()
  {
    int d, s = 0, c = 0;
    int temp = n;  // Use a temporary variable to keep the original value of n
    while (temp > 0)
    {
      d = temp % 10;
      s = s + d;
      c++;
      temp = temp / 10;
    }
    return s == c;
  }
  public static void main(String[] args)
  {
    Superspy spy = new Superspy(123);
    if (spy.isSuperspy())
    {
      System.out.println("The number is a superspy number.");
    }
    else
    {
      System.out.println("The number is not a superspy number.");
    }
  }
}
```

8.

```
class Overload
{
  // Method to display a pattern of 1s and 2s
    void display()
  {
    int r, c;
    for (r = 1; r <= 3; r++)
    {
      for (c = 1; c <= 5; c++)
      {
```

```
        if (c % 2 == 0)
          // Fixed condition to check for even numbers
          System.out.print(2);
        else
          System.out.print(1);
      }
      System.out.println();
    }
  }
  // Method to display result based on comparison of m and n
  void display(int m, int n)
  {
    if (m > n)
      System.out.println(m / n);
    else
      System.out.println(2 * n + 3 * m);
  }
  // Method to perform calculations with double values
  void display(double a, double b, double c)
  {
    double z, p, q;
    p = (a + b) / c;
    q = a + b + c;
    z = p * q; // Corrected multiplication
    System.out.println(z);
  }
  // Main method to run the program
  public static void main(String[] args)
  {
    Overload obj = new Overload();
    obj.display();
      // Calls method with no arguments
    obj.display(10, 5);
      // Calls method with int arguments
    obj.display(5.0, 3.0, 2.0);
      // Calls method with double arguments
  }
}
```

SAMPLE QUESTION PAPER
COMPUTER APPLICATIONS

General Instructions

Maximum Marks : 100

Time allowed : Two hours

Answers to this paper must be written on the paper provided separately.

You will not be allowed to write during the first 15 minutes.
This time is to be spent in reading the question paper.

The time given at the head of this paper is the time allowed for writing the answers.

This paper is divided into two sections.

Attempt all questions from **Section A** and
any four questions from **Section B**.

The intended marks for questions or parts of questions are given in brackets [ ].

Section A

(Attempt **all** questions from this section) **(40 Marks)**

Question 1

Select the correct answers to the questions from the given options. **(20)**

(Do not copy the question, write the correct answer only)

(i) Consider the given 2-D array, identify the number of row-column where minimum value is present.

2-D ARRAY	col 0	col 1	col 2
row 0	11	15	22
row 1	12	16	21
row 2	13	17	20
row 3	14	18	19

(a) (row 1, col 0) (b) (row 2, col 2)
(c) (row 3, col 1) (d) (row 0, col 0)

(ii) Name the type of error in the statement given below

`double x; y : z;`

(a) Logical error (b) Syntax error (c) Runtime error (d) No error

(iii) The number of bytes occupied by the constant 45 are

(a) Four bytes (b) Two bytes (c) Eight bytes (d) One byte

(iv) Identify the operator that gets the highest precedence while evaluating the given expression:
2a+b%c*3d-2e

(a) + (b) %
(c) – (d) *

(v) Which method returns the smallest integer that is greater than or equal to the argument?
(a) Math.floor() (b) Math.ceil() (c) Math.round() (d) Math.abs()

(vi) The output of the following code is:
```
System.out.println(Math.ceil(8.4) +Math.floor(-8-6));
```
(a) -5.0 (b) 5.0 (c) 5 (d) 4.0

(vii) What does the lastIndexOf method do?
(a) Returns the first occurrence of a specified character or substring.
(b) Returns the last occurrence of a specified character or substring.
(c) Returns the total count of a specified character or substring.
(d) Replaces the specified character or substring with another character or substring.

(viii) Which statement is true about the break statement when used inside nested loops?
(a) It breaks out of the inner loop only.
(b) It breaks out of both inner and outer loops.
(c) It continues to the next iteration of the outer loop.
(d) It has no effect.

(ix) Consider the array given below:
```
char ch[]={ 'A', 'E', 'I', 'O', 'U'};
```
Write the output of the following statements.
```
System.out.println(ch[2]*2);
```
(a) 146 (b) 138 (c) 'I' (d) 0

(x) It is a loop within a loop.
(a) Inner loop (b) Outer loop (c) Nested loop (d) Listed loop

(xi) Cell numbers of a dimensional array are also known as ....
(a) packets (b) blocks (c) subscripts (d) compartments

(xii) Write a method prototype name check() which takes an integer argument and returns a char
(a) char check () (b) void check (int x) (c) check (int x) (d) char check (int x)

(xiii) What does a method signature consist of?
(a) Method name and parameter list (b) Method name and return type
(c) Method name and access modifier (d) Return type and parameter list

(xiv) A variable that is bounded to the object itself is called as
(a) instance variable (b) class variable
(c) local variable (d) argument variable

(xv) How can you parse a string representing a number in a different base (e.g., binary, octal, hexadecimal)?
(a) Integer.parseInt(String s, int radix) (b) Integer.parseInt(String s)
(c) Integer.parseInt(int radix, String s) (d) Integer.parseInt(String s, String radix)

(xvi) **Assertion (A)** The += operator can be used to add a value to a variable and assign the result to that variable.
Reason (R) The += operator is a compound assignment operator that combines addition with assignment.
(a) Both A and R are true, and R is the correct explanation of A.
(b) Both A and R are true, but R is not the correct explanation of A.
(c) A is true, but R is false.
(d) A is false, but R is true.

(xvii) A student wants to print the numbers from 1 to 5 using a loop. He writes the following code snippet:
```
for (int i = 1; i < 5; i++)
{
  System.out.print(i + " ");
}
```

Which of the following corrections should be made to ensure the code prints numbers from 1 to 5 inclusively?

A. Change i < 5 to i <= 5

B. Change i++ to i--

C. Remove System.out.print
(i + " "); and replace with System.out.println(i + " ");

(a) A only (b) A and C (c) B and C (d) All of these

(xviii) What will happen if charAt is called with an index that is out of bounds?

(a) It returns null. (b) It returns an empty character.

(c) It throws an IndexOutOfBoundsException. (d) It throws a NullPointerException.

(xix)
```
int z = 8;                                   #1
if (z % 2 == 0)
{                                            #2
  System.out.println("z is even");           #3
} else {                                     #4
  System.out.println("z is odd, incremented by 3: " + z);    #5
z += 3;                                      #6
}                                            #7
```

Choose the correct order to get the proper output:

(a) #1,#2,#3,#4,#6,#5,#7 (b) #1,#4,#2,#3,#5,#6,#7

(c) #1,#2,#4,#5,#3,#6,#7 (d) #1,#4,#5,#2,#3,#6,#7

(xx) **Assertion (A)** Java methods can have access modifiers such as public, private, and protected.

Reason (R) Access modifiers control the visibility of methods in Java.

(a) Both A and R are true, and R is the correct explanation of A.

(b) Both A and R are true, but R is not the correct explanation of A.

(c) A is true, but R is false.

(d) A is false, but R is true.

Question 2

(i) Rewrite the following code using the if-else statement. [2]

```
int m=400;
double ch=(m>300) ? (m/10.0)*2:(m/20.0)-2:
```

(ii) Evaluate the expression when the value of x = 4 [2]

```
x * = --x + x++ +x
```

(iii) Consider the below code: [2]

```
String flavor = "CHOCOLATE";
if (flavor equals("VANILLA"))
{
  System.out.println("VANILLA ICE CREAM");
}
else if (flavor.equals ("STRAWBERRY"))
{
  System.out.println ("STRAWBERRY ICE CREAM");
}
else
{
  System.out.println("UNKNOWN FLAVOR");
}
```

The above code has error in it, identify it to produce the output "UNKNOWN FLAVOR".

(iv) Write a statement in Java for the following mathematical expression [2]

$$\sqrt[3]{ab+cd}$$

(v) Analyse the given program segment and answer the following questions [2]

```
for(int m=5; m<=20; m+ =5)
{
    if(m%3= =0)
        break;
    else
        if(m%5==0)
        System.out.println(m);
    continue;
}
```

(a) Write the output of the program segment.

(b) How many times does the body of the loop get executed?

(vi) Write the output of the following string methods: [2]

```
String x="Cat", y="Cot";
```

(a) `System.out.println(x.charAt(0) ==y.charAt(0));`

(b) `System.out.println(x.compare To(y));`

(vii) Predict the output of the following code snippet: [2]

```
char ch='D';
char chr=Character.toLower Case(ch);
int n=(int) chr-10;
System.out.println((char)n+"\t"+chr);
```

(viii) Identify the error in the below code:

```
public class AverageCalculator
{
  public static void main(String[] args)
  {
    int[] numbers = {5, 10, 15, 20, 25};
    int sum = 0;
    for (int i = 0; i
    <= numbers.length;i++)
    {
      sum += numbers[i];
    }
    double average = sum / numbers.length;
    System.out.println ("Average: " + average);
  }
}
```

[2]

(ix) Consider the below code and identify the type of constructor

```
public class Car
{
  private String brand;
  private int year;
  public Car()
  {
    brand = "Unknown";
    year = 0;
  }
  public Car(String brand, int year)
  {
    this.brand = brand;
    this.year = year;
  }
```

```
        public String getBrand()
        {
            return brand;
        }
        public int getYear()
        {
            return year;
        }
        public static void main(String[] args)
        {
            Car car1 = new Car();
            Car car2 = new Car("Toyota", 2023);
            // Output
            System.out.println
                ("Car 1: Brand - " + car1.getBrand() + ", Year - " + car1.getYear());
            System.out.println
                ("Car 2: Brand - " + car2.getBrand() + ", Year - " + car2.getYear());
        }
    }
```

[2]

(x) Consider the given array and answer the questions given below

int x [ ] = {4,7,9,66,72,0,16};

(a) What is the length of the array?

(b) What is the value in x[4] ?

[2]

Section B

(Attempt **any four** questions from this section) **(60 Marks)**

Question 3

A class **DeciOct** has been defined to convert a decimal number into its equivalent octal number. Some of the members of the class are given below [15]

Class name	DeciOct
Data members/Instance variables	
n	To store the decimal number
oct	To store the octal equivalent number
Member functions	
void getnum (int nn)	Assign nn to n
void deci_oct()	Calculates the octal equivalent of n and stores it in oct
void show ( )	Displays the decimal number n, calls the function deci_oct( ) and displays its octal equivalent

Specify the class **DeciOct**, giving details of void getnum(int), void deci_oct() and void show(). Also define a **main**() function to create an object of the class and call the functions accordingly to enable the task.

Question 4.

Define a class to perform binary search on a list of integers given below, to search for an element input by the user, if it is found display the element along with its position, otherwise display the message "Search element not found".

2, 5, 7, 10, 15, 20, 29, 30, 46, 50

[15]

Question 5.

Define a class to accept a string and modify it according to the following rules: [15]

(i) Convert the string to uppercase.

(ii) Replace each letter with the next letter in the alphabet.

(iii) Replace each digit with the previous digit.

(iv) Keep all other characters unchanged.

e.g. Input "Hello123!"

Output "IFMMP012!"

Question 6.

Write a Java program to sort an array in ascending order and array elements must be input by user. [15]

e.g. Input : 4, 5, 2, 0, 7

Output : 0, 2, 4, 5, 7

Question 7.

Define a class to accept a positive integer and check whether it is an Armstrong number or not. An Armstrong number is a number that is equal to the sum of its own digits each raised to the power of the number of digits. [15]

e.g. Input 153

Output "Armstrong number"

Question 8.

Define a class to overload the method display() as follows: [15]

void display()	to print the following format using nested loop. 1 4 1 4 1 1 4 1 4 1 1 4 1 4 1
void display(int n, int m)	to print the quotient of the division of m and n if m is greater than n otherwise print the sum of twice n and thrice m.
double display(double a, double b, double c)	to print the value of z where z=p*q and p=a+b/c and q=a+b+c.

Answers

1. (i) (d) 11 is the minimum value present at row 0, col 0.

 (ii) (b) We cannot use ; as a separator for multiple variables declaration, so it will give the syntax error.

 (iii) (a) Just use the constant 45 without specifying a data type, Java will treat it as an int, which occupies 4 bytes.

 (iv) (b) % has highest precedence than +,*,–.

 (v) (b) Math.ceil()method returns the smallest integer that is greater than or equal to the argument.

 (vi) (a) For Math.ceil(8.4), the smallest integer greater than or equal to 7.4 is 9.0, Math.floor(-8-6) is -14.0 so 9.0+(-14.0)=-5.0

 (vii) (b) The lastIndexOf method in Java is used to find the last occurrence of a specified value within a string or a list.
 It returns the index of the last occurrence of the specified value. If the value is not found, it returns-1.

 (viii) (a) When a break statement is encountered inside nested loops (loops within loops), it immediately terminates the execution of the innermost loop that it appears in.

 (ix) (a) ch[2] means 'I' from given array so I's value is 73, 73*2=146.

 (x) (c) Nested loop is a loop within a loop i.e. an inner loop within the body of an outer one.

 (xi) (c) Cell numbers of a dimensional array are also known as subscripts.

 (xii) (d) char check (int x) indicates a function named check that accepts an integer argument (int x) and returns a char value.

 (xiii) (a) Method signature consists of Method name and parameter list.

 (xiv) (a) A variable that is bounded to the object itself is called as instance variable.

 (xv) (a) Integer.parseInt(String s, int radix)is the proper syntax to parse a string representing a number in a different base.

 (xvi) (a) Both A and R are true, and R is the correct explanation of A.

 (xvii) (b) Option A is correct because changing i < 5 to i <= 5 ensures that the loop includes 5.
 Option C is depending on whether you want each number on a new line or on the same line.

 (xviii) (c) It throws an Index OutOfBoundsException as charAt is called with an index that is out of bound.

 (xix) (a) #1,#2,#3,#4,#6,#5,#7

 (xx) (a) Both A and R are true, and R is the correct explanation of A.

2. (i)

```
int m = 400;
if (m > 300)
   double ch = (m / 10.0) * 2;
else
   double ch = (m / 20.0) - 2;
```

(ii) *The expression can be written as*

x = x * -- x + x++ + x

x = 4 * 3 + 3 + 4

x = 12 + 3 + 4

x = 19

(iii) *In second line it should be if(flavor.equals("VANILLA"))*

(iv) *Java statement for* $x = \sqrt[3]{ab + cd}$ *is*

```
x = (Math.pow(a*b+c*d), 0.33);
```

(v) (a) ***Output***

5

10

(b) *Three times the body of the loop will be executed.*

(vi) (a) *true* (b) – 2

(vii) 2 d

(viii) *The for loop condition i <= numbers.length causes an ArrayIndexOutOfBoundsException because array indices range from 0 to numbers.length - 1.*

(ix) *default and parameterized constructor used in the given code.*

(x) (a) *Length-wise, the size is 7.*

Memory-wise, the size is 28 bytes.

(b) 72

3.

```
public class DeciOct
{
  int n, oct;
  void getnum(int nn)
  {
    n = nn;
  }
  void deci_oct()
  {
    int x = n;
    if (n > 0)
    {
      int rem = n % 8;
      n = n / 8;
      deci_oct();
      oct = oct * 10 + rem;
    }
  }
  void show()
  {
    int original = n; // Store the original value of n
    oct = 0; // Initialize oct to 0
    System.out.println("Number: " + n);
    deci_oct();
    n = original; // Reset n to its original value
```

```
        System.out.println("Its octal equivalent: " + oct);
    }
    public static void main(String[] args)
    {
      DeciOct d1 = new DeciOct();
      d1.getnum(25);
      d1.show();
      }
    }
```

4.
```
import java.util.Scanner;
public class Search
{
  public static void main(String[] args)
  {
    int intarray[] = new int[10];
    Scanner sc = new Scanner(System.in);
    int beg = 0, mid = -1, end = 9, se = 0, i, found = -1;
    System.out.println("Enter 10 integers in ascending order:");
    for (i = 0; i < 10; i++)
    {
      intarray[i] = sc.nextInt();
    }
    System.out.println("Enter search element:");
    se = sc.nextInt();
  while (beg <= end)
  {
    mid = (beg + end) / 2;
    if (intarray[mid] == se)
    {
      found = 1;
        break;
    }
    else if (se > intarray[mid])
    {
      beg = mid + 1;
    }
    else
    {
      end = mid - 1;
    }
  }
  if (found == 1)
    System.out.println("Found at position: " + (mid + 1));
  else
    System.out.println("Search element not found!!!");
    sc.close();
  }
}
```

5.
```java
import java.util.Scanner;
public class Main
{
   public static void main(String[] args)
   {
      // Accepting input string from the user
      Scanner scanner = new Scanner (System.in);
      System.out.print("Enter a string: ");
      String inputString = scanner.nextLine();
      // Modifying the string according to the rules
      String modifiedString = modifyString(inputString);
      // Displaying the modified string
      System.out.println("Modified string: " + modifiedString);
   }
   // Method to modify the input string according to the rules
   public static String modifyString(String input)
   {
      StringBuilder modified = new StringBuilder();
      for (char ch : input.toCharArray())
      {
         if (Character.isLetter(ch))
         {
            // Convert letter to uppercase
            char modifiedChar = Character.toUpperCase(ch);
            // Replace each letter with the next letter in the alphabet
            modifiedChar = (char) (modifiedChar + 1);
            // Wrap around 'Z' to 'A'
            if (modifiedChar > 'Z')
            {
               modifiedChar = 'A';
            }
            modified.append(modifiedChar);
         }
         else if (Character.isDigit(ch))
         {
            // Replace each digit with the previous digit
            char modifiedChar = (char) (ch - 1);
            // Wrap around '0' to '9'
            if (modifiedChar < '0')
            {
               modifiedChar = '9';
            }
            modified.append(modifiedChar);
         }
         else
         {
            // Keep other characters unchanged
            modified.append(ch);
         }
```

```java
        }
        return modified.toString();
    }
}
```

6.
```java
import java.io.*;
import java.util.*;
public class Sorting
{
  public static void main(String[] args) throws IOException
  {
    int count, temp;
    //User inputs the array size
    Scanner scan = new Scanner (System.in);
    System.out.print("Enter number of
   elements you want in the array: ");
    count = scan.nextInt();
    int num[] = new int[count];
    System.out.println("Enter array elements:");
    for(int i=0;i<count;i++)
    {
      num[i] = scan.nextInt();
    }
    scan.close();
    for(int i=0;i<count;i++)
    {
      for(int j=i+1;j<count;j++)
      {
        if(num[i] > num[j])
        {
          temp = num[i];
          num[i] = num[j];
          num[j] = temp;
        }
      }
    }
    System.out.print("Array Elements in Ascending Order: ");
    for(int i=0;i<count-1;i++)
    {
      System.out.print(num[i] + ", ");
    }
    System.out.print(num[count - 1]);
  }
}
```

7.
```java
 import java.util.Scanner;
public class Main
{
    public static void main(String[] args)
    {
        // Accepting input from the user
```

```
        Scanner scanner = new Scanner (System.in);
        System.out.print("Enter a positive integer: ");
        int number = scanner.nextInt();
        // Checking if the number is an Armstrong number
        if (isArmstrongNumber(number))
        {
            System.out.println("Armstrong number");
        }
        else
        {
            System.out.println("Not an Armstrong number");
        }
    }
    // Method to check if a number is an Armstrong number
    public static boolean isArmstrongNumber(int number)
    {
        // Counting the number of digits in the number
        int originalNumber = number;
        int numberOfDigits = 0;
        while (originalNumber != 0)
        {
            originalNumber /= 10;
            numberOfDigits++;
        }
        // Calculating the sum of digits raised to the power of the number of digits
        int sum = 0;
        originalNumber = number;
        while (originalNumber != 0)
        {
            int digit = originalNumber % 10;
            sum += Math.pow(digit, numberOfDigits);
            originalNumber /= 10;
        }
        // Checking if the sum is equal to the original number
        return sum == number;
    }
}
```

8.

```
public class DisplayOverloader
{
    // Method to display the pattern
    void display()
    {
        for (int i = 1; i <= 3; i++)
        {
            for (int j = 1; j <= 5; j++)
            {
                System.out.print((j % 2 == 0) ? "4 " : "1 ");
            }
            System.out.println();
        }
    }
```

```
    // Method to handle integer parameters
    void display(int n, int m)
    {
        if (m > n)
        {
            System.out.println("Quotient of m and n: " + (double) m / n);
        }
        else
        {
            System.out.println("Sum of twice n and thrice m: " + (2 * n + 3 * m));
        }
    }
    // Method to handle double parameters
    double display(double a, double b, double c)
    {
        double p = a + b / c;
        double q = a + b + c;
        double z = p * q;
        System.out.println("Value of z: " + z);
        return z;
    }
    public static void main(String[] args)
    {
        DisplayOverloader obj = new DisplayOverloader();
        // Calling the display method without parameters
        obj.display();
        // Calling the display method with integer parameters
        obj.display(2, 5);
        // Calling the display method with double parameters
        obj.display(2.0, 3.0, 4.0);
    }
}
```